OL'
DIZ

Also by Vince Staten

Unauthorized America
Real Barbecue (with Greg Johnson)

OL' DIZ

A Biography of Dizzy Dean

VINCE STATEN

HarperCollins*Publishers*

HarperCollins books may be purchased for educational, business, or sales promotional use. For information, please call or write: Special Markets Department, HarperCollins Publishers, Inc., 10 East 53rd Street, New York, NY 10022. Telephone: (212) 207-7528; Fax: (212) 207-7222.

FIRST EDITION

Designed by Cassandra J. Pappas

Staten, Vince
    Ol' Diz: a biography of Dizzy Dean / Vince Staten.—1st ed.
      p. cm.
    Includes index.
    ISBN 0-06-016514-6
    1. Dean, Dizzy, 1911– . 2. Baseball players—United States—Biography. 3. St. Louis Cardinals (Baseball team) I. Title.
GV865.D4S73   1992
796.357'092—dc20
[B]   91-50464

92 93 94 95 96 MAC/RRD 10 9 8 7 6 5 4 3 2 1

For my sons, alphabetically:
Adam, Kurt, Marc, and Will

Contents

1. Scoops   1
2. The Real Scoop   8
3. Turning Pro   35
4. The Old Pro   43
5. Back to the Bushes   59
6. Rookie   74
7. The Sophomore Jinx   88
8. Dizzy and Daffy   97
9. Dizzy Triumphant   137
10. Barnstorming   152
11. "The White-Haired Boy of the
    Overflowing Mississippi"   160
12. The Last Good Year   173
13. The Toe   181
14. The Trade   189

CONTENTS

15. Turn Your Radio On   205
16. The Gambler   230
17. Things Folks Ain't Seeing   238
18. A Game of the Week   252
19. 1934 Is Gone Forever   278

    Afterword   291

    Appendix A Major and Minor
    League Record of Jay Hanna
    "Dizzy" Dean   294
    Appendix B Diz in His Own
    Words   296
    Appendix C A Log of Diz's
    30 Wins in 1934   309
    Appendix D Diz on Video   311
    Appendix E Dizzy Dean's Annual
    Salaries for Playing Baseball   312
    Appendix F Dizzy Expressions   313

    Index   317

    Photographs follow pages 118 and 214

OL'
DIZ

1

Scoops

He was born Jay Hanna Dean on January 16, 1911, in Lucas, Arkansas. At least that's what he told Tommy Holmes of the Brooklyn *Eagle,* when Holmes taxied to the Governor Clinton Hotel in Manhattan to interview him September 13, 1934.

Later that same morning he confided to Bill McCullough of the Brooklyn *Times-Union* that he was born February 22, 1911, in Bond, Mississippi.

And during a lunch interview he told Roscoe McGowen of the *New York Times* that he was born August 22, 1911, in Holdenville, Oklahoma.

Scoops. The eager-to-please Dizzy Dean gave out a lot of scoops during his half century in the public eye. In addition to his changing birthplace and birth date, he often handed out scoops on his name. He was variously identified as Jerome Dean (when he first came up to the Cardinals), Jay (by his brother Paul), Jay Hanner (by sportswriters who got the "straight scoop" during the 1934 pennant race), Jerome Herman (by other sportswriters, who got a different "straight scoop" during the 1934 pennant race), and Jay

Hanna (by writers who chronicled his move from radio sportscasting to television sportscasting).

He answered to all those names, but he preferred folks just to call him Diz. He even had three different stories on how he came by the name "Dizzy."

After Babe Ruth, he may be the most famous player in baseball history. But while the New York Yankee slugger had twenty-two towering seasons, including his record-shattering sixty-home-run year in 1927, Dizzy Dean had only five and one-half good years in the big leagues, all of them in the media outpost of St. Louis.

And yet he's still remembered, still quoted today.

• When Reggie Jackson refused to slide into second and broke up a double play in the 1981 World Series by deflecting the throw with his body, *USA Today* recalled the time in the '34 World Series when Diz was plunked in the head with the ball while trying to break up a double play. "They X-rayed my head and found nothing," the paper remembered Dean announcing.

• In 1987 Brewers manager Tom Trebelhorn, irked at an English teacher who had criticized him for using the word "irregardless," recalled the time ol' Diz was criticized for his mangling of the language: "The guy said to Diz, 'Don't you know the King's English?' and Diz replied, 'Yup, and so's the queen.'"

• Recapping the 1988 Super Bowl, Detroit *News* sportswriter Dave Rossie wrote, "The hope that springs eternal had just sprang, as Dizzy Dean might have said. But it didn't stay sprung for long." He was referring to Diz's well-known declension of the verb "slide" as "slid, slide, slud."

Why is ol' Diz still a recognized name fifteen years after his death, twenty-five years after his retirement from the announcer's booth, and half a century after his retirement from the pitching mound? Because he was Dizzy Dean. He was bigger than the game, and if you didn't believe that, all you had to do was ask. Ask him.

He made his name in baseball, then added to his recognition with thirty years in broadcasting, crowned by his twelve years on CBS television's "Game of the Week."

His mangled syntax and misplaced modifiers had English teachers alarmed in four different decades, surely a record. In the late fifties they began a letter-writing campaign, asking CBS to drop Diz from its weekly broadcasts. They didn't know that a decade earlier English teachers in St. Louis had tried the same thing with the local radio station. And a decade before that language purists had been just as upset with the illiteracies of Diz, the rawboned rookie baseball player.

None of it ever bothered ol' Diz. His Depression-era response was to the point: "A lot of folks that ain't sayin' 'ain't' ain't eatin'."

And Diz was eatin', living high on the hog, as he called it.

Dizzy Dean was larger than life, a fact established in 1953 with his election to the Baseball Hall of Fame, despite a career record of only 150 wins, a total that paled next to other Hall of Fame pitchers.

Christy Mathewson had 373 victories, Cy Young 511, even Sandy Koufax, who retired prematurely, had 165 victories.

Of pitchers in the Hall only Candy Cummings and Hoyt Wilhelm won fewer games. Cummings is enshrined because he is credited with inventing the curve ball. Wilhelm was elected because of his prowess as a relief pitcher, a position where saves are more important than wins.

But Diz wasn't elected on his career record; he was elected on his career. And in addition to pitching, fielding, and hitting that career included baiting umpires, riding opponents, entertaining sportswriters, and spinning tales. Usually about himself.

Not that his pitching feats weren't star quality.

He won thirty games in 1934, a feat that has been accomplished only once since. His contemporary Carl Hubbell never won thirty. Nor did any of the great pitchers who played after him: Bob Feller, Bob Lemon, Bob Gibson, Sandy Koufax, Juan Marichal, or Warren Spahn.

And while he may have won only 150 games lifetime, his five-year total of 120 wins (1932–1936) is one of the top five-year records put together by any pitcher in the modern baseball era.

Only eight pitchers in the Hall of Fame have higher career winning percentages. Diz won 64.4 percent of his decisions, a figure bested only by Mordecai Brown, John Clarkson, Whitey Ford, Lefty Gomez, Lefty Grove, Sandy Koufax, Christy Mathewson, and Al Spalding.

But it wasn't just that he won most of his games, it was the way he did it that won him the admiration of baseball fans everywhere. He went all out, often using his country-boy humor to rankle an opponent. When a batter began to dig in at the plate, Diz would charge in from the mound, chattering as he ran: "You all set now? You comfortable? Well, get a shovel and call for the groundskeeper 'cause they're going to bury you right there."

Diz's career totals are deflated because of his early retirement: he was only twenty-seven when he came down with a sore arm. He tried comeback after comeback, but in 1941, at age thirty-one, he retired to the coaching lines.

He coached fewer than fifty games before he found his second calling: broadcasting. Two generations of baseball fans who never saw Dizzy play learned the rudiments of the game from his baseball broadcasts, first on radio, then TV. He was as big a character there as he had been on the playing field.

During World War II broadcasters were forbidden from reporting weather conditions, lest the enemy learn this strategic information. One day Diz and his Cardinals broadcasting partner Johnny O'Hara were trying to kill time during a rain delay, talking about everything except the weather. Finally, after an hour of this empty patter, Diz couldn't stand it anymore: "If you're wonderin' why there's no game, friends, just stick your head out the window."

He spent his best years on the Gas House Gang, arguably the most colorful collection of players ever assembled. But even when he was with the Cubs in the twilight of his career, he found a spotlight and swung it to himself and his new teammates.

He was an egotist, but an egotist who put team ahead of everything. In the crush of the 1934 pennant race, Diz pitched seven times in ten games, winning four of those games and almost single-handedly carrying the Cardinals to a pennant.

His opponents disliked him for his braggadocio, but his teammates appreciated what he could do for them. "Being on the team with Diz meant a better shot at a World Series check," says Johnny Vergez, a teammate on the '36 Cardinals.

Diz didn't see his poppin' off as bragging, and he would get a hurtful look when accused of boasting. "It ain't bragging if you can back it up," he would whisper. That explanation would land him a spot in quotation reference books.

From the time he pitched his first professional game on April 20, 1930, until his death on July 17, 1974, Dizzy Dean was never out of the headlines. If sportswriters didn't come calling at his locker, he would seek them out, offering his observations on everything from the pennant race to the presidential race. He learned early how to play the press. He was even spotlighted in the *New York Times* when he was still pitching in the minors.

He got a lot of ink because he was a sportswriter's dream. He was always accommodating, always ready with a scoop for each reporter, even if the scoop later turned out to be, well, not exactly true. Giving out different birth dates and birthplaces was just the beginning. When a sportswriter called during the winter of '36 to inquire how contract negotiations were going, Diz gave him a column's worth of complaints, concluding that it looked like he was going to have to hold out again if he was to get a decent wage. What he didn't mention was that his signed 1936 contract was already in the commissioner's office.

He was an athlete and a broadcaster but, most of all, a clown. "He was just always a load of fun," says Charles Mathis, Diz's longtime hunting companion and his best friend the last eighteen years of Diz's life.

Dizzy Dean, Will Rogers, and Mark Twain were perhaps the greatest natural comedians this country has produced. And, as Diz would have pointed out, ol' Will and ol' Mark neither one had much of a fastball.

For nine and a half years, from midseason '41 to '50, Diz conducted a daily radio forum during which he could discuss hunting, fishing, the weather back home, what the fellows down at the barbershop were talking about. He would sing a little, tell a few jokes, say hello to friends at home. And every now and then mention what was going on on the ball field. His radio broadcasts of the Cardinals and Browns games were a three-hour lesson in history, philosophy, current events, everything except grammar.

Howard Cosell may have claimed to be the first announcer to "tell it like it is," but Diz *was* the first. Once, while broadcasting the games of the St. Louis Browns, a pitiful team that soon moved to Baltimore because of poor attendance, Diz noted, "The peanut vendors is going through the stands trying to sell their peanuts. They're not doing so good because there's more of them than there is of customers."

Diz's honest manner would eventually cost him the Browns job. But he never missed a beat. He landed in New York in 1950, broadcasting Yankee games on a fledgling medium called television. Diz announced that it marked a new era for him. No more radio broadcasting. "I'm through talking about things that folks ain't seeing."

He wasn't, of course. He would be back in radio in a year, then back in television two years after that.

Not many people succeed on a national level in one career. Diz managed to do it in two fields. He accomplished it because of his mercurial talent, his sideshow bluster, and his small-town charm.

He was part Paul Bunyan, part Johnny Appleseed, and part Huck Finn, but with a difference. There really was a Dizzy Dean.

2

The Real Scoop

He was born Jay Hanna Dean on January 16, 1910, in Lucas, Arkansas.

Not Jerome Herman. Not Jay Hanner.

Not February 22. Not August 22.

Not Holdenville, Oklahoma. Not Bond, Mississippi.

And not 1911.

All the confusion over Diz's birth date and birthplace arose from Diz himself. He told J. Roy Stockton of the St. Louis *Post-Dispatch* how the three different versions came into circulation: "I like Brooklyn. They got good guys writin' for the papers over here. I like Tommy Holmes and Bill McCullough and that McGowen. They say nice things about me and I'm nice to them. I give 'em each a scoop last time we're here. It's funny, but their bosses all comes up with the same idea the same day. Told 'em to get a piece about old Diz. Well, Tommy come first and wanted to know where I was born, and I told him Lucas, Arkansas, January 16, 1911. Then it wasn't two minutes after he leaves that McCullough comes along, and doggone if he don't want the same piece. Now, I wasn't going to have their bosses bawl 'em out for both gettin' the same story, so I told Mack I was born at Bond, Mississippi—that's where my wife comes from—and I pick February twenty-second, which is giving George Washington a break. McGowen was next. He's with the *Times* ... McGowen wanted the same story, but I give him a break, too, and says Holdenville, Oklahoma, August twenty-second."

This story is apparently true. It was reported by the *Sporting News* publisher J. G. Taylor Spink on September 27, 1934, only two weeks after it is supposed to have happened: "On the Cardinal's recent trip East, three Brooklyn reporters went to him, one by one, for interviews. Very obliging, he gave each a different birthday and birth place. Explained he wanted each to have a scoop, so he might get a salary increase."

Stockton's version was published a year later in *The Saturday Evening Post*.

None of the sportswriters ever came forward to dispute the story.

This was not an isolated incidence of Diz giving a scoop. The fact is Diz was always playing with the truth, stretching the thin line between joshing and fibbing. But one fact that never varied in all his accounts of his early years was his birth year: "I was born Jay Hanna Dean on Jan. 16, 1911 in Lucas, Arkansas and that's the truth," he told Francis X. Tolbert of *The Saturday Evening Post* in 1951.

And on a form he filled out for the Baseball Hall of Fame in 1966 he listed his name as Jay Hanna Dean and his birth date as January 16, 1911.

But when census taker John Binning traveled down the dusty Lucas Road to the Hattie Blair farm on April 16, 1910, he found residing in the tenant house Albert and Alma Dean, their two-year-old son Elmer, and their three-month-old baby, Jay.

The facts are duly recorded on page 272 of the 1910 census book for Tomlinson Township, Logan County, Arkansas.

So Dizzy Dean was born January 16, 1910, a year earlier than his lifelong claim and a year earlier than any of the baseball reference books' record.

His real name was Jay Hanna, not Jay Hanner, not Jerome Herman. Part of the confusion over his name came from his thick Arkansas slur. The 1933 edition of *Who's Who in Major League Baseball* listed him as Jay Hanner, as did a 1935 *Saturday Evening Post* article by Roy Stockton. But just as John Kennedy would later have trouble pronouncing Cuba, spitting it out as Cuber, so too did Jay Dean have trouble with his middle name, mangling it as Hanner.

That is when he gave his real name as Jay Hanna.

Here again it was Diz who started the stories about his name being Jerome Herman, and it was Diz who kept the stories going.

When he arrived in St. Louis in the late summer of 1930, he was known as Jerome, as well as Dizzy.

Where did he get the name Jerome Herman?

John Kieran of the *New York Times* reported in a May 1931 story that Diz was named after his own brother, Jerome Herman Dean, "who died before Dizzy was born."

In 1934 he told the *Post-Dispatch*'s Stockton that he had adopted the name of Jerome Herman as a small child, when a playmate by the name of Jerome Herman died.

"I just can't help doin' favors for people," he told Stockton. "You know how people follow me around now: when I couldn't see over a cotton field, it was the same way. I was very popular with the neighbors and especially with a man who had a little boy about my age six or seven, I guess. I often wondered whether that man thought more of me or his own boy. Then all of a sudden the boy took sick. My name, in the first place, was Jay Hanner Dean and this boy's was Jerome Herman Something or Other ... This boy Jerome Herman took sick and died, and we sure did feel sorry for his dad. He just moped around and didn't care for nothin' no more. So I went to him and told him I thought so much of him that I was goin' to take the name of Jerome Herman, and I've been Jerome Herman ever since. He perked up right away, and I guess wherever he is he's mighty proud."

He told Tom Meany of the New York *World-Telegram* a different story, that he started calling himself Jerome in 1929, "Out of a friendship for a battery-mate in the San Antonio City League, Jerome Herman Harris, who looked something like him."

Wife Pat contributed a fourth version in a 1934 interview with Vera Brown of the St. Louis *Star-Times:* "He took the name Jerome Herman from another ball player on the Houston team."

During the 1934 World Series, Diz's father offered a fifth variation on the name Jerome Herman: "We went visiting once and somebody called him Jerome Herman. I guess he liked it and he's kept it ever since."

There was even a story that he'd taken on Herman as a middle name because it was Babe Ruth's middle name.

It is true that when Diz came up to the big leagues in 1930 he was known as Jerome Herman Dean. But where the name really came from is lost.

Not even Diz could decipher his past. He testified under oath in a 1934 trademark trial, "My real, correct name is Jay Hanna Dean. I was named after Jay Gould. But when I was playing down in San Antonio in 1928, there was a catcher who looked like me called Jerome Harris. So they started calling me Jerome Herman, and that's been my name ever since."

Even this version is suspect, for on his employment application at San Antonio Power Company, filled out April 9, 1929, before he had ever played with Jerome Harris, Diz listed his full name as Jay Herman Dean.

Two of the other variations can be disproved easily. Pat Dean's version can't be right because there was no Jerome on the Houston team, other than him. And the *New York Times* story that he was named after his own brother, Jerome Herman Dean, is easily knocked down. Diz's older brother is buried next to Diz's mother in Pinelog Cemetery, near Booneville, Arkansas. The headstone reads, "Charles M. Dean, son of AM & AF Dean, April 20, 1905–May 16, 1906."

But Diz did tell the gospel truth in his trial deposition: he was born Jay Hanna Dean.

Jay was for Jay Gould, a famous businessman and railroad baron of the nineteenth century. At one time Gould owned one of every ten miles of railroad track in America, and many of the train lines that ran on those tracks. Among his business interests were the Western Union telegraph system, the Union Pacific Railroad, and the Wabash Railroad. Years later Diz would make famous one of the Wabash's trains, the *Wabash Cannonball*.

Hanna was for Mark Hanna, an Ohio politician of the 1890s who was famous for settling the coal strike of 1902.

Diz was descended from the hardy pioneer stock of Tennessee, home state of Davy Crockett, another expert at creating a legend. His great-great-grandfather Moses Dean disliked the encroaching civilization, and in the early years of the nineteenth century he crossed the Ozark Mountains into Missouri, settling in what is now Phelps County, just south of the town of Rolla.

Matt Dean, Diz's grandfather, was the first Dean born in their new home in the Ozarks. Matt would later serve two terms as sheriff of Phelps County.

Diz's Aunt Mary Williams told a reporter in 1934 that the Deans had been native Americans so long that their exact previous origin had been lost in the past.

Albert Monroe Dean, Diz's father, was born in Rolla in 1872 and lived there until he was fifteen. That year, 1887, Matt Dean felt that ancestral wanderlust and moved his family south and west to Oklahoma.

Albert Monroe Dean became a timberman who did a little tenant farming to pay his rent. When the Depression of 1899 hit Oklahoma, he moved east to Arkansas. It was while working timber in the Lucas area, southeast of Fort Smith, laboring in the sawmills and hauling logs, that he met Alma Nelson, who was staying there with her aunt. They married in 1904; he was thirty-two, she was twenty-four. They moved into a frame tenant house about a quarter mile from where they met.

Their first child, Charles Monroe Dean, was born April 20, 1905. He was sickly and didn't thrive, dying only weeks after his first birthday.

A second child, Sarah May, also died in childhood.

Their third child, Elmer, who was born in 1908, would be the first to survive to adulthood. Elmer was followed quickly by Jay in 1910 and Paul in 1913.

Wiley Thornton of Dallas, who had helped Paul Dean coach baseball at the University of Texas at Plano in the forties, researched the Dean family history in 1951 for an autobiography Paul was writing called *Me 'n' Diz* that was never published.

Thornton came to the conclusion that the Dean brothers inherited much of their athletic ability from their mother, Alma. "She was a superb girl athlete with natural ability. There was little opportunity to develop but an old gentleman watching her on the school yard thought she was a splendid town ball player. [Town ball was an early variation of baseball.] Alma was apparently exceptionally good since a girl doesn't usually attract attention playing ball. The old timers [in Lucas] had seen her play town ball at school.... Much Dean athletic ability came from her."

Diz's father, Albert, also liked to claim credit for the boys' pitching genes. At the '34 World Series he told some reporters he had pitched for Fort Smith in the Western Association fifteen years earlier and others that he played third base.

There is no supporting evidence for a minor-league baseball career for the elder Dean. If he meant exactly fifteen years earlier, that would have been an impossibility. The Western Association did not operate in 1919 or 1918, according to *The Story of Minor League Baseball*, published in 1953.

It's doubtful he would have pitched then anyway. He would have been forty-seven years old in 1919.

On the assumption that he was speaking loosely, as his son often did, I made a check of Fort Smith rosters of 1914, 1915, 1916, 1917, 1920, 1921, and 1922; they list no Dean. Fort Smith had no team in 1912 or 1913. It did have a team at the start of the 1911 season, but it was disbanded on June 12, 1911. And no Dean is listed on the roster or the abbreviated roster. There was no Fort Smith team in the years 1906–1910 according to the *Reach* baseball guides. Perhaps he pitched one game sometime during the years Fort Smith had a team. Perhaps he made the story up.

The late baseball historian Lee Allen, in his book *Dizzy Dean, His Story in Baseball*, a biography published for the juvenile market in 1967, wrote that Albert Dean played for the Hartford Blues.

A check of Hartford Blues rosters for 1901 to 1912, when the team was in the Connecticut League, does not show an Albert Dean or any Dean for that matter. Nor was he on the roster in 1897 when the team was in the Atlantic League. It seems unlikely that the Missouri-born Dean would have found his way to the northeastern states to play on what were then, in the years before the farm systems, local teams.

An Al Dean did play for Tacoma in the Northwestern League in 1916 and for Aberdeen in 1918, and it was not Al "Chubby"

Dean, who would later play for the Philadelphia A's. Chubby was born in 1916. But in those years it is well established that Albert Monroe Dean was working timber and sharecropping to support his growing family. He couldn't afford to uproot his brood for a summer in Washington state. His age, forty-four in 1916, works against that theory.

In the *World-Telegram,* Tom Meany, one of many sportswriters who interviewed the elder Dean at the 1934 World Series, came away with a few suspicions about the old man's assertions.

"He passes over interruptions like a Baron Münchhausen and skips from one subject to another like a Rocky Mountain goat giving the hunters a workout. If any of his statements are questioned, he ignores the questions. Like Diz, he knows that accuracy is quite likely to rob a story of its interest.... Poppy said that he played ball until he was 45 at Fort Smith, Ark., a third baseman is what he says he was. 'Jay and Paul used to come around the park and watch the games. That's how they come to get interested in baseball,' he said. His interviewer pointed out that if this were so, Diz would have been six and Paul four at the time Poppy quit, rather young to be taking an active interest in baseball. 'I umpired for five or six years after I quit,' explained Pater Dean."

Most likely Albert Dean never played professional baseball. He might in his earlier years have played semipro baseball. But there is no evidence he was ever on the roster of a team in organized baseball.

He apparently got carried away by the media attention at the 1934 World Series and inflated those semipro experiences to another level. If that's what happened, it would surely have made his son proud.

Life was hard in Logan County, Arkansas, in the year of Dizzy Dean's birth, 1910. There was no industry to speak of, only work at the sawmill or on the farms. Albert Monroe Dean did both, sharing his crops with his landlady, Hattie Blair, a widow, and cutting timber for money. He was often away for long stretches, working in the logging industry.

His wife, Alma, stayed home, caring for young Elmer, who was mildly retarded, and newborn Jay.

"His family was terribly poor," wife Pat told an interviewer in 1934. "Many a time he did not have enough to eat. And he didn't have any clothes except a pair of overalls."

Roy Stockton reported in his 1935 *Saturday Evening Post* article that "Dizzy didn't have an entire pair of shoes until he joined the Army."

Paul would later say that both these claims were exaggerated. But if the family wasn't god-awful poor, it was for sure they didn't have much money. What they did have was plenty of love, much of it supplied by Alma Dean. Thornton said the old-timers he talked to in Lucas remarked on what a good mother Alma was.

Nobody had much in Lucas in the first years of the century. But in the close-knit community, neighbors shared what they had with each other. That's how it was that the Deans were living with Hattie Blair when the census taker arrived in April of 1910. They were her tenant farmers, working her land in return for their rent. "He was born in Hattie Blair's house," says Ray Gill, the current occupant of the farm where Dizzy was born. Gill, seventy-five, is a lifelong resident of Lucas. "The family lived in a little cabin just down from here. The old house set out back of where mine does."

Mrs. Blair had taken in her tenant farmers while Alma was giving birth and recuperating from childbirth.

Diz grew up eating the fruits of the nearby fields. "Plain grub made the boys, nothing but plain grub," his father would later call it. "They was raised on corn bread, sweet potatoes, peanuts and milk."

Ray Gill was too young to remember little Dizzy. "I was

about two when they left here." But he heard stories. "I had neighbors named Calverton. Mae Calverton, she told me about one time when Dizzy and his mother was visiting. Dizzy he kept whining and whining. Mrs. Calverton asked, 'What's the matter with that boy?' She said Mrs. Dean said, 'He wants his clothes off; he ain't used to clothes.' He was three or four. So Mrs. Calverton told her to let him take his clothes off."

Diz began school in the fall of 1916, walking about a mile with the other children of Lucas to the Pinelog School.

Even as a tot Jay displayed a trait that would become familiar to millions in the thirties. "Dizzy was always a little stubborn," his father said in '34, "but if you bragged on him he would work his head off. You couldn't, however, get anywhere with severe methods. When he was a youngster I'd tan him until his back was on fire, but he would just get white mouthed and wouldn't budge. He had to be smoothed down."

Diz apparently began playing baseball while still in Lucas. In a memoir of Logan County, John Holt of Possum Hollow in south Logan recalled playing Sunday baseball in a nearby field with the Deans and the four Holt kids.

"Dizzy and Paul, the way they learned to throw a baseball was throwing rocks at squirrels," says Ray Gill.

"Jay never wanted more than one throw at a squirrel," Albert Dean boasted in '34. "He used to carry a pocketful of rocks and he'd send Paul behind the trees to scare the squirrels out where he could get a chuck at them and that was the end of that squirrel."

The rock-throwing squirrel-hunter story has had considerable currency over the years. Diz expanded the legend even further in a 1943 pamphlet published by Falstaff Beer, his sponsor on radio. "I was choppin' cotton down in Arkansas; and because of floods, drought, and the weevils we sure was pore. So, Pa used to send me out huntin' squirrels in the woods for our supper. Since we didn't have enough money to buy no ammunition until the cotton was sold at market, I had to throw rocks at the squirrels to kill 'em. That's how I got such a blazin' fast ball by throwin' rocks at them squirrels, and I got good control, too, because if I missed 'em, we didn't have no supper, and just had to eat blackeyed peas, and dunk our corn pone in the pot likker from the peas."

A plausible story until Diz continues with the tale of a Cardinals scout who came to check him out: "When he sets out to find me, he sees a bunch of dead squirrels lyin' around and he follows this trail. I'm just killin' my last un, and fixin' to go back through the woods pickin' up the others and puttin' them in my sack to fetch 'em home for supper.... After supper he comes out to the farm with a catcher's mitt and a baseball and tells me to throw him a few. So I wind up easy like, because now I ain't bearin' down like I was when I was throwin' them rocks up in the trees. After just a couple of pitches, he says, 'That's enough, you can throw harder'n anyone I ever ketched. But I thought you was left-handed. That's the way you was throwin' in the woods.' So I tell him, 'Yeah, but I throw so hard with my right arm that I squash up them squirrels somethin' turrible and they ain't fit eatin' then. If I'm just huntin' for fun, I do throw right-handed, but when I'm out rustlin' up our grub, I dasn't throw thataway, I got to throw left-handed.'"

The exaggeration lands the story squarely in the Davy Crockett zone. Dizzy probably did throw rocks at squirrels. The story is too widespread among the old-timers in Lucas to be discounted. But his real pitching education came with a homemade ball.

Pat told an interviewer, "His dad had often told me about the baseballs Dizzy made when was a kid. He used a stone for the center and wound it with a string or unraveled an old sock to wrap the stone. That's the kind of childhood Dizzy had—no money for such things as baseballs. The bat was a stick he cut himself in the woods and whittled down smooth.... I've been pretty close to tears when I think of that little gawky boy throwing homemade baseballs at his baby brother."

Diz, in another pamphlet published by Falstaff in the forties, recalled, "My first baseball bat was a sawed-off wagon tongue and we made our first ball out of old inner tubes from automobile tires. We wrapped the twine around the inner-tubes as tight as we could and kept on windin' the string until the ball got big as we wanted it and we was ready to start a game."

With that homemade ball came homegrown instruction. "I taught Dizzy and Paul all they know about pitching and baseball," Albert Dean told one of his many interviewers at the '34 World Series. "I kept Dizzy and Paul supplied with baseballs from their cradle days. I showed Dizzy how to hold the ball and throw a curve. He got pretty good before he was out of short pants."

During the winter of 1917, when Jay was seven, his mother contracted tuberculosis. Alma Dean died in March of that year, leaving three small sons.

Diz would later tell reporters that he was only four when she died. Actually Paul was four at the time. This story seems an obvious exaggeration, perhaps created to elicit sympathy for his motherless childhood, perhaps to explain his boyish behavior even into his twenties. Certainly Diz knew when his mother died. A seven-year-old is more aware of his surroundings than a four-year-old. Diz was already in school, so he would have had that as a marker.

What is sure is that the next decade was not an easy one for the Dean boys.

Wiley Thornton says, "The toughness of those early years was very largely the result of Alma's death, three small boys left behind and no one to care for them since Mr. Dean was away from home working. Her early death grieved the [Lucas] community deeply—the people liked Albert Monroe Dean—they loved Alma."

Neighbors helped look after the Dean brothers. "The Dean boys were not mean—never any criminal activity," said Thornton. "They were lost after the death of Alma."

Albert admitted as much in a '34 interview: "I had my hands full, trying to raise my three boys, but I always tried to do what I could for them. They went to Sunday school regularly and stayed for preachin', too."

Thornton learned all the Sunday-go-to-meeting education didn't sink in. "The Dean boys did sometimes run loose and throw rocks at people after her death."

Ray Gill adds, "My uncle Ernest Gill, he said they was mean little buggers; they was apt to rock you."

It is impossible to accurately chart the Dean family's wanderings after Alma's death. Sometime before 1920 Albert Monroe Dean remarried. His new wife, Cora Parham, was a widow with three children, Herman, Claude, and Carol.

This new blended family moved to Chickalah, Arkansas, a farming town outside Dardanelle in Yell County in 1920. "They lived on my dad's place from 1920 to 1922," recalls Raymith Wilson, who was eight when the Deans moved onto her family's farm. "With all the stepchildren that made for a big family working for us. That's why my dad rented to them, because it was such a big family."

David Ferguson, Jr., says the Deans worked for his father during that same period. "My father, David Ferguson, Sr., was a cotton farmer in the Arkansas River Valley near Dardanelle in Yell County in the early twenties. He also contracted many acres of cotton to harvest and hired several families to help 'pick' the cotton. One of those families was Monroe Dean and his three sons. They worked for my dad in the fall of 1922."

Wilson remembers that the Dean brothers already had a fondness for baseball. "And I was just about old enough that when they missed a ball I could pick it up and throw it back to them."

Diz, Paul, and Elmer enrolled at nearby Mountain Springs School. "They came to school to play ball," says Wilson. "They didn't come to school to learn anything."

Wilson believes the Deans moved to Oklahoma in 1923. "They left our place and moved to Okemah. And then later to Spaulding." One thing that might have taken them to Okemah was that Monroe's brother Harry ran a store there.

Why did Monroe Dean, who had now resided in Arkansas for at least twenty years, uproot his family and head west? Dean family tradition has it that Monroe became embroiled in an argument with another Arkansas Dean over rights to a tobacco field. "That's what my granddaddy always told us," says Linda Shanks, whose grandfather Robah Dean was Dizzy's first cousin.

If we can't be certain when the Deans left Arkansas, we can be certain they lived in Spaulding, Oklahoma, in 1925 and 1926. Dizzy was listed in the 1926 school enumeration for the Spaulding schools, taken January 18, 1926.

On page 31 enumerator Riley Mayfield detailed the schoolage children of the A. M. Dean family of Bilby township:

Name of child	Color	Sex	Date of birth	Age
Elmer Dean	W	M	March 11, 1907	18
J. Dean	W	M	Jan. 22, 1909	16
Paul Dean	W	M	Aug. 16, 1911	14

As usual, Diz's birth information was completely wrong. His birthday was January 16, 1910. Monroe Dean signed the enumeration sheet, so he apparently gave Mayfield the incorrect information.

Spaulding community legend has it that the Deans also lived in nearby Greenleaf for a time, but there is no record of the boys attending school in the Greenleaf district in the middle years of the twenties.

Diz's attendance in school was sporadic after his mother's death. He often joked about his education, or lack of. On occasion he claimed he dropped out after second grade because he didn't want to pass his paw. The story, as with most Dizzy stories, changed with the teller and the tellee. Pat said in a '34 interview, "He never went beyond the fourth grade."

In his 1935 *Saturday Evening Post* article Roy Stockton reported, "His schooling was a smattering; the fourth grade was as far as he went."

When Dizzy filled out his job application at San Antonio Power Company in 1929, however, he advanced himself to a ninth-grade education. But when he completed his Baseball Hall of Fame questionnaire in 1966, he backtracked a bit, admitting to only six years of schooling.

The truth came out in 1951, after a second *Saturday Evening Post* article reported:

As a boy cotton picker in Arkansas Diz got only as far as the second grade—"and I didn't do so good in the first," he states proudly.

"Heck, it takes a college graduate to call a football game, and I just went through the second grade."

In the spring of 1919 an Arkansas schoolteacher named Ralph Dennis was trying his level best to get an eight-year-old called Jay Hanna Dean through the Second Reader.

Professor Dennis often used a hickory stick—which was a standard 1919 device in child psychology—on Jay Hanna. Professor Dennis made the big-footed child stand for hours with his nose in a ring drawn on the blackboard, as punishment for repeated classroom failures. Nothing did much good, apparently. Jay Hanna just couldn't seem to learn. And late in the spring of 1919 the Dean boy solved the whole problem by running away from school and becoming a permanent fugitive from the truant officer.

"I got as far in school as the Second Reader, only I didn't learn all of it."

J. H. Dean was easily the most backward and ornery scholar in the one-room schoolhouse at Chickalah, Arkansas, which is a village in the mountains northwest of Little Rock. And the older folk of Chickalah today will be surprised to learn that their second grader of 1919 who was figured least likely to succeed will earn the princely sum of $75,000 in 1951 as a public speaker, businessman and writer.

Paul, who was coaching college baseball in Texas at the time, decided he had had enough of Diz's exaggerating the Deans' ignorance. He told the *Sporting News,* "Diz left school in 1926, while he was in the Seventh Reader at Spaulding, Okla. Now, some folks might think that there isn't much difference in those two statements, but I think there is. There are a good many people in this country who didn't get past the seventh grade, but there aren't so many who didn't finish the second. If you stop to think about it, there's a big difference between the two. By the time a person gets to the seventh grade, he has the groundwork for a pretty good education he can read, write, spell and figure."

Diz conceded Paul's point. "I went to school off and on at Spaulding, Okla., in 1926, and played ball for Spaulding High School but I wasn't in high school. As I remember it, I was in the fourth grade. That's as far as I ever got."

Paul also challenged Diz's assertion that he was backward and ornery. "That's a lot of baloney. Just ask anyone who knew Diz when he was in school, and they'll tell you that he certainly wasn't a 'backward' student. In fact, I'd say that he was just about an average student the same as I was. I'll even go further than that and say that both of us were a good bit above average in mathematics. It's true that Diz quit school before he graduated, but he never was a 'backward' student at all."

Paul finished his argument: "Along the same line, the story says that Diz was 'almost illiterate' when he left school. That's wrong, too. By the time he quit school, Diz could read and write as well as you'd expect of the average seventh-grader. The truth is that Diz has always done quite a lot of reading, mostly magazines and newspapers. I'd say he reads at least as much as the average person."

This debate over how far Diz got in school obscures a very real fact of life: Diz worked hard during his childhood. He worked as a nomad of the cotton fields, picking crops for what was then the going wage, fifty cents a day. He went to school when he could, but because the Deans moved frequently, his schooling was sometimes interrupted. They lived in Okemah, Spaulding, Purcell, all located in the farm belt around Oklahoma City.

"The boys used to pick cotton for me at Purcell, Okla.," Albert Dean told an interviewer in '34. "Jay used to scheme about how to make money from his great right arm and used to think a lot. Paul would pick as much as 500 pounds a day, but Jay never went over 400 pounds a day. And I was only able to pick about 200 pounds cuz I had to watch Jay."

Schooling was now a sometime thing for Dizzy. "He didn't go to school much," recalls Ornie Mayfield of Holdenville. But not attending school regularly didn't prevent young Diz from pitching for the local school team in Spaulding. "Many was the time my dad went to the field to get him to play with us at school. His old man would make him work. My old man would go over there and talk him into it. He'd say, 'These boys are going to make you proud of 'em.'"

The Dean family settled in Spaulding for a time, living in a small house on Tater Hill, a neighborhood between Spaulding and Holdenville. "His dad was sharecropping for old man Gallimore from Holdenville," remembers Ornie. "It was hard times back then."

Pat said in '34: "He had always played baseball in his bare feet. He played with the Spaulding (Ok.) High School team though he never went to high school and he pitched a shutout

game against the Oklahoma Teachers' College, in his bare feet."
He didn't pitch against an official team from Oklahoma Teachers'
College in those years because the school, now Central State University, didn't field a team then. But records at the Edmond,
Oklahoma, school reveal that there was an unorganized team in
the years 1924–1928 that played a pickup schedule. The school's
1928 yearbook blamed the failure to field a team on a "shortage
of coaches" and noted that "nevertheless the team performed
splendidly" (during those five years).

When Diz and Paul were preparing to lead the Cardinals into
the 1934 World Series against the Tigers, the *Holdenville Daily
News* ("Read with interest in more than 3,600 homes") ran a
story about its native sons. Chief among his local sports exploits,
the paper mentioned a junior high baseball tournament. "Diz
won three games in one afternoon and hit a home run into the
corn patch that was never found."

His local friends recalled for the newspaper Diz's typical dress
during his Spaulding days: "Slouch cap pulled down over one ear,
ragged overalls and faded blue shirt." They claimed he never wore
shoes unless it was too cold. "He did not care for girls, being very
shy around them.... On many a wiener roast to tater hill he would
run from the girls and join a crowd of boys, cornering and lectur-
ing them on what he would do someday."

Ornie and Jay—"It was Jay then. He didn't wear that 'Dizzy'
at Spaulding"—played on the Spaulding School team in 1924 and
1925.

One factor that enabled young Diz to play high school baseball at age fourteen was his physical development. He'd grown up
fast, by necessity. "He was a kind of big, old, overgrown kid,"
remembers Fleeda Jones of Holdenville. "He was a big, old, lard-
ass kid."

Already Diz's pitching prowess was apparent. "He could play
anywhere, but he was a pitcher," says Ornie. "He could throw a

ball so damned hard you couldn't see it. He'd pitch a double-header; he was that much above anybody else."

Also apparent was his ability to stir up trouble. "Jay was big and loud and friendly. He was a cutup then; he had a big mouth. He never did get over that."

Fleeda Jones remembers one of Diz's first disappointments in baseball: "They used to have a [semipro] baseball team over at Holdenville. He went up there and wanted to play. He went up with overalls on with a nail holding the bib and barefooted and they wouldn't let him play. By looking at him they thought he couldn't be good enough."

Diz loved playing baseball. But life at home was growing more and more difficult.

One day in March 1926, Diz left home for school and never returned. "They didn't know where he was at," says Ornie, who remembers the search for Diz. "They looked all over for him. Somebody heard he'd gone into the army and they found him down there. He'd went into the army so he could play ball. He'd run away from home."

Dizzy Dean was, by his own admission, "the worst soldier in God's living world." His first sergeant at Fort Sam Houston, James Brought, agreed: "He was by every measuring stick invented the worst soldier in this or any army. Legend hell! He was a menace. There were times when I know if that .45 I was wearing had ammunition in it I'd have shot him full of holes even if he was the best baseball pitcher I ever saw."

Jay Dean didn't run away from his Spaulding home that cold March morning in 1926 with the army or the big leagues as his destination. He might have dreamed of making a living as a baseball pitcher, but the reality of his flight was much more down to earth. He'd actually taken the bus south to stay with his stepbrother, Claude Parham, who lived in Houston. It was Parham, who had already served in the army, who convinced Jay that he too should sign up: the pay was good, you got free meals, a free bed, and, what's more, no picking cotton.

"When he was 15 he lied about his age and got in the army down in San Antonio," Pat Dean told a '34 interviewer. Actually he was sixteen and big for his age. Victor Vogel, author of *Soldiers of the Old Army,* a book about the U.S. Army between the World Wars, says it was easier to join at sixteen than it sounds: "A lot of boys lied about their age. They weren't checked. It was sort of an easy-going period of time. I knew a man who enlisted at 16. Diz probably didn't have a birth certificate. I didn't have one. You had to be 18 to enlist. The minimum was dropped later but it was 18 prior to the Selective Service Act of 1940. But it wasn't difficult to join early. Lots of boys did."

Jay took the train from Houston to Fort Sam Houston in San Antonio to enlist. It was the first time he had ever ridden on a train. He was assigned to the Third Wagon Company, Second Infantry Division. He always claimed that on his first day in the army he was ordered to shovel horse manure in the fort's stables, a task he recalled reading about in second-grade mythology: "like that there Hercules." It wasn't exactly the high life: twenty-one dollars a month to clean the stalls in the horse barn.

Diz didn't find the army to his liking. It was too much spit and polish and discipline. And too much manure shoveling. He was only sixteen; he didn't relish getting up at dawn to march endlessly and pointlessly. After all, there wasn't any war going on.

"A lot of the boys he soldiered with told me about him," Pat said in '34. " 'The orneriest, laziest kid in the outfit,' they said."

But then something happened. "They put him to playing baseball," recalled Pat. "That was his first competitive game in the army. He took to it like a duck to water."

In their spare time the soldiers in Diz's outfit would often go out and toss a ball around. In the competitive atmosphere of the army the soldiers would try to outdo each other by firing the ball. Diz's fastball was uncatchable without a glove. His ability soon attracted the attention of the company's first sergeant, Brought, and he was drafted onto the company's ragtag team.

"I played my first formal baseball game when the Third Wagon Company met the Twelfth Field Artillery," Diz told Francis X. Tolbert in *The Saturday Evening Post*. "Top Sergeant Johnny Brought, of the Twelfth, liked the way I done in the game. He said if I'd transfer to the Twelfth I could play ball more and shovel manure less."

And that was just what Diz wanted to hear. "I was in trouble anyhow with an officer. This here officer had called up and asked me when I was going to haul over some manure to put on the flower beds at his quarters. And I answered, 'Right soon, sir; you are Number Two on my manure list.' He figured I was getting smart with him. My chances of getting promoted to PFC in the Third Wagon Company wasn't too good."

In addition to the fastball, Brought might have seen something of himself in the young Jay Dean. Brought had quit school after the sixth grade and worked in the Pennsylvania coal mines for a time before hopping a train to Texas, seeking a better life. He too landed at Fort Sam Houston, where he enlisted. After distinguishing himself in France during World War I, he returned home as General John J. Pershing's hand-picked color-guard bearer. Brought rode on Pershing's right-hand side as America's fighting men paraded in the capitals of Europe before returning to New York to be cheered by throngs of bystanders. He knew firsthand what the army could do for an uneducated young man.

And like Dean, his off-duty time was consumed playing baseball. In his younger days he had had his offers, money laid out before him if he would only sign with this team or that team. But Brought appreciated the stability the army gave him and rejected all the opportunities to play professional baseball. By the time Diz arrived at Fort Sam, Brought was managing a very good baseball team for the Twelfth Field Artillery, a team known around town as "Army Laundry." In no time Diz was assigned to, and pitching for, Army Laundry. He also showed up as a cook in the headquarters of the Twelfth with Mess Sergeant Obie Opalinski as his boss.

Diz's kitchen skills were completely lacking. On one occasion he cooked up a batch of biscuits for the company. When he walked into the mess hall to see how the fellows liked his dish, he was pelted by a hail of brick-hard biscuits.

But his cooking skills were no worse than any of his other military skills. The San Antonio *Light* reported, "He (frequently) showed up at formations with his wrap leggings dragging behind him." Another time at Camp Stanley he turned a caisson too sharply, hit a support pole, and dragged down a whole shed.

Twenty-five years later at a reunion with his former charge, Sergeant Brought still shuddered at the thought of Dean's dirty mess kit. A 1952 issue of *The Fourth Army Recruiter* newsletter reported that when Brought shuddered, Diz just guffawed: "Shucks, Jimmy. I didn't eat out of that blamed thing. I just used it for inspections."

Dizzy Dean's decidedly unmilitary ways caused him to be shifted around among the companies of the Twelfth, but he always seemed to wind up back with Sergeant Brought and the only jobs that seemed to suit him: loading wagons and driving the teams.

And pitching for the company team.

In the young Dean, Brought saw a diamond star in the rough. Although he had a blazing fastball, Diz lacked control. Brought adopted Diz as his special project and Diz in turn came to think of Brought as a father. Brought couldn't seem to teach Diz discipline or the army way, but he was able to teach him the art of control. That was Sergeant Johnny Brought's contribution to Dizzy Dean's career. That and Dizzy's nickname.

There are several stories about the origin of the nickname "Dizzy."

Diz's 1934 Goudey baseball card notes, "Dizzy made the White Sox dizzy trying to bat against him several years ago and so they dubbed him 'Dizzy.'" Diz's father repeated the story to a United Press reporter at the '34 series, declaring that it happened at a 1930 spring training game against the White Sox. "One of the Sox batters was having real difficulty with Dean's slants and complained, 'I cain't hit that dizzy pitcher' and the name just seemed to stick."

Roy Stockton's 1935 article in *The Saturday Evening Post* told another variation of the same story: "The nickname 'Dizzy' is a transferred epithet. He was striking out Chicago White Sox hitters in an exhibition game in Texas and had the batters groggy. He was giving Chicago a headache. He was a pitcher of dizziness. Somebody called him Dizzy and it stuck."

And Diz's 1952 film biography, *The Pride of St. Louis,* which was sanctioned by Diz, placed it in that same 1930 exhibition game. A White Sox coach tries to rattle Diz, taunting: "All right, knock this dizzy kid out of the box ... He's dizzy ... Let's get busy on Dizzy."

But the fact is it came from Sergeant James Brought. Brought's son Bob, who lives in San Antonio, tells the story as it was told to him by his father. "Dad pointed out to Private Dean that to accomplish the art [of control] you must practice and practice. One morning as Dad entered the Twelfth Field Artillery mess hall, where Dean was on KP, he heard one heck of a noise coming from the basement. After investigating the noise, he found—to his dismay—Private Dean throwing potatoes at a trash can lid which was hung from the ceiling. Dad stopped the private and asked just what he was doing at 0530 in the morning. Private Dean only smiled and said, 'You said practice, Sergeant Brought, so I am and I'm still on KP too.' Dad's only answer was, 'Why you dizzy son-of-a-bitch, but not with potatoes.' The incident was told throughout the Twelfth Field Artillery that day, and so the name 'Dizzy' stuck."

Regimental baseball games were played on Mondays. Brought knew Diz was going out on Sundays and making a few extra bucks pitching for town teams in south Texas: Castroville and Seguin and New Braunfels. And he didn't mind as long as it didn't hurt his pitching for the regimental club.

On one particular Saturday Brought called Private Diz in to remind him he was to pitch an important game Monday against the Ninth Infantry and its star pitcher, Joe Holmes. He ordered his ace to rest over the weekend. But on Monday he picked up the paper to see the headline DEAN PITCHES DOUBLEHEADER FOR CAS-TROVILLE; WINS BOTH GAMES. Brought called Diz on the carpet, threatening him with every legal form of military punishment, then sent him out to pitch against Holmes and the Ninth. Diz threw a shutout. Brought told the San Antonio paper: "What could I do to the big lug but forgive him?"

But he could do more. And soon he did.

He took to throwing him in the guardhouse for safekeeping before an important pitching assignment. Brought reasoned, "Diz loved to play baseball.... When I'd make him quit pitching batting practice, he'd get a catcher's glove and warm up Zip Myler and the others, and I had to go take the glove away from him. One of the sergeants came to me and said: 'Jimmy, this guy'll do anything in the world you tell him to but you have to tell him so many times.'"

It was around this time that the Deans' slightly retarded brother, Elmer, became lost.

Diz said he, Paul, and their father were in the first Model T in the caravan while Elmer had the bedrolls, cooking things, and the nine-foot cotton sacks in the second auto.

"We come up to a railway crossing and a big freight train was coming. Paul, driving the first car, made it across the track ahead of the freight. Elmer had to wait for the train. Paul drove on, figuring Elmer would soon catch up. But the train stopped and blocked Elmer for about twenty minutes. Then Elmer must have took the wrong turn further up the road. For he never caught up with us. That was in 1925, and we didn't see him again until 1930. We hunted for him."

Tolbert of *The Saturday Evening Post* reported, "Elmer happened to get his hands on a Sunday Dallas *News,* and while looking for the funny papers he saw Dizzy's photograph on the sports page. 'This here player favors Jay Hanna,' Elmer said. 'Reckon he could of quit cotton picking and got into ball? It is Jay Hanna! He must be right smart of a ballplayer to get his picture run in the paper. Hope he ain't got losted from paw and Paul.'"

Tolbert said Elmer, who had been put into peonage by a farmer, found a friendly druggist to write a letter to Dizzy.

Wiley Thornton, who researched Elmer's disappearance for Paul's book, contradicts the dates in Tolbert's story. In a letter to the Baseball Hall of Fame Thornton says Elmer Dean was lost from 1929 until 1934: "Paul, Mr. Dean, Elmer, and a friend were separated on the way back from south Texas after cotton-picking season when a red light held up Paul and Mr. Dean. Paul and Mr. Dean never caught up. They spent a night on the Bratos River near Waco looking for Elmer to come by. No Elmer. Elmer worked on a farm near Plummerville, Arkansas. He went into a drugstore there, saw pictures of Diz and Paul, told the druggist they were his brothers, and the druggist contacted the Deans, who had figured Elmer was dead. Reunion in Plummerville, Arkansas, after the nineteen thirty-four Series."

Raymith Wilson heard the story from Pat. "They were in Dallas and had bought a popcorn machine for him to use for ball games. They got him all new clothes and went over to pick him up. He said, 'I've been hearing about you. I knew you were playing ball someplace.' They said, 'You go to the house and get your clothes. We've come to get you.' They put him in the car: 'Toss those clothes out, we've got better things for you to put on.' And they stopped at a motel and had him change clothes."

Paul contradicted Diz's version, telling the *Sporting News,* "The *Post* story said Diz was with us when Elmer was separated from the family. Diz wasn't—he was in the Army at Fort Sam Houston, Texas.

"Tolbert stated that Elmer was 'put into peonage' while he was away from the family. That statement reflects unfavorably on Elmer, and it is not true. Elmer was working as a farmhand, and he was paid by the month—just like thousands of other farmhands are paid. He hadn't been mistreated, and Diz and I did not beat up the farmer he had been working for, like the *Post* story said we did. The only trouble we had with the farmer was an argument over $20 back pay that he owed Elmer, and there wasn't any fight at all."

Dizzy finally admitted that he was in the army when Elmer was lost.

By the winter of 1928–1929 Dizzy Dean was tiring of army life. While Diz appreciated the preferential treatment he received as the unit's star pitcher, he was still in the army and subject to army rules and army discipline.

His moans about the army brought results in the winter of 1928. According to one story Diz told, his brother Paul took nearly one fourth of his annual wages from picking cotton, $120, and bought Diz's way out of the service.

Vic Vogel confirms that in the army of that period, you could get out before your hitch was up by paying a lump sum of money.

"After 12 months you could buy your way out for $120. It dropped after the first year to $100. Then it dropped ten dollars a month down to $30. It was a routine matter. Conditions were entirely different prior to World War II."

But it wasn't Paul who bought Diz out of the military. Nor was it his father, as another story went. It was none other than the San Antonio Public Service Company.

3

Turning Pro

Dizzy told the story a hundred times in a hundred different ways. This was the version he told in "The Dizzy Dean Dictionary," a pamphlet published by Falstaff Brewing Corp. in 1943.

In them days it was easy to git out of the army 'cause we wasn't fightin' nobody. And I figgered the Twelfth Field Artillery could git along without me. After all I had given them mules three of the best years of my life.

I was way ahead of them army sergeants. I started lookin' for some kinda easier job. After several months I heard about a soft job in San Antonio in the meter-readin' department of the Public Service Company.

A fellar tole me that readin' meters was the easiest work a man could do without actually bein' unemployed.

After talkin' to the boss at the company I figgered maybe meter readin' was just about the easiest job I knowed anything about.

The only bad thing about it was you had to bend over once in a while.

Finally I ask the boss if he was sure they ain't got a easier job than meter readin'.

Well, he said there was only one job any easier. That was assistant to a meter reader. That's the job I took.

Dizzy told the story a hundred times in a hundred different ways. One time it would be Paul who would slave away in the fields, saving his hard-earned dollars to buy unhappy Dizzy out of the army. Another time it would be Pa who came up with the money.

In a 1938 *Liberty* magazine article Diz claimed that when he told his father he was joining the army, "It was a shock to me to see tears come to his eyes as he shook my hand and to hear his voice tremble as he said, 'I'll buy you out, son, the first good cotton year I get.' He made good on that promise, and not long afterward. Made good on it, although it took almost every dollar he got out of his first good cotton crop.... He'd sold his cotton crop prematurely and at a low price so he could buy me out."

It was a great story: hardworking family member saves pennies earned picking cotton, pays Dizzy's way out of army so he can embark on pro baseball career.

Diz told it so many times that he may even have begun to believe it.

But it wasn't exactly the way it was. Let Fonce Burkhardt of Type Creek, Texas, tell the story. He was there.

"I was playing on the San Antonio Public Service Company baseball team in nineteen twenty-nine. I was first baseman. Before the league opened, we would schedule preseason games. Our manager, Riley Harris, scheduled a game with Post Laundry out of Fort Sam Houston. Being the visiting team we gave them first hitting, then we got our batting practice. We looked at 'em and thought it was going to be a warm-up. But it took us ten or eleven innings to beat them, two to one. Dizzy was pitching for them. After we went back to the bench, we'd tell Riley, 'Get that s.o.b. on our team.' So they bought him out of the army, although they denied it. San Antonio Public Service Company

36

bought him for one hundred and fifty dollars, and we got him on our team."

It was an open secret in San Antonio at the time. The power company bought Diz out of the army and gave him a job so he could pitch for their company team. It was not an uncommon occurrence. Many company teams in that era had semipro and former pro players on their rosters, guys who worked for the company so they could play on the company baseball squad.

Diz filled out his San Antonio Public Service Company job application on April 9, 1929.

He listed his name as "Jay Herman Dean," his birth date as "16 day Jan. 1911," and his birthplace as "Holdenville, Oklahoma." Of course none of that was correct.

He noted that he was living with his father and that his current address was "412 Ash St. Sanantian [sic] Texas."

He was, he told his prospective employer, single, with a ninth-grade education and no debt.

In the space marked "If unmarried and parents are not living, name and address of nearest relative," he listed his stepbrother, "Claude S. Parham, Houston."

His only reference was James Brought, his old army sergeant.

According to the company folder he was hired that day as a "Helper Elec. Dist."

"When we got him, we put him in the meter department," recalls Burkhardt. "He was what they call a helper. We had three journeymen, on a crew of five, and he and I were the helpers. That's an aide—grunts they used to call them. We were working downtown, putting up meters at night, new meters. He said, 'They charge these people for this electricity?' That's how naive he was."

Diz's pay almost quadrupled in his new job. In the army he'd made twenty-one dollars a month. "They'd start you off at three-fifty a day and after six months go to four-fifty a day," says Burkhardt. Diz was now making almost as much in a week as he'd made in a month in the army.

His new job wasn't shoveling manure. But it wasn't a piece of cake either. "We worked every cotton-picking day till five o'clock," says Burkhardt. "There wasn't no sloughing off 'cause we were ballplayers."

Burkhardt remembers the first major work assignment his crew had after Diz came on board: "We had to cut the downtown network from a two-circuit to a one-circuit system. We had to change the meters out because of the connections. We'd have to work all night long."

And that was when Diz first showed his true colors.

"In these big office buildings old Diz'd always be missing. We'd find him in one of the offices asleep in a swivel chair. One time we couldn't find him. He'd gone out to the old Model T truck to get materials and never come back. We finally found him. What he'd done was he'd took the front seat out and was laying in the backseat."

The workers were a little unhappy with their shiftless new colleague: "One of the journeymen said to go to the underground boys and get a magneto-ringer. I found the guys in underground and borrowed a magneto. There was three of us. One held the case of the magneto itself, one held the electrode to one of Diz's hands—he was spread-eagled with his arm out. And I held the other electrode to the other hand. The guy with the magneto started cranking it. It gave Diz a little shock on his hands, and they started twitching. The second time the guy cranked it, Diz jumped up and ran across the parking lot; he ran so fast he even sprained his ankle. He ran around, and when he finally came back he said, 'Oooo, it eeetches.' He said, 'What are you son of a bitches doing?'

"We were working, sweating and all, and he run off. That's what that stinker would do. He would gyp us, so we fixed him with that magneto. Incidentally, I don't think we never had any more trouble with him sleeping on the job."

Even if Diz did reform his work habits, he knew his future was not in rewiring buildings. It was in winning baseball games. And there was no sloughing off when it came to that.

"We played every weekend, Sundays," says Burkhardt. "We had three more pitchers, but when we went up against a tough team, he started." And finished. Diz would later recall that he won sixteen games that season, not bad for a weekend pitcher.

The San Antonio Public Service team was the terror of the city league. "We went all the way to the state and should have won that."

And Diz was the star of the team.

Says Burkhardt, "He'd tell us sometimes when we were through hitting, he'd say, 'You stay on the bench I don't need you.' We'd say, 'Rules and regulations call for us to.' But then he'd strike out the side. You could call it bragging, but it was like that guy in the movies, 'No brag just fact.'"

Burkhardt recalls a trip the team took west to the border town of Del Rio to play its semipro team, the Cowboys. "They were a bunch of minor leaguers who couldn't make the big leagues. They got their jobs because they were ballplayers; course, I did, too. So did Diz. It was prohibition. We'd go across the river to Ciudad Acuña and eat Mexican food and drink beer. One night Riley was watching Diz because he knew somebody had to take care of him. Diz got away from him, and when he found him, he was in one of these bistros where these gals would get you in and get you to pay two dollars a beer for them. We got him out of there fast."

The only team that gave Diz any trouble that season was the touring Cuban All-Stars. They played San Antonio Power Company a doubleheader, splitting the two games, knocking Diz out of the box in the game he pitched.

Diz's pitching prowess was well known at the time. Not so well advertised was his hitting. "Diz was a good hitter," recalls

Burkhardt. "Once we were playing Oakland, Texas, and they had beaten everything on the east end of Texas. They had a pitcher name of Lynn hadn't even lost a game. Dizzy singled to left field. The ball got by the left fielder so Diz kept running, around third, and the shortstop in short left had the ball as he rounded third. The third-base coach was trying to stop him, and he wouldn't stop. He was going to get a home run out of it. The catcher had the ball, and Diz was about ten feet away. He was going to slide, he jumped instead, caught his spike shoe, flew up in the air, and sprained his ankle."

Despite the injury Diz continued to play. Against the advice of his manager.

"The next week we went to Yoakum. Diz wasn't supposed to be able to play because of his ankle, but he talked Riley into going on the bus. He smuggled his uniform on."

Diz's competitive fire wouldn't allow him to miss a game, even though his ankle was swelled up as big as a softball.

"Diz pitched the second game with that sprained ankle and won, six to one. And Yoakum was a good team. They had Beau Bell—who later played with the Browns. He was a college boy at the time. And Slim McGrew, who'd played for the Senators, was on that team. Beau Bell popped a home run over their short right-field fence. But that was all they got, and with that sprained ankle Diz pitched and won. Beat 'em so bad the Yoakum fans were hanging cow bones on the screen, they were so disgusted."

The fastball was there, along with the control. Only one element of the Dizzy Dean of the thirties wasn't yet fully formed: the sense of humor. "He wasn't any more of a clown than the rest of us. He had his fun like everybody else."

But what Burkhardt says he remembers most about his old teammate was his emotions, which he wore on his shirtsleeve: "He didn't have much of an education, but he had a heart as big as a house. I remember we got paid twice a month. There was a little old lady, kind of a recluse, who lived near the plant we all worked at. She knew when paydays were, and she'd come and beg for money. She came in once—she got mixed up and came a day early. Diz was wearing striped overalls—that's all he wore. He was six-three, and she wasn't five feet. She was begging for money, and all he had was change. Back then there was a café down the street where you could buy lunch for thirty-five cents. He put thirty-five cents back in his pocket for lunch and gave her the rest. He had a big heart."

And soon he would have a fat billfold.

Diz told the story of his signing with the Cardinals this way: "A friend of a big league scout seen me on the mound one day and started burnin up the telephone lines between San Antonio and St. Louis. The Cardinals number one scout came down to Texas and ask me to throw a few balls. I throwed four balls and the guy sez that's enuff. That ended my career as assistant-meter-reader. They signed me up to a contract for three hundred bucks a month."

Don Curtis was the name of the scout, but he was far from the Cardinals number-one scout. In actuality, he was a railroad man, a brakeman on the Katy line, the Kansas-Texas Railroad, that ran between Waco and San Antonio. His scouting was strictly part-time, and it was for the Houston Buffaloes of the Class AAA Texas League, not the big-league Cardinals.

Fred Ankenman, then president of the Buffaloes, wrote in his memoir, *Four Score and More,* "A Katy railroad conductor mentioned Diz to Don as he knew Don was looking for young player prospects. Dizzy was pitching on Sundays for the San Antonio Public Service team, which was managed by a man named Riley Harris whom Don had met some time previously. At the first opportunity, Don went out to the park to see Dizzy pitch."

Curtis would later recall, "After seeing Diz pitch less than a dozen fastballs, I knew he had what it takes. I called Riley Harris to one side and asked him if he could have Diz in his room at the Mailton Hotel that night. The three of us met at the hotel as I had requested and before I left, Dizzy signed a contract with the Houston Club calling for a salary of $100.00 per month and no bonus."

Fonce Burkhardt says, "Our manager acted as an adviser to Diz so he wouldn't get whopped." Diz didn't get whopped but one hundred dollars a month was not a mammoth raise from the eighty-some dollars a month he was earning working for the utilities company. But it was a contract with a professional baseball team. No more fetching tools for electricians and pitching on weekends. Now he could do what he loved and get paid for it.

Curtis sent the contract to Ankenman. There was a minor error and it was sent back for a correction, but there was no hold-out by Diz, who would later become famous for such tactics. The second contract was returned intact to Ankenman and forwarded on to the Cardinals' office in St. Louis, since Houston was a Cardinal farm club.

It was a standard baseball contract between J. H. Dean of 412 Ash Street, San Antonio, and the Houston Base Ball Association, with Ankenman signing for Houston. Don Curtis witnessed the contract. The contract date was May 25, 1929, but because the pro season was already well underway, Diz was not required to report until the spring of 1930.

The signing happened quickly and simply, but over the years Diz would embellish his end a bit. Detroit *Free Press* columnist Doc Green wrote that Dizzy told him the people who scouted him thought he was left-handed: "That was because they seen me killing squirrels with stones th'owing left-handed. If I'd of th'owed right-handed I would have squashed them." The story was straight out of Paul Bunyan, pure Dizzy and pure hogwash.

4

The Old Pro

On March 10, 1930, Jerome Herman Dean, as he was now calling himself, reported to the Houston Buffaloes' training camp at Buffalo Stadium in Houston. The Buffs were a St. Louis Cardinal farm club, but they didn't train with the major-league team in Florida. Instead, they saved money by training at home. Times were hard for the minor leagues. Only a decade before there had been forty-three recognized minor leagues. By 1930 that number had shrunk to twenty-one.

The Cardinals and their general manager, Branch Rickey, had pioneered the concept of a farm system in the early twenties as a method of competing with the wealthier teams in the east. They signed young ballplayers by the truckload and threw them into the fray of the lower minor leagues. The survivors worked their way to the top, where the major-league team benefited from this grand-scale competition. The system worked, and by the spring of 1930 the Cards had won pennants in two of the last four years and would win again in '31. Houston was loaded with these combative young farm hands and Jerome Dean was not expected to make an impact. In fact he was scheduled to be farmed out to Shawnee in the Class C Western Association.

But Diz attracted attention almost from his first day in camp. Not with his mouth, as would later be the case, but with his arm. Legend has it that Branch Rickey arrived for an inspection and was told by a veteran minor-league catcher named Abbott, "I've been warming Dean up, and he has more stuff than any pitcher I've ever caught."

There was a veteran catcher named Abbott in the Cardinals' farm system that year, Charles Abbott. But if this actually happened, it didn't happen in the Buffaloes' camp, because Abbott wasn't in the Buffaloes' camp. He reported to St. Joe's camp in Shawnee, Oklahoma, on April 5, "straight from the oil fields," according to an account in the *St. Joseph Gazette*. Diz had reported two days earlier.

Rickey told *Liberty* magazine in 1938 that the first time he saw Dizzy was at the Saints' camp in Shawnee. "He pitched sixteen balls, striking out three batters. [I] told the manager to work the boy another inning. Dean repeated his strike-out performance with eighteen pitches."

Another legend has it that Diz's first taste of big-league hitters came in an exhibition between Houston and the major-league Chicago White Sox. He supposedly faced such established big leaguers as Willie Kamm, Carl Reynolds, a lifetime .300 hitter, Bennie Tate, and Johnny Watwood, and fanned eleven with his fastball. This was also said to be the game in which Diz got his nickname. One report had exasperated White Sox coach Mike Kelly telling his humiliated players, "That kid is making you look dizzy." The Sox did train in San Antonio that spring, and they scrimmaged a number of area minor-league clubs. But there is no record of a game between the Sox and the Buffs. And Dizzy was already Dizzy by the spring of 1930.

What actually happened, as Buffs president Fred Ankenman reported in his autobiography, was that in training camp young Dizzy caught the eye of one Eugene Bailey, an ex-Dodger outfielder who had managed the Buffs in 1929. "Dean, inexperienced, was not ready for the Texas League," Ankenman wrote. "And so he was one of the youngsters to be optioned to a lower classification. Bailey was impressed with Diz, having seen him during our spring training season, and urgently requested that we option him to the St. Joseph Club." Bailey had a reason for the request. He was to be the manager of the new St. Joseph club, which would be playing its first season in the Class A Western League.

Bailey was not the only one to notice Diz that spring. Lloyd Gregory, the *Sporting News* Houston correspondent, wrote of the Houston spring camp: "Two of the rookies showing exceptional promise are: Dizzy Dean from San Antonio, and Roger Traweek from Mexia, both right-handers. These young twirlers lack polish but each has a lot of natural ability and a season in class D baseball would do wonders for them."

But Diz didn't go to Class D, the bottom rung on the professional baseball ladder. He had too much stuff for that. On April 1 the Buffaloes announced they were sending Dizzy, along with two other farmhands, outfielder Vernon "Lefty" Deck and shortstop Blaine Kunes, to the Class A St. Joseph Saints.

It was apparent from the day Diz reported that he was the most talented pitcher on St. Joe's staff. In an unbylined story the *Gazette* reported he had "probably the fastest ball in the Western League since Bullet Joe Brown was with Oklahoma City several seasons ago." Diz was even selected to pitch St. Joe's first exhibition game April 6 against Shawnee, another Cardinal farm club.

A mediocre showing in that game—Diz pitched six innings, allowing five runs on ten hits—probably cost him the opening-day pitching assignment. "Dean did not do so good today but it was his first contest in organized baseball and he was nervous," reported the *Gazette*. Diz came back four days later in a relief appearance but was even less effective. He gave up three runs and

six hits in just three innings of work. That cinched his demotion
to the number two spot in the pitching rotation.

The Saints broke camp on April 14, heading home in antici-
pation of an April 19 opening game.

The return of baseball was a big event in St. Joseph, and the
town was preparing to celebrate its new team with a parade and a
picnic. The night before the season opener the players were treated to a movie at the Missouri Theater: *They Learned About
Women,* which, the newspaper was quick to point out, despite its
title "had a baseball theme."

In the week leading up to opening day the *Gazette* ran a daily
feature called "Introducing 1930 Saints." Each column profiled
two of the ballplayers. Diz's profile, which ran April 14, was a
doozy, a mix of fact and fiction that would set a standard for
future Dizzy Dean stories:

J.H. (Dizzy) Dean might well be called the long end of the St.
Joseph Western League club. He stands 6 feet 4 inches tall in his sock
feet. Dean is having his chance in professional baseball but with a
world of speed, control, change of pace and a knuckle ball which
hops a foot, he appears to need only experience to be able to toss 'em
up with the best of hurlers in the Western League this season. Dean
pitched the San Antonio Public Service team to the semi-pro championship of the city last season and immediately went into the state
tournament, from which the aggregation emerged champions.

Dean, who had accomplished the stupendous task of pitching and
winning five games in one week, was signed by the St. Louis Cardinals for a tryout. He spent a month in the camp of the Houston Buffs
and then reported to St. Joseph in good shape.

Dean also holds a record of thirty-nine consecutive scoreless
innings, made last year with the San Antonio club. Joe Schultz, manager of the Houston Buffs, finally broke his string of consecutive tal-
lyless innings with a two-base hit which scored a runner.

The lanky hurler is a native of Oklahoma. He graduated from St. Joseph's High School of Oklahoma City in 1925 after having participated in several sports. Dean ended three years play with the Independent Oil Company baseball team in 1926 and continued to hurl semipro ball for Spaulding, Okla. He went with the Public Service Company team at San Antonio in 1928 and won seventeen and lost only two games that year. Last year he doubled the number of wins of the previous season, emerging victor in thirty-four contests, but lost only two.

The Public Service baseball team not only won the San Antonio championship but the organization's basketball squad copped a title. Dean was a member of that aggregation, playing center. The club won twenty-one games and wasn't on the short end of a score in any melee.

The newly minted high school graduate Dizzy Dean made his professional debut on April 20, 1930, in the first game of a doubleheader against the Denver Bears. The *Gazette* reported that 3,000 fans braved cold weather to witness Diz's professional debut. It was the Saints' second game of the season; Mace Brown, who would later become a relief specialist for the Pirates, had pitched and won the season opener the day before.

Dizzy was triumphant, allowing three runs and four hits in an extra-inning affair won when the Saints scored two runs in the bottom of the tenth. The final score was 4–3.

The *Gazette* observed, "Dean deserves lots of credit for that 4-hit game. Had it gone only nine innings he would have made his professional debut with at least a 1-bingle game. That hit, by Vargas in the seventh, was a fluke and could have been called an error."

It was an impressive debut. Diz struck out eight while walking only one. He didn't allow a hit until the seventh. Denver scored two runs off him in the third but all three were unearned. He did give up a home run to Jimmy "Choppy" Adair in the tenth, and he also hit two batters.

Three days later Diz was back on the mound, but this time his fortunes weren't so good. He was pounded by the Pueblo team, 13-6; in addition Diz got pounded in a fistfight with Pueblo first baseman Vic Shiell. Shiell took exception to an inside pitch in the eighth inning, he and Diz had words, and soon they were locked in mortal battle. Shiell was cut up badly enough in the ensuing melee to require hospital attention.

The *Gazette* reported:

> The Pueblo club had been "riding" Dizzy Dean, starting Saints hurler, throughout the game. In the ninth Frey beat out an infield hit. Shiell, first sacker for the visitors, coaching at the initial bag, is said to have called Dean a rather foul name and the elongated Saint twirler made for him. Before the pair had been separated Dean's lefts and rights had inflicted considerable punishment on the husky Puebloan. Both were chased from the game by the umpires. They will be fined and possibly suspended.

In only his fifth professional appearance Diz made history by starting a triple play, the first in the history of the Western League. The opponent was again Pueblo, and Diz was called on in the ninth to relieve. With St. Joe up by two and men on first and second, nobody out, Diz caught a weak fly off the bat of a McIsaacs, whirled, and threw to second baseman Dewey Bondurant, who whipped the ball to first baseman Chief Wano for a game-ending triple play. The Saints won, 8-6. Diz would later claim this happened in his first professional game, an error that was probably as much a mistake in memory as an intentional exaggeration.

Diz won three in a row in May, quite a feat considering the ineptitude of his own team. The Saints would finish the season dead last in the Western League.

The Saints didn't just play badly, they looked bad. Sec Taylor, sports editor of the Des Moines *Register,* wrote after the May 11 game between Des Moines and St. Joe: "The St. Joseph team does not make a presentable outfit for one owned by a major league club. Gray, brown and white outfits were in evidence. The team looks like Pumpkin Center's high school nine instead of one in a professional league."

Branch Rickey attended St. Joe's May 14 game at Omaha. The *Gazette,* noting the June 1 deadline for cutting the roster to sixteen, speculated that Rickey would make wholesale changes "to bolster the team with new players." The paper said there was only one player who definitely would not be cut. "Dean will remain, that is a certainty."

Box Score of Diz's First Professional Game

Denver at St. Joseph, Missouri, April 20, 1930

Western League

DENVER	AB	H	O	A	E
Adair, ss	5	1	3	4	0
Granada, lf	4	1	2	0	0
Metz, 3b	5	0	2	2	0
Parker, rf	3	0	2	1	0
Cheeves, cf	3	0	1	0	0
Crawley, 1b	2	0	11	0	0
Palmer, 2b	4	0	4	2	1
Vargas, c	4	2	3	1	0
Piercy, p	1	0	0	1	0
Jolley, p	3	0	0	7	0
Totals	34	4	28*	18	1

*One out when winning run scored.

HOUSTON	AB	H	O	A	E
Honea, cf	4	1	2	0	0
Glassgow, 2b	4	1	3	1	1
Kunes, ss	5	1	2	1	0
Cotelle, lf	3	1	2	0	0
Wano, 1b	4	1	9	0	0
Hall, rf	2	0	2	0	0
a-Ferguson	1	0	0	0	0
Mueller, 3b	4	0	3	4	0
Abbott, c	4	1	7	0	2
Dean, p	3	0	0	4	0
Deck, rf	0	0	0	0	0
Totals	34	6	30	10	3

a-Batted for Hall in eighth.

Denver   002 000 000 1—3 4 1
St. Joseph 002 000 000 2—4 6 3

Two base hits—Kunz, Granada. Home run—Adair. Stolen bases—Hosea 2. Double play—Mueller and Glagow.

At the end of June Diz's record was 12-5. But the team was mired in the cellar and manager Bailey was fired, replaced by Everett Booe, who'd played one season in the Pirate outfield before jumping to the old Federal League for a couple of years.

Diz was dazzling during July too, winning another five games and improving his record to 17-8. He was nine games over .500 pitching for a team that was twenty-four games under .500.

One night at Topeka he struck out eleven batters. But Diz was still a young pitcher learning his craft, and another night in

Omaha he would walk ten batters, though he did hang in and win the game.

In addition to his pitching prowess, Diz was also hitting his counterparts on the other clubs pretty good too. He batted .279 for the half season, knocking in twelve runs and even stealing a couple of bases.

The only area the local sportswriters could find to criticize was Diz's fielding. "Dean, anxious to win, fields balls frequently he should leave to the infielders," wrote an uncredited *Gazette* reporter. "Frey [the Pueblo centerfielder] got a hit on a slow grounder down third base when 'Dizzy' cut in on Mueller, who was on the ball."

St. Joe would finish the season dead last with a record of 53-92. Diz would account for one-third of those wins, despite the fact that he would be called up to Houston on August 5.

But he was creating as many headlines off the field as on.

Shortly after he arrived in St. Joe, or so the story goes, he had a run-in with Earl Matthews, the chief of police. Diz was driving his jalopy sixty-five mph, going the wrong way on a one-way street. When he was stopped by the chief, he feigned ignorance of the law and tried to talk his way out of the ticket. "Why I was only going one way." He blushed. When asked who he was, he replied, "I'm Dizzy Dean, who beat up that big Pueblo first baseman the other day." It didn't work, and he was hauled into court and fined. But Diz didn't hold a grudge, and the next time he saw Chief Matthews, he slapped him on the back and said, "How you doing, Chiefie boy?"

Diz also displayed an ignorance of modern ways by registering for rooms at the YMCA, the St. Francis Hotel, and the Robidoux Hotel. He didn't know you had to check out when you weren't in attendance and used each as a convenient crashing pad, depending on whichever was closest when he got tired.

It's doubtful the one-way street story really happened. Ray "Peaches" Davis, Diz's teammate on the Saints, says he never heard the story. And if anyone heard it at the time, it would have been Davis. A Sportslog column in the April 10, 1930, St. Joseph *Gazette* called Peaches and Diz "inseparable."

But Davis confirms the accuracy of the multiple-room story. "He kept an apartment and rooms in two hotels so that when he wanted to go to bed he could go wherever he was."

Davis also says all those stories about Diz borrowing and losing clothes are true. "Dizzy didn't have any baseball shoes and days he pitched he'd borrow my shoes. One time I gave him some of my clothes. He had plenty of clothes but he'd leave 'em somewhere. He went somewhere with a suitcase of clothes and came back without it so I gave him some clothes."

On August 5, when the call came, Diz was moving up. The Cardinals wanted him to finish the season with the Triple A Houston Buffaloes in the Texas League. He was 17-8 and had won four in a row.

The Sporting News reported it this way:

HOUSTON OBTAINS HURLER

Houston, Tex., August 5—Dizzy Dean, promising righthander, who has been with St. Joseph of the Western League most of the season, has been obtained by the local club of the Texas League. Dean won 17 games and lost eight for the weak St. Joseph entry.

Houston was a big step up for Diz. He was skipping Double A ball entirely and jumping to a league that was only a notch below the big leagues. In the Triple A Texas League he would be facing the most promising young batters, many of whom were destined to win big-league jobs the next spring, and fading veterans with something to prove, men who only weeks earlier had been hitting against the likes of Carl Hubbell and Lefty Grove. He would play against men who had roomed with Babe Ruth, lockered next to Walter Johnson. It was a heady experience for a twenty-year-old who pitched in the second professional game he ever saw.

Diz arrived in Houston at a propitious time. The team had moved into a new stadium only two years earlier, a stadium with a decided pitcher's bent. The new Buffalo Stadium was mammoth; it was 344 feet from home plate to left field, 323 feet from home to right field, and 434 from home to center. And even if a hitter did tag a pitch in the heavy Houston night air, chances were the ball wouldn't escalate above the twelve-foot-tall fences that guarded the outfield.

The palatial park seated 14,000 and cost $400,000 to build.

(It was demolished in '63 and is now the site of Finger Furniture Company. There is a plaque in the furniture store marking where home plate was.)

Diz broke in with a smash, pitching the very night he arrived in Houston. He faced San Antonio and won, 12-1, striking out fourteen. But he didn't get the publicity he deserved for the feat because the same night Waco outfielder Gene Rye hit three home runs in one inning in a 20-7 win at Beaumont.

Diz won his first six starts in the Texas League before losing to Fort Worth. His season climaxed on August 29, when he struck out sixteen batters in an 8-1 win over Beaumont.

He was beginning to create a legend, but, as usual with Diz, the legend wasn't just for pitching.

George Payne, his Houston roommate, told reporters that Diz would borrow his shirts and ties and then leave them in hotel room wastebaskets. He also recalled the time Diz started a road trip carrying a large suitcase containing only a pack of cigarettes.

And the St. Louis *Post-Dispatch* would report on January 1, 1931:

With Dizzy Dean stories becoming as numerous and as widely told as those of the Great Art Shires, Joe Schultz, manager of the Houston Buffs of the Texas League, has come to bat with one.... Dean played with Schultz' team the latter part of the past season before joining the Cardinals.

Dizzy is a pretty fair hitter as pitchers go, and during one game in which the Buffs were plastering the Fort Worth Cats, Dean drove a clean hit down the left field foul line. Ordinarily, it would have been good for two bases, but Dizzy pulled up at first. However, a runner, who was on first at the time, made third on the blow.

On the next pitch, Dean bolted for second. His act crossed up the entire Houston team as well as the Forth Worth players. In the excitement the catcher made a bad throw to second, which made no difference anyway, for no one was covering the bag. The ball shot into the garden and caught the center fielder unawares. Dean and the man on third scored.

When Dizzy got to the bench he found Schultz spitting spirits of nitre.

"Diz," said Skipper Joe, "what were you trying to do? Did you think you got the steal sign on that pitch?"

"No, Mr. Manager," Diz replied. "But I should have got to second on my hit so I decided to get there somehow and even things up."

Diz finished his abbreviated Texas League campaign 8-2 and was named to the league's all-star team. It was his second all-star selection. Earlier he had been named to the Western League all-star team.

He had succeeded spectacularly on two levels in the minor leagues. He had scorched Triple A hitters, ringing up ninety-five strikeouts in only eighty-five innings.

There was only one place left for him to prove himself.

* * *

Dizzy Dean was called up by the parent Cardinal club on September 10, 1930. The Texas League season was at an end, and his call-up was part of a big-league tradition, bringing in talented minor leaguers to get a taste of the big leagues at the tail end of the season. It was the proverbial cup of coffee.

But Diz was not well versed in the ways of the world. He'd ridden a few more trains since that first trip to enlist in the army. And he knew a team bus inside and out. But he didn't know about such things as hotel laundries and room service. The *New York Times* reported, "When Dean was informed at Houston towards the close of the season that he was to report to the Cardinals in New York, he sought to route himself through his home city of San Antonio, explaining that he needed several shirts before going to the big town. So sincere was he about his preparedness that it was only after Dizzy had become thoroughly convinced that shirts could be purchased and washed in New York, that he was persuaded to forgo his trip to San Antonio and report to the Cards in the East, promptly."

The parent club was in the midst of a heated pennant race when Diz arrived. They had been in fourth place, twelve games back, on August 9, but finished the month with seventeen victories in twenty-three games. By the time Diz arrived they were in second place with the first-place Cubs in their sights.

Upon joining the team in New York he had taken one look at the third-place Giants and informed manager Charles "Gabby" Street, "I can beat those clowns." But there was no place for bravado in a pennant race, and Street let the untried Dizzy Dean languish on the bench while the pennant was on the line.

The Cardinals were even hotter in September, winning twenty-one and losing only four. They clinched the pennant on September 27, the next-to-last day of the season, when Jesse Haines, called "Pop" because of his age, thirty-seven, pitched the Cards past the Pirates, 10-5.

There was still one game left in the season, so manager Street called on Diz.

Diz remembered that first game this way in *Dizzy Dean's Dictionary:* "As I'm warming up before the game, the Pirate players think they are goin' to have an easy time of it, since I'm a rookie. Larry French, who has 17 wins to his credit, is their pitcher and he gets a bonus of $1,000 if he wins 18 games. Larry probably thought that bonus was in the bag for sure when he learned he's opposin' a ganglin' kid like me."

Diz got the same treatment any rookie pitcher starting his first game would have gotten. "While I'm warmin' up, the Pirate players start throwin' insults like, 'Busher, you won't last long against us.' And 'We'll send you right back to the sticks where you belong.' When they keep ridin' me, it gets my dander up. So I yell at 'em, 'Yeah, you get me mad now and you won't get no more 'n' three hits off'n me today."

In the first inning it seemed the Pirate players had the rookie rattled. Diz, who was pitching in ill-fitting shoes he borrowed from the smaller (5'10") Burleigh Grimes (Diz was 6'3"), walked the first two hitters, right fielder Gus Dugas and center fielder Paul Waner, before coaxing second baseman George "Boots" Grantham to line out to second. Then third baseman Pie Traynor singled sharply to center, scoring Dugas, and Diz looked to be in trouble. But he composed himself, striking out Adam Comorosky and getting Gus Suhr on a weak grounder to first.

Pitching against the same Pirate lineup, which only twenty-four hours earlier had threatened to keep the Cards out of the World Series, Diz was masterful. He allowed only two hits the rest of the way, finishing with a three-hitter, while striking out five and winning 3-1. Paul Waner, called "Big Poison" because of his hitting prowess (he had 3,152 career hits), failed to muster even a scratch single.

Diz even aided his own cause by singling in the third and scoring the go-ahead run on a steal of home.

After the game, Diz moaned to sportswriters, "Those bums got three hits off'n me."

Box Score of Diz's First Big League Game

Pittsburgh at St. Louis, Sept. 28, 1930

PITTSBURGH	AB	R	H	RBI
Dugas, rf	3	1	0	0
P. Waner, cf	3	0	0	0
Grantham, 2b	3	0	0	0
Traynor, 3b	4	0	2	1
Comorosky, lf	3	0	0	0
Suhr, 1b	4	0	0	0
Sankey, ss	3	0	1	0
Bool, c	3	0	0	0
French, p	3	0	0	0
Totals	29	1	3	1

ST. LOUIS	AB	R	H	RBI
Douthit, cf	4	0	1	1
Adams, 3b	4	1	1	0
High, 2b	4	0	1	1
Bottomley, 1b	2	0	0	0
Orsatti, 1b	1	0	0	0
Hafey, lf	2	0	0	1
Blades, rf	3	0	0	0
Smith, c	3	0	0	0
Gelbert, ss	2	1	1	0
Dean, p	3	1	1	0
Totals	28	3	5	3

OL' DIZ

| Pittsburgh | 100 000 000—1 3 0 |
| St. Louis | 002 001 00x—3 5 0 |

2b—Douthit
BB—Dean 3, French 2
K—Dean 5, French 1
WP—Dean

5

Back to the Bushes

Diz was at his insufferable worst after the '30 season. He'd tasted success in the major leagues and thought it would be his for the taking from then on. He didn't even hang around St. Louis for the World Series, heading immediately south to Charleston, Missouri, where he was to winter with the St. Joseph club's business manager, another avid hunter, Oliver French. Living with French was Branch Rickey's idea; it was for Diz's own protection. He spent most of the winter in the Missouri boot heel, hunting and hanging out. He did venture into Texas in the late fall for a barnstorming tour on a team led by Philadelphia A's slugger Jimmie Foxx.

That winter Diz penned a letter that bordered on the obnoxious to Ken Chilcote, the sports editor of the St. Joseph *Gazette:*

Show me another pitcher in the majors who has never been defeated. I didn't go to the series. Sure, they begged me to come along. I told Mr. Rickey I would wait until next year and win him three games in the World Series. I signed for $700 a month for next year and I guess I can live on that because they make me room with a coach, Joe

Sugden, and his idea of a good time is getting up at seven in the morning and going to bed at ten each night. In two years I'll be of age and maybe Mr. Rickey won't think I need a nursemaid then.

Right after Christmas I guess I'll start training. You see I've got a 16-year-old brother that I'm going to take to camp next year so I've got to kind of coach him on a few pointers about the majors. Next to me I think he will be the greatest pitcher in the world. They tell me I've got the fastest ball of any pitcher. Well you ought to see him lob 'em over.

That winter J. Roy Stockton, the St. Louis sportswriter who would chronicle Diz's career for the next decade, motored down to Charleston, in the southern part of the state near the Kentucky border, for an interview with Dizzy the Great, as Diz had now taken to calling himself. He found Diz, not at the French home, but instead at the Russell Hotel, three blocks away. He'd been too tired to walk home the night before, Diz explained, and had checked in, informing the desk clerk he was to send the bill to "Mr. French, my secretary." Stockton accompanied Diz to his daytime hangout, Ellis Drug Store, where the budding great one chatted with the local high school girls, buying them sodas and swapping flirts. "I personally believe I'm going to win 30 games for the Cardinals but that would sound braggy, so let's make it 25. They're in the bag right now because I'm in swell shape and am going to stay that way," he expounded.

Despite the fact that they had placed Diz with a full-time winter baby-sitter, the Cardinals were still concerned about their youthful pitcher. Rickey told Stockton, "Dean is like an oil burner without a governor. If we could get a governor for him, he would be the greatest pitcher in the world."

Word of the team's concern made its way the 151 miles down to Charleston and Diz reacted, "I'm in good condition and I'm going to stay that way. I'll be the hardest worker on the team. No sir, I'm not going to misbehave. I've never done anything very wrong and I realize that baseball is a great opportunity for me."

Diz would soon contradict that statement.

He reported to Bradenton, Florida, for spring training in early March with the rest of the Cardinal pitchers. Despite his obvious talent and his season-ending success the year before, he was no shoo-in for the staff. After all, the Cardinals were coming off a pennant year. United Press's Leo H. Petersen reported Diz would have to beat out one of the team's veteran pitchers: Burleigh Grimes, Jess Haines, Flint Rhem, Bill Hallahan, Jim Lindsey, or Syl Johnson. Gabby Street told reporters he had one spot open on his pitching staff, and he expected it to be between Dizzy and another gangly rookie right-hander, Paul Derringer. Still, Street was favorably disposed to Diz, calling him his "most promising rookie pitcher and one of the best prospects I have seen in years."

Diz agreed, telling Joe Williams of the New York *World-Telegram*, "I can't miss being a great star because I've got everything."

The first sign of trouble came out of the blue: suddenly IOUs came floating into the Cardinal office from various Bradenton merchants. Dizzy was spending his salary faster than the Cardinals could dish it out. Sportswriters reported the rumor—probably from Branch Rickey—that Dizzy had already spent three-fourths of his 1931 salary and it wasn't even April yet. Rickey called in the pitcher he had labeled "somewhat of a nuisance" and told him he was on a strict budget: $1 a day, to be disbursed by club secretary Clarence Lloyd. He'd sign a sheet: "Received today—$1—Dizzy Dean."

Diz didn't like it but after a two-hour conference with Rickey, he agreed. Rickey and Lloyd then began broadcasting a message to local merchants: no more charge accounts for Dizzy Dean.

If that had been the only problem with Dizzy that spring, he would probably have spent the '31 season in St. Louis. But Diz had trouble getting up for 10:00 a.m. practices. He also ignored direct orders from Street. The final straw probably came on March 29, when Street sat Diz down for a lecture: no more disobeying orders, no more skipping practice. Street explained there were pitchers making three times what Diz was who were able to do as they were told. Diz nodded in assent, promised to walk the straight and narrow, and missed the next practice only a half hour after his dressing-down. Street hit the ceiling: "This kid can't stay in our camp if he is going to disobey all orders. I don't want him to associate with my law-abiding players. If Dean is going to worry anybody this year, it will be the manager of Scottsdale or one of the other farms."

But when the Cardinals broke camp, Diz actually accompanied the team north. The club opened the season with a four-game series in Cincinnati, beginning April 14. They followed with a four-game set in Chicago before opening at home April 22 against the Reds. The Pirates followed the Reds into town. Diz saw no action those first two weeks of the season. It was on May 2, during a three-game series against the Cubs, that Diz got the word: he was going down to Houston.

There was no moaning among Cardinal regulars. There was, if anything, derisive joking. Rookie shortstop Billy Myers asked his roommate, pitcher Jim Lindsey, if he had ever heard of a team losing thirty games in one day. When the befuddled Lindsey asked what he meant, Myers replied, "Dizzy Dean just got sent down."

Ankenman would later recall, "As soon as Joe Schultz and I heard that Street did not wish to carry him on the Cardinal Club, we requested he be optioned to our club. This was satisfactory to everyone, and Diz was happy to come back to Houston. This was a great break for the Houston Club but trouble and worry for me."

When Diz joined the Houston club, they were already sixteen

games into the season. But Diz got off on the right foot. He blanked Wichita Falls, 6-0, on three hits in the opener of a doubleheader his first day back. "You can tell the fans of Houston that the Buffs will win the flag," he told a local reporter. "Despite my late start, I'll win 25 games."

His next outing was just as impressive: he shut out Shreveport, 4-0. Before the month was out he had won five and lost none. Well, none in the box score. He did lose a fight in his fifth victory, a 7-1 triumph over Dallas on May 23.

The newspapers reported: "He knocked down Al Todd, a big, tough catcher. Todd jumped to his feet and shouted, 'You do that again and I'll punch you in the mouth.' When Dean wheeled in another one at Todd's head, the batter charged the mound."

Years later Diz would recall, "Al got the idea I was throwing at him, just because he got a base hit. I didn't throw at him, honest I didn't. Oh, maybe I was trying to move him back from the plate just a little. Next time up he charges out to the mound. I figure I could outtalk him but he didn't say a word. I was waiting and I had a good wisecrack to let him have but he popped me without a word. I kept picking myself up and he kept knocking me down."

Fighting was but one of many ways Diz would exasperate his new manager, Schultz. But unlike Street, Schultz was able to take it in stride. He would later tell Joe Williams another story of Diz's Houston escapades: "Houston was playing Fort Worth and Mr. Dean, who always fancied himself an excellent hitter, got a home run in one of the earlier innings. But along about the fifth or sixth he got into a jam and filled the bases and the manager, one Joe Schultz, took him out. Instead of going to the showers Mr. Dean went directly to the score board, climbed a ladder and removed the one-run marker he had contributed. Then he returned to the dugout. 'And just what was all that funny business about?'

demanded the manager. 'Twarn't no funny business,' groused Mr. Dean. 'If I can't pitch, you can't have my run.'"

And off the field he was as dizzy as ever. Fred Ankenman often told of the times Diz put him on:

"One morning the Houston *Post* carried the story that it would be ladies' night with Dizzy pitching. About ten o'clock that morning, my secretary, Andrew French, answered the phone and said a doctor wanted to talk to me. I took the phone and a gentleman said he was Doctor Morris, a chiropractor, in the Binz Building. He stated that pitcher Dean was in his office with a badly injured shoulder, but he thought, with proper treatment, he could have him ready to pitch again in about thirty days. First, however, he needed my consent for him to go ahead with the proper treatment. This came as quite a shock as Diz was in good shape the night before. I told the doctor to have Diz come to the phone. I asked him 'Diz, what in the world is wrong with you?' He started moaning and telling me how bad his arm was and how he had injured it the night before at the stadium. I told him to get out of that chiropractor's office and go to our club doctor, Dr. J. R. Bost. 'Okay,' he said, 'but I am in awful bad shape.' You can imagine how I felt with him due to pitch that night and to think of losing him for an indefinite time. The game started at eight o'clock. At about seven-thirty, I heard Diz out in the office lobby asking for me. He walked in my office with a big grin. I asked him what his trouble was. He raised his right arm up, felt of his muscle and said, 'Watch me go out and shut those birds out tonight.' I asked him about the doctor who had called me, and he said, 'That was no doctor, it was just a friend of mine, and we wanted to have some fun with you.' He went to the club house, uniformed, and then pitched a shut-out."

Even marriage didn't squelch Diz's practical joking. Ankenman recalled, "On another occasion, Mrs. Dean called me one morning and said Diz would not be at the park that night as he had a bad leg, and she had been putting hot towels on it from time to time. I told her to have him go to Dr. Bost. I do not think he ever went, but he reported that night at the usual time and showed no signs of any leg trouble. It was the practice of Mrs. Dean to get to the park just shortly before game time, coming through one of the ramps leading to the box section. On this particular night, just as she was entering through the ramp, here came Diz running a foot race from left field with one of the visiting players. I was standing in the ramp at the time and when she saw Diz running in a race, she said, 'Can you beat that? Here I have been putting hot towels on his leg all morning and here he is running in a race.' This was just another case of his having a little fun. This time the fun was with both his wife and me."

Diz would later say, "Being sent down to Houston was probably the best thing that ever happened to me." And he was right. Not only did he solidify his pitching reputation with a spectacular season, but he also met the woman who would stabilize his off-the-field life.

It was one of the great whirlwind courtships of all time.

Patricia Nash and Jay Dean were married on June 15, 1931, only days after meeting. "We met on a Monday afternoon and got married the next Monday," Diz would later say. Actually it was a little longer than that. But it was less than two months. He didn't arrive in Houston until May 2. He announced their engagement to the newspapers June 1. And two weeks later they were wed.

The Cardinals were not at all keen on Diz's engagement. They thought it was another impetuous act on the part of their impetuous pitcher. But Diz didn't care what the Cardinals thought; this was true love.

The standard version of the Diz-meets-Pat story—one certified by Diz's authorized movie biography *Pride of St. Louis*—had

Diz meeting her in a department store, where she managed the hosiery department.

Raymith Wilson, one of Diz's childhood friends, says that's not the way Pat told it to her. "She told me the story many times. She said she was in school in Houston and had a room in the apartment building where a bunch of the ballplayers stayed. She said she promised one of her girlfriends she'd have a date with him before he left."

She not only got a date, she got a marriage proposal.

He had big plans for the ceremony: they would get hitched at home plate before the Houston–San Antonio game and then he would throw a no-hitter. Pat vetoed that spectacle. And, ironically, Diz would never throw a no-hitter in his career.

Diz would later claim that it was Ankenman and Schultz who insisted he be married at home plate. "[They] figured it would be swell publicity. I refused point blank."

But Rickey and Breadon in a 1938 *Liberty* magazine article refuted Diz's statement. They told writer Harry Brundidge, "It is a matter of record that the Cardinal management opposed his marriage, that he demanded the right to be married at home plate just before he started pitching and that Ankenman refused to let him."

They were married by Dr. Harry Knowles, pastor of the First Christian Church of Houston, in the church office with a handful of people present: Fred Ankenman, club secretary Andrew French, local businessman Sam Becker, and three sportswriters, Kern Tips, Lloyd Gregory, and Andy Anderson. Ankenman told the inside story in his memoir. "Quite a number of years later, Dr. Knowles called me on the phone and said he had something quite funny to tell me. 'If you ever tell it to the press, I will deny the story,' said Dr. Knowles. Continuing, Dr. Knowles said, 'Fred, you know what Diz gave me for marrying him and Patricia? He gave me $2.50, and I believe he thought he was over-paying me at that.'"

Diz also saved on the ring. Pat wouldn't let him buy her one. "I said no ring until our home was paid for," she later recalled.

Diz was twenty-one, Pat, a month shy of twenty-five, although in later tellings that three-and-a-half-year age gap would shrink. During the '34 World Series, she would tell a sportswriter, "I'm two years older than he, and to me he seems like a little boy." And that was the way she always treated him, as if she were his mother. She would later tell an interviewer, "When he comes to the door, I get him right to bed. In one game this summer he lost 12 pounds. Whenever he pitches, I make him rest at least an hour before he has supper. I have to watch every mouthful he takes and make him eat. I sit over him at breakfast until he has cleaned up his plate, and I feed him cod liver oil all the time." Lucky Diz.

She spoiled him, she admitted to the interviewer, because she felt sorry for him. "When I first knew him he had no affection at all. Nobody had ever done anything for him. He had been dragged up, not raised up. He had a stepmother at home and was put to picking cotton as soon as he was big enough."

The courtship may have been brief, but the marriage was to last a lifetime. The strength of the union was that it was more than a marriage; it was a partnership.

"I don't know anything about baseball strategy," she told Vera Brown of the St. Louis *Star-Times*. "That's Dizzy's business. But I do know how the money is to be got and what to do with it. That's my part of this partnership. When one member of the firm is lacking in practical sense it is a good thing the other member has it. That's where I come in. A baseball player's life is so short. Three big years. That's the record nine times out of 10. Sometimes only one big year. Sometimes only one big moment. Sport fans are the most fickle people in the world, especially in professional sport. They may make allowances for amateurs, but when they pay their money they want their money's worth. I've heard cheers change to jeers almost in one breath. The higher you go, the harder you fall. That is the law of gravity. Well, when the crowd starts booing Dizzy instead of cheering him, I want him to be able to retire gracefully with money in his pocket."

She vowed to save $1,500 of his $3,500 salary that first season, and by all reports she did.

She told another interviewer, "I am determined Dizzy shall not end his career on a park bench. If we have to retire to a little patch and dig our living out of the ground, at least it will be our own ground. I want to take what we get and salt it down in Government bonds. I simply won't allow it to be thrown away."

By all accounts the marriage was healthy, happy, and prosperous. And it may have been a lifesaver for Diz, who was squandering every penny he earned and had lately taken up smoking and drinking.

Diz's father told *The Saturday Evening Post* in 1951, "Jay Hanna was the troublest boy I had until he married Pat. He ain't give no trouble much since." Fred Ankenman concurred, "Patricia appeared to be a good financier, and soon after marriage, their financial problems appeared taken care of."

Not that the marriage didn't have its ups and downs. There was a much publicized incident in 1940 in New York when Pat threw a lamp at Diz when he headed out of their hotel room for a little fun at Jimmy Kelly's nightclub. She was as accurate a hurler as her husband, and the gash on his left arm required stitches. (She explained it a little differently: "The telephone rang in the middle of the night ... Jerome reached out in the dark to answer it. His arm hit the glass top of the telephone table and knocked over a lamp. The lamp broke the glass top and Jerome cut his arm on the broken glass.")

Of course domestic life with Dizzy was no picnic: "Dizzy never pretends to pick up anything. Leaves his shoes in the middle of the floor. Drops his shirt where he takes it off. I am forever picking up after him. On the diamond he may be a hero, but at home he is just a husband."

She also revealed that much of his public bluster was an innocent act: "All the popping off at the mouth he does which is always getting him into scrapes is because he doesn't think of the effect it may have on some people. He can concentrate on his game, but he does not concentrate on himself, in spite of what people say about his egotism. He is a natural showman, and is always showing off, but he never attaches serious consequences to his clowning. Windy talk? That's just his line. He pulls it at home, too. 'You're a lucky girl to be married to a great guy like me,' he'll say. He doesn't get away with that with me, of course. He is a great teaser and kidder and practical joker, but he does not waste much of that stuff on me."

And as for the notorious temptations of fame, Pat was decidedly not worried. "I always know what Dizzy is up to because I am always with him." It was a habit Pat would maintain throughout their marriage. Where Diz went, she went.

A year earlier Albert Dean's lame back forced him to quit work. He was fifty-eight and the years of stooping over in the cotton fields had taken their toll. His boys were now his sole means of support. Paul was working at a San Antonio gas station at the time. Diz was just beginning his baseball career. "I've never wanted for anything," Pa Dean would tell a reporter at the '34 World Series. "They've sent money promptly when I asked for it, when I've run a little short."

Actually, the elder Dean didn't have to ask for it. Money was automatically deducted from Diz's check and sent to his father, the result of a deal Fred Ankenman struck with Monroe Dean in exchange for the elder Dean's signature on Diz's first St. Louis contract. Ankenman remembered, "At the time Diz signed his first Houston contract, very little, if any, attention was given to the requirement that contracts signed by a minor should also carry the consent of the parent."

In 1929 Diz was nineteen, two years away from majority, but he was claiming his birthday as 1911, making him three years away from legal age. Two years later, when Diz signed his 1931 contract with the Cardinals, he was of age. But there was already some confusion over Diz's birth year. Ankenman wrote in his memoir, "At that time, there was a question as to his age. Anyhow, I was in St. Louis for a meeting and Mr. Rickey gave me Dizzy's contract and had me go to San Antonio and get Mr. Dean to sign with Diz, who had already signed."

The elder Dean was then living in what Ankenman termed "a shack that was one of about eight or ten others located in what looked more like an alley than a street.... I could hardly believe that Mr. Dean could be living in such a terrible place. I took a few minutes to look the place over. I looked through the windows of the three small rooms and inside, they were in such an unkempt state."

Mr. Dean wasn't home. Ankenman found him walking down the road and gave him a lift. It was during this ride that the old man gave Ankenman a scare. "He started talking about Diz and how great a year he had at St. Joe. He then told me that some Captain over at Fort Sam had told him that any contract signed by Dizzy was no good without his signature." Mr. Dean then began rambling how Dizzy hadn't sent him any money since he started playing ball.

Seeing an opening, Ankenman jumped in: "I then brought up the contract matter. I asked him if he would sign the contract if I would give him a written agreement in which we would assure him that we would have Dizzy agree to send him $50 per month, and further, if Dizzy refused, the Cardinals or Houston would make the payments. He said that would be fine and he knew Dizzy would do it. I gave him an agreement as indicated and he signed the contract."

The arrangement continued through the end of the '31 season. But when Diz joined the Cards in '32 the clause was no longer in his contract. In fact, Pat Dean tried to get the money back from the year before. Ankenman wrote, "Mr. Rickey sent me a letter written by Mrs. Dean in which she said I had taken this money out of Dizzy's check without authority, and she wanted the total returned to Diz. Dizzy apparently had told Pat that I had sent this money to his Dad without agreement by him. I sent a copy of the agreement, signed by Diz, and that closed the apparent misunderstanding. Just another case of Diz pulling off another one of his jokes and enjoying a little fun out of it. I wondered at the time what Pat said to Diz when she saw his signature signed to the agreement."

She probably had some very choice words, but history has not recorded them.

The Buffaloes won the first- and second-half pennants in the Texas League's split-season format before heading to the Dixie Series, a minor-league version of the World Series, matching the champion of the Texas League against the winner in the Southern Association in a best-of-seven set. Their opponents, the Birmingham Barons, were a powerhouse team that had won the Southern title by 10½ games.

But that didn't matter to Diz, who boasted to reporters, "Beating those Birmingham Barons will be like taking candy from a baby.... My conscience hurts me every time I think of what those Birmingham galoots have coming to them. If my conscience prods me much more, I will strap my pitching arm behind me and pitch with the other hand."

He said that if he didn't beat Birmingham every game he pitched against them, he would run off to Benton Harbor, Michigan, grow a beard, and join the barnstorming House of David baseball team: "That beard would help me hide my blushes of shame."

All this was dutifully reported in Houston—and in Birmingham. The match began in Alabama on September 16, with Diz squaring off against forty-three-year-old Ray "Old Man" Caldwell, who had once thrown a no-hitter while with the Boston Red Sox. Diz's popping off produced the desired results: a record crowd of 20,074 turned out to see the game, and they weren't disappointed. It was a barn-burner that wasn't decided until the eighth, when the Barons squeaked across a run on singles by Zack Taylor and Caldwell and a double by Billy Bancroft. The Barons held on to win, 1-0. Afterward Barons manager Clyde Milan, who'd spent sixteen years in the Senators outfield backing up fastballer Walter Johnson, praised Diz: "I expected him to use blinding speed against us, but he showed me a brainy exhibition of pitching."

Zipp Newman wrote in the next day's Birmingham *News*, "Give Dizzy Dean credit for 10,000 of that crowd." Police had to rescue Diz from the mob after the game, but not because his safety was endangered: "Everybody swarmed him for his autograph which he smilingly wrote."

By the time Diz took the mound again September 19 his Buffaloes held a 2-1 advantage. He faced off again with Caldwell. This time Diz came out on top 2-0. But Birmingham battled back, and the series went to a seventh game. The veteran Caldwell was unable to pitch—the first two games had worn him out—so Diz went against Bob Hasty, a 6′3″ right-hander who'd pitched for Connie Mack's Athletics in the early twenties.

Diz struck out five of the first six batters he faced, but the toil of a long season—he'd pitched nearly 350 innings in four and a half months—took its toll in the last three frames. Diz allowed five runs in those three innings, and the Barons won the game, 6-3, taking the series.

Still, Diz had nothing to be ashamed of. And after the season he received the award for most valuable player in the Texas League: a $100 cash prize and a trophy.

In Houston life had been a big game for Diz. He would have greater seasons and play to greater acclaim, but because he was outside the intense media glare that would later both invigorate him and wear him down, he would never have more fun than he did that second season in Houston.

He led the league in victories with 26, in shutouts with 11, and in strikeouts with 303, and tied for the earned run average lead with 1.53. Demonstrating his characteristic workhorse habits, he also led the league in innings pitched (304) and complete games (28) despite his late start.

And in the heat of July, when the Buffs were battling Beaumont for the first-half pennant, Diz pitched—and won—three games in four days, including both ends of a doubleheader.

But perhaps the most telling statistic of all was the number of customers, 229,540, who paid their way into Buffs games. It was a new club record and topped the number who attended Cardinals games.

The folks in St. Louis took notice.

6

Rookie

When spring training for the 1932 season began, Dizzy Dean knew the facts. Despite his most-valuable-player season at Houston in 1931 Diz was not guaranteed a spot on the Cardinal roster in '32. In fact, as sportswriter Roy Stockton ran down the pitching prospects in a spring training column, it looked as if Diz might be in a fight for his career:

"Jess Haines is the only veteran.... [Bill] Hallahan is still young and strong.... [Paul] Derringer will get more work during the coming season.... [Syl] Johnson and [Flint] Rhem look like regular starters and if Tex Carleton continues to shine on the trip northward he will have the distinction of being a member of the Big Six. Allyn Stout ... probably will be used again to rescue faltering mates.... Jim Lindsey will be given a chance as a starter."

The Big Six, plus Stout and Lindsey, made eight. And manager Gabby Street had already announced his intentions of going with a nine-man staff.

Stockton concluded, "Dean and [Ray] Starr still must be considered, too, as candidates for regular places on the roster."

It wasn't as if the Cardinals were desperate to find a spot for the rookie right-hander. As Diz knew all too well, they had won pennants the last two years without him.

Diz had reported out of shape. Wintering in Danville, Arkansas, not far from his Lucas birthplace, he had picked up a flu bug that felled him for a couple of weeks and knocked fifteen pounds off his already thin frame. But his mouth was still the same size. "We can start training in earnest now because I'm here and everything is all right," he told reporters when he arrived February 22. He also predicted he would win twenty to thirty games, depending on how many games he got to pitch.

His mouth, and his poor practice habits, had cost him a roster spot the previous spring, when he had a seeming inability to make it up in time for morning workouts.

His late hours had led L. C. Davis to practice the art of newspaper doggerel in the St. Louis *Post-Dispatch:*

> You admit that you're a star, Dizzy Dean,
> And at that perhaps you are, Dizzy Dean,
> But the customers opine
> If you want to make the "nine"
> You had better rise and shine, Dizzy Dean.

But 1932 looked to be a different story. He was up for 10:00 A.M. sessions. And he gave Gabby Street no back talk.

But he hadn't been in camp a week when trouble erupted: he was threatening to jump the club. "My wife is ill in Gulfport, Mississippi and the Cardinal club won't let me have her come to training camp. If they insist on that order, I may pick up and leave. I can't go on worrying like this. They tell me it don't look right for a young fellow trying to make a place on the ball club to have his wife down here but I don't like that. I'd rather dig ditch-es and be happy than be on this ball club and be unhappy."

The Cardinals might have condoned a little whining. But Diz knew they wouldn't keep him if he didn't pitch effectively. And he got off to a horrible start. The Athletics pounded him in Miami on March 6; then when the club returned to Bradenton March 9 to open their home exhibition season, he was hit hard by the Reds. His worst outing was on March 21, when the Yankees tattooed him in the third inning of an exhibition. He'd retired the side in order in the first and second and got Frank Crosetti on a grounder to second baseman Sparky Adams to open the third. He walked second-string catcher Arndt Jorgens and then his defense collapsed behind him. Adams misplayed pitcher Lefty Gomez's grounder into a hit; two men on. Then right fielder Jodie Hunt let a one-hopper bounce off his head; Jorgens scored, men on second and third. The misplays rattled Diz and before the inning was over, he had given up six runs, three on a home run to dead center field by Lou Gehrig. He showered after the inning, replaced by another of his competitors for the last pitch-ing slot, veteran Tony Kaufmann.

Manager Street later took him aside and consoled him, "Don't get downhearted about those two games.... You were unfortunate in being picked to work on the two worst days we've had down here. But forget them. I believe in you and I'll string along with you. You've shown an inclination to work and play fair with me."

But Diz wasn't to be consoled. Sitting in the lobby of Bradenton's Dixie Grande Hotel, he told Stockton, "I'll bet you $5 or $50 that I'm sent to Houston or Columbus or Rochester.... I wish they would send me. I'd like to have one more good year at Houston and then the Cardinals would have to keep me."

This was not the voice of the self-proclaimed Dizzy the Great. It was the wimpering of an insecure rookie fighting for the last roster spot on a championship team.

Behind the bombast, the booming challenges, and the pompous bluster, Dizzy Dean was really just an uncertain country boy in the big city, an innocent kid who found that "popping off," as boasting was called then, could get him attention. And he liked attention.

This time Diz was afraid, afraid that maybe he wouldn't get a chance to prove himself in the big leagues. It wasn't that he had lost confidence in his ability. "If they'd give me a chance in this league and start me as often as they did at Houston, I'd win as many games."

Diz didn't know anything about sampling techniques, but he knew that the six-week spring training period wasn't long enough for the Cardinal brass to see all his capabilities. He knew he need-ed a full season. And fortunately for the Cardinals, he got it.

The Cardinals' season got under way April 12 at home against Pittsburgh. Street had decided to start Diz out in the bull pen: "Until he gets his feet on the ground. I haven't quit on him. He hasn't recovered his strength yet, after his attack of flu. But he'll come along."

In the *New York Times* the Cardinals were even money to repeat as champs. Wall Street speculators made them eight to five favorites, with the hometown Giants second at 2 to 1. In St. Louis, local odds maker Tom Kearney made them the 3-2 choice.

Diz may have had an uncertain spring, but the team was com-ing off a strong training campaign. Their record of 15-8 was sec-ond best in the National League, behind the Giants' 20-8. So when they stumbled out of the gate, losing five of their first seven, it was completely unexpected.

Diz was called on for the first time on April 23 in Pittsburgh. The Cardinals had lost five games in a row, but on this day they rallied from six runs down to tie the score in the top of the eighth. Dizzy was given the assignment of holding back the Pirates. He started strong, striking out all three hitters he faced in the eighth: Lloyd Waner, Adam Comorosky, and Pie Traynor. Then slugger Gussie Suhr led off the bottom of the ninth with a booming home run into the upper deck in right field.

"It was a shock to Dean," Stockton wrote. "Dean stood there on the mound for several moments after the home run drive clattered among the empty seats. Then he saw the other Redbirds making for the clubhouse with their sweaters and paraphernalia and he departed too, stunned and disappointed."

Diz was on the team, but his place was not secure and the team's slow start couldn't have helped his confidence. Nor could the statement made by owner Sam Breadon, who met the slumping club in Cincinnati April 26. He told reporters he would farm out a couple of players before the team returned home: "I am not worrying about the Cardinals and their poor start. Every championship club has to learn that it can't win games on its last year's reputation.... I am glad that the slump has come so early as there is plenty of time for the Cardinals to readjust themselves."

When the cuts came a day later, Diz was passed over. He was safe. For now. And soon, for good.

Diz got his first start on May 3 and made the most of it. He shut out the Reds, 9-0, allowing eight hits while striking out four. He even singled and scored a run for his own cause. The Reds were no powerhouse—they would finish the season in the cellar—but at the time they were in fourth place, a half game ahead of the Cards.

His next start was five days later in the second game of a doubleheader against the powerful Giants. The McGrawmen, as newspapers called the Giants, drawing the nickname from their legendary manager John McGraw, won the opener, 4-1, and the crowd was not happy. But Dizzy redeemed the Cardinals with a strong pitching performance and an amazing base-running display.

He would later describe it this way:

"Since I'm a rookie they haven't learned yet what a great hitter and daring base runner I am. So I lays down a bunt, and beats it out at first. From the corner of my eye, I see Bill Terry jugglin' the ball, and so I break for second. He's so surprised that he throws wide to the second baseman and it gets by him. So I just keep right on tearin' for third, and I'm goin' so fast I lose my cap. The shortstop's throw to third is ahead of me, but I slide in hard and upset the third baseman. Before they know what's happened, I'm up and a chargin' for home. As I cross the plate one of my socks has fell down over my shoe, and all the fans is cheerin' wild, because it's the winnin' run.

"The great John J. McGraw, who's only been managin' ball clubs for 33 years, retires as manager of the Giants that night. When he sees a pitcher get a home run on a bunt, that's just too much for him, and he makes Terry the new manager."

It was the winning run, but from the *New York Times* description, it sounded more like a swinging bunt: "With Gelbert on first, he tapped the ball over the bewildered Vergez, who was tearing in to field an expected bunt. This so confounded the Giants that Koenecke's wild return got away from the infielders and not only Gelbert, but Dean had scored as well."

And McGraw didn't retire that night; he waited another three weeks to conclude his long managerial career. And it wasn't just Dizzy who finished him off: a serious sinus infection had kept him at home while his team toured late in May. And it probably made a difference that the Giants were 17-23 and residing in last place when he called it quits.

* * *

By the middle of May the Cards had climbed to .500 and Diz had won three starts in a row.

He lost his first big-league game May 22 when the Pirates pounded him for five runs in five and two-thirds innings. A week later the Pirates beat him again, 8-6.

As June arrived Diz was back on track, shutting out the Cubs on five hits in a rain-shortened seven-inning game. He was now 4-2. But the Cardinals were 20-24 and sinking slowly in the west.

A spring of too much goodwill was beginning to get to Diz. The second week in June he began grousing about his status on the team. They weren't treating him fair, he complained to sportswriters, who soon learned from club officials that what Diz meant by unfair treatment was the team's refusal to raise his salary. When the club turned him down, Diz, as always, took it personally.

On June 15, he abruptly left the team in the middle of a road trip and took the train home from Philadelphia to St. Louis.

Street learned of Diz's departure from sportswriters. "He'll be back with us," Street said, shaking his head. "He's a hard proposition to handle."

Back home in St. Louis Diz announced that he was going to petition the commissioner for his unconditional release from his contract on the grounds that he was not of age when he signed his 1932 contract: "My father did not sign this contract for me as he had done in previous ones. I am not 21 yet and therefore the contract has no value. I am entitled to my release."

Diz, of course, was not underage. He was actually twenty-two when he signed his contract. But he was going to try and change his birth year again, sliding it back to 1912.

Commissioner Kenesaw Mountain Landis had already declared a number of players free agents because they were underage and didn't have their parents' countersignature on their contracts.

The Cardinal front office—Branch Rickey in particular—was in an uproar. Had they slipped up? Had Rickey, the lawyer, let a legal nicety escape him?

Fred Ankenman recalled in his memoir, "Mr. Rickey called me on the phone and said that Dizzy had applied to the Judge for free agency.... Even in those days, Diz would have brought several hundred thousand dollars on the open market. Mr. Rickey was frantic and wanted to know if I knew how old he was. I told him I thought he must have been at least twenty-one when he signed the Cardinal contract. He wanted to know if I could prove it. I told him I would check and try."

Ankenman remembered Diz had been married in Houston, so he went to the courthouse to check the marriage license: "In the application, Diz had signed his name Jerome H. Dean and his age was shown on a date that put the Cardinals in the clear. I called Mr. Rickey and he was just as happy an individual as one could imagine. I mailed him a copy of the marriage license immediately."

What the marriage license showed was that Dizzy was not only of age when he signed his '32 contract, he was actually twenty-two and Rickey immediately told the press, "He was 22 years old when he signed the contract this year. If Dean leaves the city and does not rejoin the club, he will be severely punished."

This was the first time Diz's true age was ever reported, but the discrepancy somehow eluded the press and his age continued to be reported incorrectly even in his obituaries.

The case went all the way to the hearing stage. Ankenman, a close friend of Rickey's, repeated the story of that hearing as told to him by Rickey: "First, Judge Landis interrogated Diz at great length. Diz testified positively that he was not twenty-one years old when he signed the Cardinal contract. When he finished, the Judge asked Mr. Rickey if he wished to ask Dizzy any questions, that Diz's statements appeared rather conclusive. Mr. Rickey said yes, that he did have a few questions to ask. He asked several questions, each time the answer was the same and that was that he was under twenty-one when he signed. Then Mr. Rickey brought up the marriage question. In answer to questions, the answer was the same. He was asked if he took out a marriage license when he got married and he said, 'I did not have to have one because everybody in Houston knew me.' He said he was never requested to apply for a license. 'Are you quite sure and positive?' 'I signed absolutely nothing,' he said. At this point, Mr. Rickey pulled the copy of the marriage license out of his inside coat pocket, showed it to Diz and asked, 'Is that signature Jerome H. Dean yours or somebody else's and also is the date correct?'"

Rickey, the University of Michigan–trained lawyer, had managed to outbluff Dizzy, the Ozark con man.

Ankenman writes, "Diz just looked at the license a minute and then with a big grin said, 'You got me, Mr. Rickey, you got me.' That ended the hearing but not until the Judge had given Diz the lecture of the century."

Diz flew to New York to rejoin the team, and as a face-saving measure the Cardinals agreed to refund $225 that had been taken from Diz's check and sent to his father, a payment that was part of the agreement Ankenman had worked out with Pa Dean two years earlier.

The Cards began to see what a box-office draw Diz could be on June 26 when he pitched—and lost—the second game of a home doubleheader against the league-leading Cubs, 4-3. The loss was easy for owner Breadon to stomach because 31,000 fans, a new Cardinal record, turned out to watch Diz pitch. And by scheduling Diz for the second game, the Cards insured that the crowd would stay the entire afternoon, consuming more hot dogs and sodas, putting more money in the coffers. In fact, Diz would pitch every Sunday the Cards were at home for the remainder of the season.

Diz had an up-and-down July. On the first day of the month he beat the Pirates, 5-3, ending their seven-game winning streak and knocking them out of first place.

A week later he suffered a tough loss at the hands of the Boston Braves. He went seven innings, allowing only four hits but left trailing, 2-0.

He proved his versatility two days later in a doubleheader against the Phillies. The Cards won both games with Diz relieving in the first and pitching a five-hitter in the second. The twin killing, as the sportswriters called it, enabled the Cards to pass the Phils and Dodgers and jump to fourth place. When the team won its next two, it appeared that perhaps the defending champions were awakening, ready to reenter the race.

Then on July 14 Diz faced the Giants in St. Louis. The game was tight until the seventh, when the Giants batted around, scoring four and sending Diz to the showers. The Cards would lose, 6-3.

On July 17, still smarting from the battering he had taken from the Giants, Dizzy nearly precipitated a brawl when the Dodgers were in town. He had gone into the eighth leading, 5-1. But the Dodgers began teeing off on his fastball, and soon Diz found himself in a tie game. To get back he nailed second-string catcher Clyde Sukeforth with a fastball to the top of the head, rendering him unconscious. When he came to, Sukeforth charged the mound. A number of the Dodgers took offense at Diz's beanball. They pointed out that Sukey was a good five inches shorter and considerably lighter. Street removed Diz between innings and the inspired Dodgers went on to win, 8-5.

Diz was only following the lead of his fellow pitchers on the Cards. Years later he would explain, "When I was pitching, or some of those old fellows like Pop Haines or Pat Malone, we'd walk in there and tell that batter, 'I'm glad to see you dug yourself in there so good, because I'm gonna bury you right there.' You didn't all the time like to do it, but that was when you'd put the ball in here [in one ear] and out up here [the other ear]. That's when it was time for the 'purpose' pitch."

Nine days later Diz found himself facing the Dodgers again. Diz had developed a habit of wetting his fingers with his lips, and the Dodgers, already angered by his knockdown pitches, used it as a weapon. Each time he went to his mouth they complained to umpire Ernie Quigley that he was throwing a spitter. Quigley reacted by throwing out the ball. In the seventh Quigley issued a final warning, and Dizzy, rattled by all the commotion, lost his composure. They pounded him, racking up eight hits in seven and two-thirds innings. Diz left with no decision, but the Cards went on to lose, 5-4.

And just three days after that, in front of a disappointing crowd of 3,000 at Ebbets Field, the Dodgers beat Diz again, knocking out eleven hits and seven runs in seven innings. Hack Wilson did most of the damage with a homer and double. The loss dropped the Cards into sixth place, behind the Dodgers.

Diz continued in his tailspin the next week. He gave up thirteen hits in six innings against Boston on July 31.

He was sent to the bull pen the next day. On August 2 in a game at Boston he relieved Allyn Stout, who had relieved Jim Lindsey. He allowed four hits in one and one-third innings and was the losing pitcher when Boston rallied to win, 4-3.

He righted himself the next weekend at the Polo Grounds. He won the second game of a doubleheader, 10-2, allowing only seven hits and driving in two runs. Two days later, he beat the Phillies in the second game of a doubleheader, striking out seven in the process.

He continued his success back home against the Cubs, winning the second game of a Sunday doubleheader, beating the league leaders, 2-1, in ten innings. He allowed only six hits and struck out eight, six of them in a row. That streak was only one short of the then major league record of seven.

This was the third Sunday home doubleheader Diz had pitched, and he was beginning to complain that the Cardinals were saving him for the weekends to draw a crowd.

Thus, on Thursday, August 18, they started him in the first game of a charity doubleheader against the Phillies. The 15,000 who were on hand to benefit the St. Louis Tuberculosis Society saw him give up five hits and five runs in only three innings. So it was back to the Sunday doubleheader schedule. On Sunday, August 21, he came on in the eighth in relief of Bill Hallahan. It was a strong performance: he gave up only four hits in six innings and struck out ten, but he lost when the Braves scored two in the top of the fourteenth.

Next began an incredible five-day stretch in which Diz would win three games, going the distance in the first two and leaving in the eighth of the third after spraining his ankle.

As September dawned the Cards were in fifth place, thirteen games out of first. There was no talk of another pennant charge when the Cards visited the first-place Cubs for a weekend series. The Cubs were on a roll; they'd won twelve in a row and ran that string to fourteen before facing Dizzy in the second game of a Saturday doubleheader. Diz ended the Cubs streak, winning, 3-0, striking out seven in the process.

Diz got into trouble during a Labor Day doubleheader

against Pittsburgh, even though he didn't pitch. Roy Stockton reported, "There was an outbreak of razzing on the Cardinal bench and [umpire] Quigley, spying Dean sitting outside the dugout, had reason to believe the gay young man was doing most of the horn blowing. He made two steps toward the pitcher, who hastened to his feet and in all seriousness shouted to Ernie: 'Please please don't, Mr. Quigley. I'll go out peaceably.' Quigley laughed, but the next day Dizzy received notice of a $25 fine from [National League] President [John A.] Heydler."

The Cardinals were on a downhill slide and not even Dizzy could stop it. He lost starts in Philadelphia and in New York, before closing the season with four straight wins to finish 18-15.

Before the '32 season Diz had written a letter to a Russellville, Arkansas, sportswriter, boasting, "If I have only a fair year, I should win 20 games, but of course I expect to have a good season. I am sorry you bush league sports writers are not going to the big parade with me but am glad you guys will get to read about me if not write about me. You know Dean, always good even when I am having an off day."

So according to his own calculations Diz didn't even have a fair year. He didn't win twenty games, a total that was not quite the benchmark in 1932 that it is today. A total of seven pitchers in both leagues won at least twenty that year, and two pitchers won twenty-five or more. (Lefty Grove had won thirty-one the year before.)

Diz won eighteen, which tied him for fourth in the league in wins, while losing fifteen, sixth in the league. He'd led the Cardinals in wins, but he had also led the club in losses. His 3.30 ERA was only second best on the club, to Bill Hallahan's 3.11, and didn't rank in the league's top ten.

But Diz did have some numbers to be proud of: he led the league in strikeouts (191, a whopping fifty-four more than second-place Carl Hubbell) and in innings pitched, and he was only one behind Pittsburgh's Larry French, the league leader in games with forty-seven. He had proved he was a durable pitcher with a fastball that was, at times, unhittable.

But one thing obscured every statistic: the championship Cards of 1931 had slipped to seventh place in 1932.

And Dizzy actually played before fewer paying customers than he had the previous season in the minor-league outpost of Houston.

7

The Sophomore Jinx

There's an old baseball belief that a rookie phenom will slump in his second season. It's so ingrained in baseball tradition that it even has a name: the sophomore jinx.

It's rooted in reality: a number of the greats of baseball history slumped badly in their second seasons. Hall of Famer Willie McCovey actually went back down to the minors during his sophomore year. And some rookie phenoms never regain that freshman form. Joe Charboneau, Rookie of the Year with Cleveland in 1980, batted only 194 more times in the big leagues after that superseason.

So old baseball men were watching Diz with a jaundiced eye in '33, silently hoping that he would get his comeuppance, that all his mouthing off would come back to haunt him.

As the season opened Diz didn't do anything to dash those hopes.

For the first time he was given the assignment of pitching opening day, but he lost in Chicago, 3-0. A week later he made his second start, the home opener in St. Louis. Again the Cubs were his opponents, and again they defeated him, this time, 3-1.

The Great Dean was 0-2. And the Cardinals, at 1-4, weren't much better. Cardinal fans were restless. They had come to expect much more from their team. After all, it had been '24–'25, eight years, since the club had gone two consecutive years without a pennant. But the slump continued. By the beginning of May the club was 6-9 and in seventh place. And *then* they went on a losing streak, losing six of their next seven.

The Cards had started the season without their regular short-stop in '32, Charley Gelbert. Gelbert had nearly lost his leg in a winter hunting accident. In fact, he would miss two full seasons while recovering and would never regain the form that allowed him to set a fielding record in the '31 Series. Soon Branch Rickey became convinced that the Cardinals couldn't win with their rejiggered lineup.

The team had tried Pepper Martin at short in spring training and found him wanting. They even brought back the aging Rogers Hornsby, now thirty-seven, to play the position. On April 16, Street told the *Post-Dispatch*, "If Hornsby does fail us and I have to get more batting power, I'll switch Adams to short and use either a first baseman, Pat Crawford, or an outfielder, Pepper Martin, at third. Crawford was a third baseman for me for two years at Greenville, South Carolina when the South Atlantic was a real league."

In late April, Street tried flip-flopping Hornsby and Frisch, moving Hornsby to second and Frisch to short. That didn't work either.

And on April 26 *Post-Dispatch* columnist L.C. Davis penned an ode to the Cardinals' infield problems:

> Variety's the spice of life
> And that is why the Redbirds play
> When in the hottest of the strife
> A different infield every day.

Rickey tried to swing a deal with the Cards' regular trading partners, the Reds, for twenty-seven-year-old shortstop Leo Durocher, a fielder the equal of Gelbert and a leader to boot. But to get Durocher Rickey would have to give up pitching. The rapid development of Paul Derringer in 1931 had allowed the Cards to ship Diz back to Houston for another year of seasoning. Derringer had won eighteen games in that world championship season. But he had slipped to 11-14 in '32, and now it was he who was expendable.

So on May 7 the Cards sent Derringer, relief pitcher Allyn Stout, and veteran utility infielder Sparky Adams to the Reds for Durocher and pitchers Dutch Henry and Jack Ogden. It was the classic "deal that helps both teams." Durocher would become the captain of the Gas House Gang. And Derringer would help the Reds win pennants in 1939 and 1940.

Shortly after the trade the Cardinals were in Cincinnati for a series. Before the final game on June 6 Diz and Derringer, now opponents, were shagging flies during batting practice when suddenly Derringer jumped Diz. The two pitchers wrestled to the ground, each flailing away. Dazzy Vance ran over and pinned Derringer to the ground. Teammates then separated them, but the emnity remained.

Diz would claim, "I was just going after a fly when Derringer said to me, 'What's this you're saying about my courage.' I told him I meant every word of it, and he swung at me. I'm pretty clever so I ducked under the punch. Then he grabbed me and I caught him around the neck and threw him to the ground. He said that was no way to fight, so I let go right to the side of his head. By this time three fellows had hold of me—and the fight was over."

Derringer told a different story. He said Diz had been taunting him all during the series and that he tired of the verbal jabs and challenged Diz to fight like a man.

* * *

Diz continued the workhorse habits he had adopted his rookie season. He would never turn down an assignment—unless he was "on strike," of course—and he would often volunteer for extra duty. On Friday, June 30, he pitched the Cards past the Giants, 1-0, at the Polo Grounds and then came back on Sunday to face the Giants again, this time losing, 1-0.

On the way back to St. Louis the team was scheduled to play a Monday exhibition game in Elmira, New York. Diz boarded the train with the rest of the team but when they debarked in Elmira, he was nowhere to be found. He said he slept through the stop. "Imagine my surprise to find myself in Pittsburgh. I must have got on the wrong car."

But this time Diz's high jinks didn't amuse Gabby Street, already on the hot seat because of the team's mediocre record. "We advertised Dean to be there in Elmira, and his absence embarrassed the club," he told reporters. "I am going to have to fine him a hundred."

In July stars of the American and National leagues gathered in Chicago for what was being billed as the Dream Game, an All-Star contest between the two leagues. The game's sponsor, Chicago *Tribune* sports editor Arch Ward, envisioned it as a one-time event, and it was held in conjunction with the Century of Progress Exposition. The "All-Stars," selected by a vote of the fans, made it truly a Dream Game, matching such heroes as Babe Ruth, Lou Gehrig, and Al Simmons against Paul Waner, Pie Traynor, and Carl Hubbell. Legendary manager John McGraw came out of retirement to lead the National League squad against Connie Mack's American All-Stars.

The fans didn't vote for pitchers. They were chosen by the managers, and National League manager Bill Terry, from the Giants, passed over Diz, selecting instead Cardinal stalwart Bill Hallahan. It was a fair selection. That first All-Star squad had only four pitchers, and at midseason Hallahan was having a much better year than Diz. Terry also chose his own pitchers Carl Hubbell and Hal Schumacher along with Cub right-hander Lon Warneke. The Cardinals were also represented on the team by Frankie Frisch, Pepper Martin, and Jimmie Wilson.

Diz was interviewed the week before the game by Bob Thomas, a sports announcer at St. Louis station KWK, about his choices for the National League team. Without hesitating he named Ripper Collins, Frankie Frisch, Leo Durocher, Pepper Martin, George Watkins, Ernie Orsatti, Joe Medwick, and Jimmie Wilson, all eight of the Cardinal starters. He didn't sound at all bitter about not being selected. He was young, he would have other chances. On the radio show he also did something he had resisted in spring training, predicting he would win eighteen to twenty games in '33 and his teammates, his eight All-Star selections, would win the pennant.

The American League won the All-Star game, 4-2. Frisch salvaged some prestige for the Nationals with a home run. Hallahan was the losing pitcher, but his lack of success was understandable: he'd pitched nine innings only two days before.

At this, the first All-Star break, the Cards were 40-34 and in second place, only 5½ games behind the league-leading Giants and in good position to make a run at the flag.

But over the next two weeks they dropped eleven games. By July 24, with the team 46-45 and languishing in fifth place, eight games back, Branch Rickey felt he had to make a move. Street, who had led the club to two pennants and a world championship in his four seasons as manager, was out.

Many of the regulars were hoping the job would go to catcher Jimmie Wilson. Instead, Rickey named second baseman Frankie Frisch the new skipper.

The disappointed Wilson slumped in the second half, and after the season he was traded to the Phillies, where he was named manager.

But the change had the desired effect. The Cardinals went on a tear, sweeping three games from the Reds, then three more from the Cubs. And Dizzy probably did as much to cement Frisch's hold on the managerial position as anyone else. In the first game of a July 30 doubleheader against the Cubs, he struck out seventeen batters, the first pitcher in the modern era to do so. He had only eleven strikeouts going into the eighth, but he struck out the side in the final two frames to break the record of sixteen, which had been set by Noodles Hahn of the Reds in 1901 and equaled by Christy Mathewson in 1904, Rube Waddell in 1908, and Nap Rucker in 1909. His feat tied the all-time record, set by Thomas (Toad) Ramsey of Louisville in 1886.

Diz would later describe the record-breaking strikeout this way: "With me havin' 16 strikeouts already, Charlie Grimm sends in Jim Mosolf as a pinch hitter. As this Mosolf steps up to the plate (catcher Jimmie) Wilson gives him the needle, 'Jim, you sure are in a tough spot. Ol' Diz just hates pinch hitters, and you better look out!' While Wilson is poundin' his fist in his big mitt right behind Mosolf's ear, I just breeze three right across the plate for Strikeout No. 17."

Between games Diz changed into his street clothes and went to the press box to watch the second contest. But the tiny confines of press row gave him the jitters, and he returned to the clubhouse after the second inning, put his uniform back on, and sat on the bench in case manager Frisch needed him to strike out a few more, he said.

There was an exhibition game the next day, but Diz didn't sleep through his stop this time. It was in Columbus, Ohio, against the Cardinals' farm team there, a red-hot bunch led by a fireballing right-hander named Dean, Diz's little brother, Paul Dean.

The Columbus papers advertised a duel between Deans, and 8,000 turned out. Diz pitched the first two innings against his brother, and it looked as if the younger Dean would triumph when Diz gave up a two-run homer to Columbus first baseman Mickey Heath. But the Cardinals rallied to defeat Paul and the farm club, 4-3.

Paul would finish the season 20-7 and the object of several bids from other clubs. But the Cardinals had plans for the Dean brothers in 1934.

The Dodgers were in town in late August and Diz was chomping at the bit to throw his fastball past Brooklyn's bantamweight second baseman Tony Cuccinello. Diz's catcher, Jimme Wilson, warned that Cuccinello was a fastball hitter and would murder Diz's hard one. But Diz kept whining. So finally, in the sixth, Wilson called time and went to the mound. Diz would later recall Wilson's conversation this way: "Diz, you think Cuccinello can't hit your fastball. Let's try it. Just throw that hard one in there and see what happens." Diz was delighted. "I throw one past him but the next one he hits four miles over the left field seats." A chastened Diz walked in to his catcher as Cuccinello rounded the bases. "Jimmie, I guess you're right. That one Cuccinello hit wasn't no change of pace."

Diz was already developing a reputation for having fun with members of the opposing team. Frank Graham of the New York *Sun* would describe Diz as "a flagrant offender against that commonly accepted rule that there shall be no fraternization between rival players before a game. Dizzy except when he is pitching is a friend of every other player in the league and observes all the amenities whenever he meets up with them."

The following story has been told in various forms, but Graham's version, published September 12, 1934, and attributed to the '33 season, is the best known. Diz was scheduled to pitch a game at Ebbets Field when, before the game, he took a notion to visit the Dodgers' clubhouse. He walked in, according to Graham, "just as [manager] Max Carey was calling a meeting to go over the Cardinal hitters.... He sat down and listened to every word Carey had to say. When Max was through talking, he turned to Dizzy. 'Was I right about how to pitch to you fellows?' he asked, with a smile. 'Yep,' said Dizzy. 'And now I'll tell you how I am going to pitch to these muggs.' To the astonishment of the Brooklyn players he went right down the batting order, telling each what his weakness was and being so accurate about it his listeners knew they weren't being kidded. 'Now that I've told you what I am going to pitch,' he said, 'come on out and let's see you hit it.' He picked up his glove, stalked from the clubhouse and shut the Dodgers out."

In another telling it was the Giants' clubhouse and reporting the intrusion was utility infielder Byrne James, who would tell reporters, "Ole Diz strolled in and [manager Bill] Terry, who was conducting the meeting, said, 'What do you want?' And Diz said, 'Well, I belong in the Cardinal clubhouse, but they're having a meeting, and none of them know what they're talking about, so I thought I'd come over here and visit you all.' 'All right,' Terry said, 'but we're having a meeting too, and right now we're discussing the weaknesses of the various hitters on your club.' 'That's okay,' Diz replied. 'Go right ahead. I know them all too, so you won't be telling me anything.'"

The Cards continued to surge under Frisch, but the Giants were finishing even faster. And even though the Cards were 36-26 with Frisch as manager, they lost a game and a half to the streaking Giants.

During the final home series of the season the Cardinals staged Dizzy Dean Day and presented their ace with a shiny new Buick, five squealing piglets, and a crate of baby chicks. But just calling it Dizzy Dean Day didn't make it so. The league-leading Giants beat Diz, 4-3, behind Mel Ott's double and home run.

The loss dropped the Cards into fifth place, a half game behind the Boston Braves, their second second-division finish in a row. Team historians had to go all the way back to '23–'24 to match that.

There was no sophomore jinx for Diz. He had moved up the statistical ladder a notch, winning twenty while losing eighteen. He led the majors in strikeouts with 199 and in complete games with twenty-six and led the National League in games pitched with forty-eight. In the process he became the first Cardinal to win twenty since Wee Willie Sherdel's twenty-one victories in the championship season of 1928.

Three years earlier, in announcing that Dizzy would pitch the final game of the 1930 season, the St. Louis *Post-Dispatch* had noted, "Dean has a young brother, 16 years old, who will be at St. Joseph next year. They call him 'Little Dizzy' because he's taller than Herman and Herman says the kid has a fast ball and curves that make his stuff look childish."

No one paid any attention at the time, but in the winter of '33, Cardinal brass were looking north to Columbus, where the now nineteen-year-old Paul Dean had had a bang-up season, finishing with a record of 20-7 and a league-leading 197 strikeouts.

Branch Rickey now seemed satisfied with his everyday lineup. "We've got the arms and legs," Rickey told a reporter. "If we had ten Dizzy Deans, then we would be all set."

He wouldn't have ten Dizzy Deans in 1934. But he would have two Deans.

8

Dizzy and Daffy

No one called them the Gas House Gang during that dazzling
pennant season. In fact the term Gas House Gang wasn't used in
the St. Louis papers until August 1935. But the Cardinals of 1934
were the gassiest bunch to ever play the game: expending more
hot air—at each other and at their opponents—than a bland
bunch like the Boston Braves would do in their history.

The name Gas House Gang was apparently coined in New
York, but its origins are confused. One popular story of the time
had the Cardinals in the Polo Grounds preparing to play the
Giants. Leo Durocher was supposedly chatting on the bench with
New York *Sun* columnist Frank Graham when the Great One,
Mr. Dean, wandered by and ventured the opinion that the Cardinals could win the pennant in any league, the American League
included. Durocher shot back, "Yeah, but they'd never let us play
in the American League. They'd say we were just a bunch of gas
house players."

Paul Dickson offers three different possibilities for the name's
origin in *The Dickson Baseball Dictionary*. In one the team arrived

in New York from Boston, where they had played a particularly messy affair in the rain. With no day off for laundry they were forced to play in dingy uniforms, making them look, a reporter said, like "the gang from around the gas house."

If that were true, the date would have been either May 20 or July 23. Those were the only two days during the '34 season that the Cardinals played in New York a day after a game in Boston. The problem is that both those contests in Boston were played under clear skies, with not even a trace of rain, according to weather information published in the Boston *Globe*. In fact, the second occasion, July 22, was so hot and dry across the country that the *New York Times* published a story about the heat wave on its front page, sandwiched between stories about a bus crash and the police slaying of mobster John Dillinger.

Dickson's second possible origin is a variation on the conversation between Durocher and Graham.

He also attaches credence to a story in Durocher's autobiography, *Nice Guys Finish Last*. It's the same series in New York and the same dirty uniforms, but Durocher credits New York *World-Telegram* cartoonist Willard Mullin for the name: "[Mullin's cartoon] showed two big gas tanks on the wrong side of the railroad track and some ballplayers crossing over to the good part of town carrying clubs over their shoulders instead of bats. And the title read 'The Gas House Gang.'"

In *Frank Frisch: The Fordham Flash,* his autobiography, written with Roy Stockton, Frankie Frisch, the manager and second baseman on the Gas House Gang, credited the Chicago *Herald and Examiner's* Warren Brown with using the phrase in print in July 1935: "[Brown], one of the wittiest wags in the business, climbed aboard the Cubs' train, New York bound. Curtains were drawn. All the little and big Cubs apparently had turned in for the night. 'What's the matter?' Brown wanted to know in a loud voice. 'Are you boys afraid that Pepper Martin is on the train?

You all had better stay on your side of the tracks, or the Gas House Gang will get you.'"

Bill Corum of the New York *Evening Journal* is generally credited with popularizing the name by using it in his widely read column, although others claim it was spread by Brown or Graham.

If no sportswriter had coined the name, surely someone else would have because it fit the Cardinals to a tee. Gangs at the gas house were a dirty, crude bunch and the Cardinals of 1934 were a baseball mirror image: they didn't mind getting dirty, they didn't mind playing dirty, and they didn't mind talking dirty. The only thing they minded was losing.

Durocher, in *Nice Guys Finish Last,* tells some of the dirty tricks they would use: "I used to file my belt buckle to a sharp edge. We'd get into a tight spot in the game where we needed a strikeout, and I'd go to the mound and monkey around with the ball just enough to put a little nick on it. 'It's on the bottom, buddy,' I'd tell the pitcher as I handed it to him. I used to do it a lot with Dizzy Dean. If he wanted to leave it on the bottom, he'd throw three-quarters and the ball would sail varoom! If he turned it over so that the nick was on top, it would sink. Diz had so much natural ability to begin with that with that kind of an extra edge it was just no contest."

Durocher also revealed how Frankie Frisch would aid the pitcher's cause: "Frank chewed tobacco. All he had to do was spit in his hand, scoop up a little dirt, and twist the ball in his hand just enough to work a little smear of mud into the seam. Same thing. My nick built up wind resistance on one spot; his smear roughed up a spot along the stitches, and the ball would sail like a bird."

Dirty was the key word, in both its senses, for the Gas House Gang.

The Gas House Gang members were all for one and one for all. Most of the time, anyway. There was a little incident in August that sharply divided the team, an incident precipitated by Diz and pulled off by the brothers Dean. But in the end even that helped to rally the team. Although there is no question that that was the furthest thing from Diz's mind when he staged the famous Dean brothers walkout.

But we are getting ahead of the story.

The '32 and '33 seasons had been particularly disappointing ones in St. Louis. After winning four pennants in six years, the Cardinals had suddenly fallen on hard times.

Two mainstays of those pennant years, Chick Hafey and Sunny Jim Bottomley, were gone. Hafey had been sent to Cincinnati during spring training 1932 in exchange for infielder Harvey "Gink" Hendrick, pitcher Benny Frey, and cash. Bottomley was sent to Cincinnati in December of '32 for pitcher Ownie Carroll and outfielder Estel Crabtree. None of the pickups would see much action with the Cards. Crabtree got the most playing time, twenty-three games in '33.

Dizzy Dean was a member of those '32 and '33 teams, but despite his durable right arm and his competitive spirit, he couldn't pitch the Cardinals into the World Series. He couldn't even pitch them into the first division. Not by himself.

He needed help.

The Gas House Gang had begun assembling in St. Louis in 1931 when John "Pepper" Martin, the Wild Horse of the Osage, broke in with a bang, hitting .300. He capped his remarkable rookie campaign by running wild in the World Series, hitting .500 and stealing five bases in six attempts, effectively snatching the fall classic from the mighty Philadelphia Athletics of Connie Mack.

Frisch believed the team's character derived more from Pepper Martin than any other player: "Barrel-chested, broad-shouldered, with a great competitive spirit, [Martin] is a picturesque figure as he charges down the base line like an express train, or takes off in a flying leap on one of his hands-first slides. After one time at bat on a sultry summer day, he is grimy from spiked shoes to finger tips. He looks like a member of a Gas House Gang."

Diz too picked Pepper Martin as the very embodiment of the Gas House Gang. Years later he would tell his radio audience, "[Pepper was] the top man in that Gas House Gang business. He looked like a gashouser. You could pretty him up in the clubhouse but after five minutes on the field he'd be dust from head to foot."

Also arriving that '31 season was first baseman James "Ripper" Collins, an old rookie at the age of twenty-seven. He'd gotten a late start on a baseball career, turning to the sport only after a strike forced him out of the Pennsylvania coal mines. Too short by most standards for first basemen, the 5′9″ Collins compensated with deadly power.

Dizzy Dean, who had had a cup of coffee at the end of '30, arrived to stay in '32. And in September of that year, the Cardinals called up slugger Joe "Ducky" Medwick. Medwick, whose full nickname, "Ducky-Wucky," was his wife's term of endearment for him, took over the left-field job, moving Ernie Orsatti to center and sending Pepper Martin in to play third. The muscular Medwick had a reputation among opponents as a bit "chesty." "Why shouldn't he be?" a teammate asked the Philadelphia *Inquirer*'s "Old Sport" columnist. "If I could hit as far and as often as he does you would have to send your name into the office boy before I would speak to you."

When regular shortstop Charley Gelbert was injured in that winter hunting accident in '33, Branch Rickey made yet another trade with the neighborly Reds, obtaining the Reds' feisty shortstop Leo "The Lip" Durocher, who would become the captain of the Gas House Gang, the first man to throw a punch in a rhubarb, the last man off the field in a fight. Durocher, who had once said if his grandmother was in the base path and wouldn't get out of the way he'd be forced to run over her, was the last piece in the puzzle. Well, almost the last piece.

The regular lineup for the Gas House Gang was in place at the beginning of the '33 season. But that club would finish only 82-71 in fifth place in the National League. Something was still missing. Leadership.

Durocher provided plenty of that on the field. But if Leo made them yell, it was left to Frankie Frisch to make them jell.

Frisch had come to the Cardinals in '26 in an unpopular trade for Rogers Hornsby. Hornsby, The Rajah, was a St. Louis favorite, for good reason: he had won six consecutive batting titles from 1920 to 1925. When his batting average "collapsed" from .403 in '25 to .317 in '26, Cardinal general manager Branch Rickey exercised his pet theory: it is better to trade a player a year too early than a year too late. Hornsby was only thirty and only a year removed from a batting title so his trade value was still high. Rickey shipped him to New York for Frisch and hurler Jimmy Ring. Frisch was only two years younger and had never come close to .400 during his eight years in the big leagues. But he was a natural-born leader. He would be the solid, if unspectacular, second baseman for the Cards' pennant-winning teams of '28, '30, and '31.

"Frank'd win a game for you all by himself," Diz would later say. "He'd beat out an infield hit, steal second, third if he had to. Then he'd score on an infield out. There wasn't anything Frankie couldn't do."

And in the middle of the '33 season, with the Cardinals languishing in fifth place, Rickey acted, replacing Gabby Street at the helm with his little second baseman, Frank Francis Frisch.

The Cardinal team that arrived in Bradenton, Florida, in March '34 was a second-division bunch. But their final finish in '33 was misleading. They had been fifth, yes, but they had been only nine and a half games out of first. And in the final two months under Frisch they had played almost .600 ball. This was Frankie Frisch's team.

Dizzy arrived for spring training 1934 before the rest of the team, well before.

He and Pat went to Bradenton on December 22, 1933, and Diz began his usual winter activities: hunting, fishing, playing golf.

On January 18, the St. Louis *Star-Times* in an unbylined story related Diz's thoughts about the upcoming season: "Dizzy believes that he and his young pitching brother Paul, who is expected to become another ace on the Cardinal staff, will lead the team to the National League pennant.

" 'How are they going to stop us?' he snapped. 'Paul's going to be a sensation. He'll win 18 or 20 games. I'll count 20 to 25 for myself. I won 20 last season, and I know I'll pass that figure.' "

This was the first of Diz's many predictions about the '34 campaign. He would later be quoted as predicting anywhere from forty-five to fifty wins for "me 'n' Paul," but this was the first: a prediction that he and Paul would win between thirty-eight and forty-five. In later years Diz would sometimes claim that he never made the original prediction, that it came from Branch Rickey.

The fact that the story has no byline does make it suspicious. If it had come from the *Star-Times'* beat writer, Sid Keener, it almost certainly would have carried his name. There also is no Bradenton dateline and no mention of a telephone conversation, hinting that perhaps the prediction came not from Diz, but, as Diz claimed, from the Cardinals' office, from Branch Rickey through the Cardinals' new public relations man, Gene Karst.

Four weeks later Diz spoke again on the upcoming season. The Independent News Service, a wire service, reported on February 15 that Diz was pleased with the changes the league was making to the ball. Again there was no dateline or byline. " 'Watch the fast ball pitchers make that white apple sail this season,' Dean predicted. 'I have averaged 20 victories a season with the old ball. With the new ball I feel certain I will win 25 games.' " Was this Diz talking or a Cardinals' press release?

The Cardinals opened camp on March 5. Diz walked in weighing 200 pounds, a good ten pounds over his 1933 playing weight. But it wasn't from winter chicken-circuit bingeing. He was just following orders. When he first came up to the Cardinals in '32, he carried 180 pounds on his 6'3" frame. But the heavy work load combined with the midsummer heat in St. Louis saw him drop to 165 by midseason. Rickey had advised him to ease up and add some weight. Rickey thought more weight would give him more velocity on his fastball. His second summer in St. Louis he got up to about 190. When Diz arrived in camp as a 200-pounder, Rickey told reporters the bulk would make Dizzy's fastball surpass that of Walter Johnson and all other famous speed pitchers.

Diz had been boasting about his little brother almost since the time Diz made the big-league club. "I'm great," Diz would say, "but Paul's going to be even better, if that's possible."

Following a 20-7 season for Columbus of the American Association during which he lead the league in strikeouts, Paul earned an invitation to the Cardinals' spring training. He arrived March 4 but not to pitch. Paul wanted $1,500 more than the Cardinals had offered, Diz disclosed, and his little brother was prepared to work in a common mill if the Redbirds didn't meet his terms. "Yes, sir, Paul has a job all lined up, and he's not going to pitch unless the Cardinals pay him," Diz told the *Post-Dispatch*'s Roy Stockton. "The club offered him a raise over what he got at

Columbus, but it wasn't enough for a man of his skill. It was the same salary the club offered other young pitchers, and Paul ain't an ordinary pitcher. He's a great pitcher.... And Paul is willing to gamble on his ability. He sent back his contract and Mr. Rickey sent him another exactly the same, and threatened to make Paul pay for the postage if he sent that one back. But that didn't scare brother Paul. He shot it back, too. But he told Mr. Rickey he'd pitch for nothing until he won a certain number of games, say 15, and then let the Cardinals pay him $500 for each victory. And the club turned that offer down! You can't tell what a club's going to do nowadays."

Diz acted as Paul's agent and PR man throughout the spring holdout, extolling Paul's virtues and complaining about the Cardinals' stubbornness. Paul remained stoically at his side.

Because Paul was the flip side of the coin from Dizzy, the sportswriters had a hard time getting a fix on him. They tried out a number of nicknames for him: "Harpo" because he never talked; "Nutsey" as a complement to Dizzy; even "Little Dizzy." They eventually settled on "Daffy," a nickname that was the furthest thing from quiet Paul's personality. But the sporting press liked it because it went well with Dizzy. Dizzy and Daffy.

Paul hated it.

Paul seldom talked, but he did tell the St. Louis *Globe-Democrat*'s Martin J. Haley how he became a pitcher: "Dizzy and I played on the same semipro team when we were kids, but he was a pitcher and I played shortstop. I was still playing short when I went to high school for two years, but in 1930 I became a pitcher all of a sudden. I was playing a semi-pro game. Our regular pitcher was knocked out. The coach asked me to go in. I did, and have been pitching ever since."

On March 11, after a holdout of only a week, Paul signed his 1934 contract. Diz ended his holdout at the same time. Branch Rickey was out of town, so the Deans hammered out the final details with owner Sam Breadon. It was one of the Deans' short-est holdouts because camp was in full swing and Paul needed to be out there proving his worth. Diz had a job; Paul still had to win one.

The stories varied on whether or not Paul got more money. Leo Durocher thought perhaps he got another $500; others doubted he got any pay boost.

Durocher thought Diz should have held out even longer because he was making so much money on the golf course: "All the time he had been holding out he had been playing golf against a fellow named Mort Bright, who owned the inn where we were staying. The higher the stakes go, the surer you can be that [Diz's] going to win. By the time he put the uniform on, he had beaten Mort Bright for $16,000 or $17,000. Twice his salary. And I told Diz then not to play the guy any more. 'Because boy,' I said. 'You've got the uniform on now and that putter won't be the same in your hand.'"

Diz, sure he knew what he was doing, declined Leo's advice. "Mort Bright followed us north," Durocher recalled. "Every morning, wherever we were playing, they'd be out at the local links. Bright followed us all the way to St. Louis, and got all his money back."

Diz and Paul weren't the only Cards talking of quitting. Out-fielder Ernie Orsatti, angered at having to take a 25 percent pay cut, was threatening to retire and become an actor. It wasn't as farfetched as it sounded. Orsatti had been Buster Keaton's dou-ble and frequently worked in film during the off season.

After the Dean brothers' settlement Diz declared to Martin J. Haley, "We're going to win between us 40 or 45 games this year."

When Haley asked, "How many will Paul win?" Diz replied, "I don't know but I guess he'll win more than me." In later retellings of this story, Diz's answer would change to: "Why all that I don't."

Paul actually had similar feelings. When pressed on the matter by Haley, he shrugged, "I wouldn't want to say how many we might win, but I've got confidence in Dizzy."

Durocher and some of the other infielders were playing a game of pepper on another occasion when Diz made another of his famous forty-five wins predictions to sportswriters. "[We're playing] right in front of them, with our backs to the bleachers, and we're all on the ear because everybody on the team got a kick out of Diz."

When Diz announced he and Paul would win forty-five, Durocher wrote, "We could hear the sportswriters snicker, which was all right because we were snickering too.... So I started to laugh. I looked at Frisch and said, 'Well, let's go fishing for a month and a half. We've got forty-five won. We don't have a worry in the world.' Frank looked at me sourly. 'Let's win them first. Then we'll talk about it.'"

Paul quickly showed his stuff, and on March 17 Sid Keener reported, "The real hot tip in camp is Paul Dean, and they say Paul will be a better pitcher than Dizzy in 1935. According to the inside dope, Paul will be another Walter Johnson, just as fast as the former smokeball king of the American League."

After only a week Frisch had Paul penciled in the starting rotation. "Pennants are won, however, largely on pitching, and we have plenty of that," he told Joe Williams of the New York *World-Telegram*. "First, there is Dizzy Dean, and, second, there is Paul Dean.... Behind the Deans come Bill Hallahan, Bill Walker, Tex Carleton and Jim Mooney."

The Deans were going to be the deans of the staff.

The Cardinals wound up their Florida training schedule Sunday April 8 and headed for St. Louis the next afternoon on the A.C.I. train for their annual spring series against the Browns.

The Cards opened the season April 17 against the Pirates. The starting pitcher was, of course, Diz. A crowd of 7,500 was on hand to see Diz hold the Pirates to six hits and one run in winning his first of the season, 7-1. There would be many more.

Paul didn't have as auspicious a beginning to his career—and to this season—as his older brother. He started the second game of the year and gave up four runs in only two innings. But young Dean was off the hook for the decision; the Cards tied the score in the seventh, but lost in the eighth when Cookie Lavagetto, younger than Paul by a year, homered off reliever Burleigh Grimes. The final was 7-6.

The Cardinals didn't exactly bolt out of the gate. At the end of the first week they were 1-6 and tied for sixth place with the hapless Reds.

Diz and Paul both took a shellacking from the Cubs on Monday, April 23. Diz started, if you could call it that, giving up six runs in three innings. In relief Paul gave up two runs in two innings. A week later in Chicago Diz was pounded again. It was the second time this season and the fourth in a row that the Northsiders had Diz's number.

The Cardinals finished the month of April 3-7, wedged in seventh place. Diz fared no better for the month: he was 1-2.

But the Dean brothers were able to turn it around as spring arrived in the Midwest. Paul beat the Phillies in relief May 3; two days later Diz beat them, 7-1. Diz shut out the Giants, 4-0, May 9; two days later Paul bested ace Carl Hubbell, 4-3, in a ten-inning game.

By the middle of the month the Cards had righted themselves and were 15-9, in third place, only a game and a half back of the Pirates.

When Diz won his fifth game on May 20, a 9-5 victory over the defending world champion Giants and Hubbell in New York,

Jimmy Powers of the New York *Daily News* wrote, "The merry madcap, that zany, that belligerent buffoon, Dizzy Dean, methinks, is as looney as Br'er Fox. Leastwise, he is too smart for our Giants. He slit the sleeves of his undershirt, waved his flapping arms above his head and kept pouring that little white onion in there yesterday and coasted to a victory."

He noted Diz's propensity for coasting after his teammates staked him to a big lead. "After that [lead] Dean relaxed. He grinned good humoredly into the glowering face of Manager Bill Terry, impudently capered at the plate, and passed the time of day with the umpires. He strutted, he boasted and he dominated the diamond before 40,000 fans, the largest crowd yet this season."

Diz might have been happy on the mound, but off the field he was still fuming over Paul's salary. On May 23, he led a two-man strike—with Paul—for higher wages. The strike of the Dean brothers ended as quickly as it started. When it came time for Diz's next scheduled start in Philadelphia two days later, he took the mound and beat the Phillies, 5-2. "That's just Dizzy popping off," explained Sam Breadon.

St. Louis *Post-Dispatch* sports columnist John E. Wray actually praised the Deans for their shenanigans: "The Deans love to complain, but they love to pitch better. And it's the heart they have for the game, their real zest for playing, that makes fans and owners forget their popping off. Too bad there are not a few more players with the Dean heart and spirit."

Also joining the chorus of approval was Joe Williams: "Mr. Dizzy would be getting twice as much pitching for the Giants, and he would be worth it. And he is worth it in St. Louis, but because salaries have never been high there he doesn't get it. Mr. Nutsey was started at a beginner's pay as it is figured in St. Louis. By now it is apparent that he is a real pitcher worth much more than $3,000. I am glad the Deans struck, and I think this sort of striking should be encouraged. I see no reason why a young ball player should have to wait a full year for adequate recognition at the cashier's window."

But the *Star-Times*'s Sid Keener scorched the brothers, Diz in particular, in his column: "My opinion of the affair is that the Deans were putting out more of their ballyhoo. The senior member of the Dean firm thrives on publicity. And when things become too quiet for his showmanship he can be counted on to pop up with something. On the field, Dizzy is a tireless worker, loyal to the cause and a pitcher extraordinary. I have never seen a player, except possibly Ty Cobb, put more vim and energy into his labors than Dizzy. Besides being an artist on the hill, Diz will run his fool head off in an attempt to sneak an extra base, and, unlike the average hurler, he's a hitter of considerable power. Why can't Dizzy cut out his comedy and confine his bid for fame to his performance on the field?"

As May came to a close the Gas House Gang seemed to be running on all cylinders. They were in first place, twelve games over .500. While the team was in Philadelphia Frisch hit upon an idea to keep the players' attention on the matter at hand. He began posting the league standings on the inside of the door of the Cardinals' dressing room. At the bottom in huge red letters the trainer scribbled WIN TODAY'S GAME.

Catcher Virgil Davis thought it was a good idea: "That's Frankie Frisch's battle cry so the trainer printed it on the card so we would see it just before going on the field."

With the team living up to Diz's expectations, and predictions, the clubhouse was loose and carefree. The Philadelphia *Inquirer*'s Old Sport columnist painted a picture of the Gas House Gang at leisure: "Dizzy Dean, reaching in locker 13 (he always insists on No. 13 locker) uttered a shrill mock cry of anguish. 'Hey, who took that dirty sock out of my locker? I can't pitch unless I find it. I can't pitch unless I find it. Haven't worked a game this season without having it in my pocket.'

"For three minutes the clubhouse was in turmoil as Dean turned lockers upside down in an effort to locate the missing sock.

"'You never had more than two socks in your life,' growled Frisch. 'You'll probably find it on your foot.'

"Dean looked at his right leg and then looked sheepishly at the charmed dirty sock hiding his No. 12 foot."

But things were not as tranquil as they seemed, at least not as long as Dizzy was around. On June 1, just as the Cardinals arrived in Pittsburgh from Cincinnati, Diz announced that the Dean brothers would pitch no more until their salary differences were settled.

Dizzy, who was scheduled to face the Pirates in the opening game of a four-game series, met with Frisch and informed him that he had a "sore arm." Paul joined in; he too had a sore arm.

Frisch had talked with Branch Rickey during the Cards' series in Cincinnati about Diz's strike in New York. Diz was again seeking a pay boost for Paul and when Frisch declared that he would not intercede with club president Sam Breadon, Diz pitched a fit. The meeting ended with the exasperated Frisch telling Diz, "If you don't want to pitch, go home."

"If Paul had my nerve," Dizzy told Ray J. Gillespie of the St. Louis *Star-Times*, "we'd both be back in St. Louis. I don't need a second invitation to leave when I'm not appreciated. Paul must get $1,000 cash in the hand, and there will be no compromising. When Paul and I went on strike in New York, Frisch promised he'd go to the office in St. Louis and plead our case. Now Frank has turned his back on us. Paul and I aren't running out on the other players. We'd do everything possible to help win the pennant and an extra $5,000 apiece, but we feel that we're getting the run-around by the club, and if the management doesn't care about the extra money, why should we?"

Dizzy then brought up a point that would not endear him to his colleagues on the pitching staff. He noted that his salary ($7,500) and Paul's ($3,000) together didn't equal the pay of certain other pitchers who would be lucky to win half as many games as one of the Dean boys. Then Diz mentioned a teammate by name. "Hallahan gets $12,500," he complained, insinuating that Wild Bill Hallahan, who'd won sixteen games as the Cards' number-three starter in '33, wouldn't win as many as Paul, the rookie.

"I'm satisfied with my own pay which is what I got last year, but Paul must get $2,000 more, or the Cards won't win the pennant." Diz concluded, "Neither Paul nor I will pitch any more under present circumstances."

Frisch called the Deans to his hotel room that night to hear their complaints. First Paul appeared before Frisch and his informal arbitration board of traveling secretary Clarence Lloyd, coaches Mike Gonzalez and Buzzy Wares, and veteran pitcher Jesse "Pop" Haines. Frisch would later remember the meeting this way: "Paul said that he had no complaint, that he had signed his contract and was going through with it, and that he wasn't going to go on any strike. I summoned Dizzy to hear that, and it struck me that it ought to be convincing. But after listening to it all and saying that everything was all right, Dizzy decided that Paul really didn't mean it, and he guessed he'd better keep on with his strike for Little Paul."

But by morning the strike—this strike anyway—was over. "My arm's getting better fast," Diz told Roy Stockton. "Tell Frank that I'll throw this arm off for old Frank and the boys."

The next day Diz, true to his promise, downed the Pirates,

13-4, with Paul providing relief in the eighth. The Dean boys were back.

As summer's heat arrived in St. Louis the Cardinals began to wilt. They played twenty-one games at home that month and lost one more game than they won, slipping from first place to third. But the slump couldn't be blamed on the Deans. They had pitched magnificently during the month, winning in lockstep, first Diz, then Paul. The Cards won only thirteen games during the month, Diz and Paul each winning five.

And on Sunday, June 18, they almost single-handedly carried the Cardinals on their shoulders to a doubleheader victory over the Phillies. Paul won the opener, 5-0; Diz, who had pitched eight innings in a losing cause Saturday, came on to relieve in the seventh inning of the second game, with the Cards trailing 5-4. He shut the Phils down while his teammates overcame the stalling tactics of Phils manager Jimmie Wilson, who saw dark clouds on the horizon and used four pitchers on four batters in an attempt to wait on the storm. The tactic backfired when the tying run scored on a windblown single. The Cards wound up winning 7-5.

On June 28 Dizzy got a bit of good news that would become even more significant at the end of the season. National League president John A. Heydler announced that he had changed the original scoring decision for the Cardinals' June 23 victory over Brooklyn. Bill Hallahan had been improperly credited with the win even though Diz had been the pitcher of record when the winning run scored.

It came on the heels of another controversial scoring decision and gave Diz twelve wins on the season. Only the day before, June 27, the Cardinals' official scorer, Martin J. Haley of the *Globe-Democrat*, had awarded Diz the victory in an 8-7 win over the Giants, even though Diz was no longer the pitcher of record when the winning run scored in the bottom of ninth. Diz had pitched eight and two-thirds innings but gave up three straight singles in the ninth that produced a run and tied the score. He was replaced by Lefty Mooney, who retired the final batter. The Cardinals won in the bottom of the ninth on a homer by Bill DeLancey, but scorer Haley gave the victory to Diz.

Those two scoring decisions didn't add up to much in June but come September they would be the difference between twenty-eight wins and Diz's benchmark thirty-win season.

Even though Dizzy had won five games in the seventeen days since he returned from his strike, resentments still simmered among his teammates. "Some of them resent the acclaim and applause heaped upon the Dean brothers, insisting that their own part in the success of the Redbirds has been ignored," wrote Garry Schumacher in the June 29 New York *Evening Journal.* "The Deans are all the St. Louis fans talk about. When anybody else starts on the mound, the fans chant in unison, 'We want Dean.' This attitude is supposed to explain much of Hallahan's recent ineffectiveness."

The *Sporting News*'s Dick Farrington supported this claim: "Alas, there is a drawback with the Deans. When they are winning, the other members of the hurling staff sulk in their tents. Curbstone gossip would have us believe that Frankie Frisch is not getting 1,000 percent out of some of them.... Not all the Cardinal hurlers like the Deans for what they are worth in a material sense. They resent the publicity diverted from them to the Deans. And there was that 'crack' Dizzy made in Pittsburgh about himself being more valuable to the ball club than Hallahan, who was getting about 40 percent more pay. This didn't help the Hallahan morale any, and there have been reports that Bill would like to be traded."

The Cardinals' front office fueled some of this resentment with the tub-thumping they gave Diz's performances. Ads that

114

once would have trumpeted "Giants vs. Cards at Sportsman's Park today" now read "Dizzy Dean in person vs. the Giants today."

"Farmers come out of the distant Ozarks and Mid-West traveling salesmen arrange their itineraries to catch him," Jimmy Powers wrote in the June 29 New York *Daily News*. "Sam Breadon told me that had Dean pitched last Sunday it would have meant 15,000 extra admissions."

As hard as they played on the field, the Gas House Gang members played even harder off the field, and tales of the Gang were legend and legion.

For fun Dizzy and Pepper Martin would frighten little old ladies at the hotel by staging fights. They would put unpopped popcorn in their mouths and begin swinging at each other, spraying kernels around the lobby as if they were flying teeth.

In the years of the Gas House Gang only one man could match Diz joke for practical joke: Pepper. Pepper carried sneeze powder everywhere he went and never failed to spray it in the air on New York's subways. Once in a New York hotel lobby he climbed up on the mezzanine and dropped sneeze powder on some old man's newspaper. The man promptly began sneezing. "It was red hot July weather in New York," Diz later told his radio audience, "but the man's wife turned to him and says, 'I told you, Roscoe, that you should have put on a heavier suit than that.'"

Agnes Schuble, whose husband, Heinie, was a utility infielder on the 1936 Gas House Gang, remembers, "They would play tricks all the time. One time they dressed up in overalls and went into a room at the Democratic convention and acted like they were painting things. And they gave the rookies a hard way to go. They used to put sparrows in their rooms and when the rookies would open the door, they would think bats were flying around."

No one was immune. Ethan Allen, a substitute outfielder on

the '33 team, recalls a stunt Dizzy pulled on him: "One stop at Detroit, I was taking a bath. We didn't have showers in those days. He kept telling me to hurry up so finally he just jumped in on top of me with clothes and all."

In his autobiography Frisch told about an incident from one evening in Boston: "I was standing in front of the Kenmore Hotel [where the Cardinals were staying] ... drinking in the fine New England air, when something exploded at my feet, drenching me and several other persons who were standing with me. It was a paper bag full of water that had been tossed from an upper window. If it had scored a clean hit, we could have dried off by jumping into the Charles River. It must have been a laundry bag." Frisch never did find out which of his prankster players tossed the water bag but Diz later told his radio listeners: it was Pepper.

In late June Jimmy Powers caught up with Diz in one of his quieter party moods, at a St. Louis amusement park: "In an outdoor pavilion our hero was dancing with his wife. He wore a white polo shirt, open at the throat, and a night wind tousled his handsome head until his hair sprayed out in all directions like a busted whisk broom. The orchestra was playing a waltz, and Jerome was singing softly to his wife, cheek to cheek, his lips close to her ears. She is a very pretty woman, Mrs. Jerome Dean, and when you see her you realize what a great wave of love swept through the heart of the farmer-boy-rookie when he first met her."

The Cardinals' reign at the top of the National League was brief, one twenty-four hour period in June. By the All-Star break they were in third, four games behind the Giants and two behind Chicago.

And as summer's dog days approached The Old Sport columnist in the Philadephia *Inquirer* found a dour Frankie Frisch at the Cardinals' helm: "Frisch isn't smiling much these days, not even at the antics of baseball's greatest clown, Dizzy Dean. When a man can't laugh at Dean, the thunder clouds are hanging low and the lightning is about to strike. Frisch looked as if he hadn't shaved for two days when we saw him peering out of the Cardinal dugout yesterday. Maybe the fact that he had 'charley horses' in both legs had something to do with his fierceness of face. The fact is, however, that the brilliant Redbird cast is in third place, and in the last 37 games has lost 19, certainly not a pennant stride."

The Cardinals were in a tailspin in early July, a slide that could cost Frisch his job if he didn't turn things around. After all, Branch Rickey had fired Gabby Street in the middle of the '33 season, when the team still had a winning record.

The slump was taking its toll. In Cincinnati on July 8 Paul charged the Reds' dugout, irritated at the riding the Reds' bench jockeys—aged pitcher Ray Kolp in particular—were giving him. Diz loped over from his dugout seat to protect his baby brother, inviting any takers to come out and fight. Coach Mike Gonzalez interceded, and soon things were calm. But the damage had been done. Paul was shaken and gave up two more runs that inning. Cincinnati coasted to an 8-4 win.

During one particularly trying period, when the Cards couldn't seem to buy a hit, Frisch received a phone call from one of his friends, Bernie O'Shea, who was all excited over a kid pitcher he had watched throw a no-hitter that afternoon in a semipro game. Diz would later tell his radio audience that O'Shea jabbered, "Kid was so good only one loud foul was made off him. Don't you want me to bring him around for a tryout?"

Frisch paused a minute, then told his friend, "The way my club's been hitting just get me the name of that kid that hit the loud foul."

Frisch blamed injuries and bad breaks for the fall, but the fact was the Cards just weren't playing well. Except for Dizzy. Even Paul was having his troubles, losing three in a row.

"It's too bad in a way that [Paul] hasn't Dizzy's happy-go-lucky disposition," Frisch told The Old Sport. "Paul is more serious. Dizzy is just plain crazy, but a fellow has to be crazy to be a good ball player. If you aren't cuckoo when you start, you soon get that way."

As Frisch spoke, Diz was out in the opponents' bull pen, making eyes at "Southie," the famous lucky rabbit of the Phillies.

Dean bounded into the dugout, shouting, "I've got it. I've got it," and The Old Sport reported the rest of the conversation like this:

" 'You got what?' asked Virgil Davis.

" 'I have the secret of how to eat grass, get fat and enjoy it,' replied Dean.

" 'How is that?' queried Davis.

" 'Just become a bunny.' "

The team was still playing badly the first week in August, losing two of three at Chicago and splitting a four-game series at home with the Pirates, but Diz had a solution: "This country may have needed a good five-cent cigar," he told Roy Stockton one morning. "But what the Cardinals need is more Deans."

Diz may have known something because the next day, August 9, the Cardinals' office announced the "purchase" of another Dean, Elmer Dean, elder brother of Dizzy and Paul, from Houston.

"Credit for scouting Elmer, is being taken by Blake Harper, head of Sportsman's Park concessions," said the *Post-Dispatch*, tongue firmly in cheek. For Elmer wouldn't be joining the pitching rotation. He would be selling peanuts.

Actually it was Houston Buffaloes president Fred Ankenman

Young Diz: The earliest known photograph of Diz in a baseball uniform. He was eighteen years old and pitching for the San Antonio Public Service Company baseball team. (Courtesy of National Baseball Library, Cooperstown, NY)

Dizzy Dean Birthplace: The site in Lucas, Arkansas, where Diz was born. The house he was born in has been torn down. It was located about ten feet behind this house.

Crossroads of America: In the thirties, forties, and fifties tourists drove miles out of their way to see the Lucas, Arkansas, general store, the community center in the tiny town where Diz was born, and talk to the old-timers there about baby Diz.

The Smoking Gun: Diz fudged his age his entire life. But census records don't lie. Here is the listing from the April 1910 census of Logan County, Arkansas, listing little Jay Dean, age 3 months.

Burial Ground: Diz finally 'fessed up to his real birth year for his tombstone.

Diz's Field of Dreams: Spaulding, Oklahoma, ball field where Diz starred in the mid-twenties. At that time this was right field, where Diz hit a home run that became lost in the weeds.

School Daze: Spaulding School, where
Diz attended on Fridays only. This building has been torn down. (Photograph
courtesy of Johnny Mayfield)

Dean Homeplace: The remains of the Dean family's sharecropping home on Tater Hill outside Spaulding, Oklahoma. The Deans lived here in the mid-twenties. (Photograph courtesy of David Ferguson)

APPLICATION FOR EMPLOYMENT

SAN ANTONIO PUBLIC SERVICE CO.
SOUTH TEXAS DEPT.   COMAL DEPT.

INSTRUCTIONS—Applications must be made in own handwriting.

I hereby apply for employment during your or my own pleasure and if accepted agree to observe all rules and regulations; to pay my bills promptly each month; to maintain strict integrity of character; to perform my duties to the best of my ability, and any wages earned by or owing to me shall not be due and payable until the regular pay day of the Company.

1. Name in full _Phil Herman Dunn_
2. Date of birth _16 day Jan 1911_ Place of Birth _Kerrville, Tex._
   Address _412 Ash Street Sanantion Texas_ Phone _9605_
3. Name of wife, if living (if unmarried, so state) _Single_
   Education _9th_ Grade School _9th_ High School _9th_ College _no_
4. Name and address of father and mother, | _Albert Dunn Living_
   if living, if either dead so state | _Mother dead_
5. If unmarried and parents are not living, name and address of nearest relative _Claude J parham Houston Tex_
6. Names and addresses of any person dependent on you for support, or to whose support you are contributing _father albert Dunn_
7. When and by whom were you last employed? Explain nature of employment? _U S army_
8. Have you any relatives now employed by this company, if so, give their names and the departments in which employed? _None_
9. Give particulars and amount of any debt you owe, or liabilities you are under _None_
10. What is your vocation or trade _Machinist_
11. The following persons would most likely know my whereabouts should I leave the service of the Company
    Name _____
    Address _____
12. Fill in the following blank, giving date of your employment and names and addresses of employers during the last five years.

FROM WHAT DATE	TO WHAT DATE	EMPLOYER	AT ADDRESS

13. Give names and addresses of as many persons as possible for references, who are not related to you and not former employers:

NAME	OCCUPATION	ADDRESS

ALL QUESTIONS MUST BE ANSWERED

Get a Job: Diz's employment application, filled out April 9, 1929. Note his spelling of San Antonio: "Sanantion." He was also claiming a ninth-grade education.

who had found Elmer. He remembers, "As a result of the Dixie Series in 1931 which Dizzy pitched, we discovered a brother of Dizzy's living in Arkansas. We had already signed Paul Dean, who had the earmarks of another outstanding prospect. We thought what a great thing it would be to have three brothers as pitching greats. We had Elmer, the brother referred to, come to Houston for a try-out. As a pitcher or a ball player, he proved to be a complete failure. He wanted a job so we put him to work as a vendor in our concession department … selling cold drinks."

Elmer was a sensation at first, thanks in large part to being a Dean brother. But soon his sales dropped off precipitously.

Ankenman discovered the problem in a conversation with Houston fire commissioner Allie Anderson: "Allie said if I would just watch him for a while I could see the reason. Well, I did. In those days, cold drinks were sold in bottles, and the vendors would have a towel tied to the side of the trousers which they would use to wipe the tops of the bottles after removing the caps. I watched a sale being made by Elmer to a couple close by. He removed the caps, wiped the tops off with the towel, and then, using the same towel, he wiped the sweat off his face. We took him off selling cold drinks and changed him over to selling peanuts. He turned out to be the greatest peanut salesman you can imagine."

Ankenman credits Branch Rickey with Elmer's "call-up": "Mr. Rickey came to Houston once for a doubleheader and when he saw what a great job Elmer was doing at selling peanuts, he suggested he be taken to St. Louis where Mr. Rickey said Elmer would make a 'cleanup' in Sportsman's Park. So, we sent him to St. Louis. He was doing great, but after about three days, Mrs. Dean came to Mr. Rickey and demanded that Elmer be discontinued as a vendor in Sportsman's Park. She thought it very unethical and embarrassing to her and Dizzy with Diz out there on the field doing a great pitching job for the Cardinals."

So Elmer's big-league career was short-lived.

The St. Louis *Star-Times* reported on August 10 that "upholding the reputation and tradition of the Deans, the elder brother of Dizzy and Paul 'jumped' the club today."

Elmer returned to his job in Houston, selling peanuts at Houston Buffaloes baseball games. The *Globe-Democrat* quoted Elmer as saying the big league "ain't what it's cracked up to be." He added he didn't "like the looks of St. Louis."

He was welcomed back by Ankenman: "We were glad to have him."

The brothers Dean got in hot water again during an August homestand. After an August 12 doubleheader against the Cubs, the Cards were to train up to Detroit for an exhibition game against the Tigers on August 13. The Deans somehow missed the train.

Dizzy told the *Globe-Democrat*'s Haley that he and Paul just decided not to make the trip. "I did not see any reason to make the trip. Besides, I hurt my arm Sunday. That's why I lost my fast ball. I pulled something loose in my right elbow in the fourth inning. I didn't have my stuff after that."

Paul offered a different excuse: "I hurried out of the clubhouse Saturday after the game without reading the notice about the trip to Detroit. Then I went to the park Sunday morning without a coat or grip. I returned to the hotel for them after the double-header and waited around, thinking Jerome would pick me up. He did not show up, and when I called the station they told me the train had left. I'm not passing the buck to Jerome, 'cause I'm not sorry I stayed in St. Louis. I was really tired and needed a rest."

Neither's absence was excused, so Frisch fined the brothers, Dizzy $100 and Paul $50.

"There must be discipline on a ball club," Frisch told Roy

Stockton. "I played 18 innings on Sunday, and so did the other regulars. Paul pitched 5 innings and Dizzy 7 2/3. So they didn't do as much work as lots of others. When the Yankees schedule an exhibition game, Babe Ruth is always present. So I see no reason why the Dean brothers should not be on hand when the Cardinals play an exhibition. That was a great show at Detroit, and it should have meant a lot to the players. The park was crowded with boys and girls, future customers and the ball player owes something to a crowd like that. There's no hardship in a train ride. People pay money to take train rides. Baseball is our business, and the mere fact that we worked Sunday is no excuse for running out on a Monday game just because it's an exhibition."

The next day, after Frisch announced his fines, Dizzy was dressing for the game against the Phillies and asked Frisch, "Do those fines stick, Frank?"

When Frisch replied, "Sure they stick," Dizzy got angry. "Well, then, we'll take off our uniforms."

Paul me-tooed, "Yeah, we'll take 'em off."

As the rest of the team ran out for batting practice, Dizzy stretched out on the rubbing table in the trainer's office, refusing to move. Paul sat nearby, dressed only in his uniform pants.

Ray Gillespie described the escalating confrontation in the *Star-Times:* "Manager Frisch returned to the clubhouse and said, 'Come on, boys, this is a big league ball club. Let's go.'

" 'We're not a-goin' out on the field!' Dizzy replied defiantly.

" 'You're not?' Frisch shouted. 'Well then, take off those uniforms. You're both suspended!'

"Dizzy leaped to his feet, shouting, cursing and announcing to one and all that he would never pitch again for the Cardinals.

" 'This will be the end of my Cardinal uniforms!' he yelled as he tore his white 'home' shirt and his traveling gray paraphernalia to shreds and scattered them over the floor.

"Cooler heads tried to intervene. Tex Carleton and Ripper

Collins warned the boys that they would be sorry later for whatever hasty action they might take. But Dizzy and Paul only stamped up and down the clubhouse, kicking benches, throwing cushions, and upsetting the place in general."

The brothers and Diz's wife watched the Cardinals-Phillies game that day from the press box. In the fourth inning, Pat Dean got up and said, "Come on, Diz, let's go."

When asked where they were going by the writers, Diz winked, "To Florida."

But they didn't leave town immediately. Instead they announced they would hang around until August 23, when the league-leading Giants arrived for an important three-game series at Sportsman's Park.

They were staying, Diz told Gillespie, because "Then we figure the Cards will ask us to rejoin the club. Now, while they are playing the Phillies, they don't have to worry about us. Anybody can beat the Phils. But it'll be different when the Giants come to town. It takes Diz and Paul to stop the Giants, and the Cards know it!"

Dizzy issued an ultimatum to the Cardinals: that their fines be returned to them and that they not be "docked" for being out of uniform for two games.

But the Cardinals' position was hardening. "One set of rules applies to all the players," Frisch told the *Globe-Democrat.* "The Deans had no excuse for not going to Detroit, so I fined them, and after they wouldn't play I suspended them. They can put on their uniforms any time they care to, but the fines stick."

Sam Breadon told reporters that Dizzy's fine was larger than Paul's because he was older and received more salary. Breadon also noted that it was Paul's first offense and that he was influenced by Dizzy.

It is almost unthinkable that the two top pitchers of a baseball club would desert their team just as the season headed into the home stretch. But that's exactly what Diz and Paul were doing. If it seems callous and selfish, that's because it was. Diz was playing the part of the impetuous kid, and Paul was doing what he always did, following.

It was a face-off, and management wasn't giving in. On August 15, the regular payday, Dizzy and Paul were each given their last paychecks, less the fines and less two days' salary. Diz was charged an additional thirty-six dollars for the two uniforms he had ripped up. The first uniform was torn up in a fit of rage at Frisch. Diz destroyed the second one for the photographers' benefit.

"I appreciate the fine pitching the Deans have done," said Frisch, "but that doesn't give them the privilege to do as they please. Even if it costs me my job, I'm standing pat. I won't give in because that would be unfair to others who have been fined and have taken it like men."

The situation was rapidly deteriorating into the Deans versus the Cardinals, all the Cardinals. Frisch told reporters, "Yesterday my players gathered around me and gave me a vote of confidence and said they'd give the best they have."

The next day the parties met to try and iron things out.

Diz announced that if the fines were rescinded and the wages restored, he and Paul would be back on the field in a minute.

"Those fines stay," Frisch insisted. "Take it or leave it. Go to Florida if you want and stay there. I don't want you back unless you meet my terms."

When Diz announced that he and Paul were leaving for Florida immediately, Branch Rickey offered to pay their transportation.

Despite the obvious bitterness on the Cardinals' side, Diz was optimistic. He felt sure Cardinals would refund his thirty-six dollars for the uniforms he destroyed. "I think I can get them patched up," he said.

Meanwhile, the Cardinals weren't missing the Deans as much

as the Deans had hoped they would. They had whipped the Phillies four straight and topped Boston in the first game of a four-game set.

It looked like a break in the impasse when Pat Dean told United Press she thought both Diz and Paul would be back with the Cardinals "in a day or two." She offered a new explanation for Diz's absence in Detroit: "Diz will never admit it but the reason he didn't go to Detroit was that he was heart-broken over that double-header Sunday. [The Cards had lost both games to the Cubs.] Dizzy was so disgusted he simply didn't want to see anyone. He wouldn't even have a soda with me after the game. Diz hates to lose. It hurts his pride. If he had won, he could have gone to Detroit a hero, but losing, he felt he would be a heel."

She opened the door to a settlement: "It was expensive, $100 for a day's vacation, but I feel that if he wanted the vacation he should accept the fine and go back to the club. He wasn't trying to flaunt any rules; he was just heart-broken."

But her most convincing argument for an early return by Diz and Paul was: "The Dean family needs the money."

Diz told his own story in an open letter printed in the August 17 *Post-Dispatch:*

As a favor to me I want you to print this letter. I want to present my side of this argument. I realize I made a mistake in not making the trip to Detroit. Had I known what the game was all about I would not have disappointed those kids for anything in the world. But I was so disgusted about losing that double-header Sunday that I didn't care if I never saw another game or not.

You know how bad I hate to lose. And when Paul and I both lost before that crowd of loyal St. Louis people I was downhearted. It's bad enough to lose when I am away from home, but to go out there and pitch my heart out in that hot sun and still lose, well, you can imagine just how I felt.

Then, Tuesday, when the team came home I went out to the park expecting a fine. I realized I had made a mistake. When I went into the clubhouse I expected Frank to call me over and tell me I was fined. But it seems as though everybody on the team had been told about it before I was. So when they all, from the bat boy up, got through telling me I was fined I wasn't in any frame of mind to be jumped on. So I blew up. One word brought on another, and when the storm was over I had torn up my uniforms.

The ball club announced I was suspended until I would accept the fines and that I could return when I was ready to. I wanted to return today, and I agreed to take the fines, suspension for two days without pay and to pay for the uniforms. But after I agreed to do that, the "powers that be" informed me that I would get an extra ten days' suspension, because Paul does not care to return. Paul is 21 years old and a man with his own mind.

I have apologized and admitted I was wrong, and I want to go back to work now, not ten days from now. I'll leave it up to you and all the sports fans, what else can I do?

> Sincerely,
> "Dizzy" Dean

It was an attempt to win the fans to his side. And it might have worked if the fans hadn't been reading the Deans' changing stories in daily newspaper dispatches.

The matter came to a head on Monday, August 20, when the warring parties met in Commissioner Kenesaw Mountain Landis's office for a hearing.

Diz admitted he had told a radio interviewer, "Yes, I'll be glad to pitch for the St. Louis fans but not for the Cardinals" …"I said that, but I was sore at the time, and I'm sorry about it."

The Cardinals presented evidence that Diz had been a problem employee since he joined the Cardinal organization, dating back to his stints in St. Joseph, Missouri, and Houston.

When Rickey was questioning a witness from the Cards' office, Dizzy interrupted, "Sure, they'll say what you want. They'd be a fool if they didn't."

In the end Diz was the losing pitcher. Landis ruled the Cardinals were right in fining and suspending the Deans.

Diz posed afterward for pictures with Breadon, Rickey, and Frisch, but when photographers asked for a smile he pretended not to hear them.

On Friday, August 24, Diz and Paul returned to the team. They had missed nine games, at least two starts apiece, in the thick of the season. Diz played the role of returning prodigal son to the hilt. The New York *Evening Journal*'s Garry Schumacher described this new Dizzy Dean: "He allowed his shoulders to slump and hung his head, focusing his eyes on the ground as though anxious to avoid the gaze of the crowd. Whenever Manager Frisch offered a word of advice he listened with studied attention. The crowd got the impression he wanted them to get—that here was a man sorry for his sins and anxious to make amends. As the game progressed, and his pitching won storms of approval, his attitude changed. He straightened his shoulders, became his old aggressive, assertive self. He began to talk to the Giant batters, taunt them as they came to the plate."

Diz shut out the Giants, 5-0, on five hits for his twenty-second win of the season. Schumacher concluded that Dizzy Dean was back: "Yes sir, it was Dizzy's day, his show. If St. Louis didn't kill the fatted calf in his honor last night, it is truly ungrateful."

Diz was back and not an inning too soon. The Cardinals needed him if they were to have any chance of overtaking the Giants. Time was running out. The Cardinals were seven games back with only thirty-six games to go.

Diz's fans were still behind him too.

The next day, when Tex Carleton was being slapped around by Dodger hitters, the 3,000 youngsters in Sportsman's Park's left-field bleachers began a familiar chant: "We want Dean! We want Dean! We want Dean!" Reliever Jesse Haines received the same treatment later in the game, and when Lefty Mooney came on in the ninth, instead of Dizzy or Paul, the knothole gang actually booed him.

The repentant Dizzy was gone. The braggart Dizzy was back: "I know for a fact that the St. Louis club was offered $100,000 and a few good players for me, and several teams have been trying to buy Paul for $50,000," he told Bill McCullough of the Brooklyn *Times-Union*. He was already beginning his salary negotiations for next season. "I don't care where I pitch so long as I get the salary I'm entitled to. And that goes for Paul, too."

Then, after boasting to McCullough that no hitter in the league could touch him when he was in stride, he turned around and claimed he didn't like publicity: "[Dizzy] maintains that they can't keep him out of the headlines. He claims he's just a bashful boy from Oklahoma whom the big town sports pages thrive on because without a Dizzy to write about they would pass out of existence."

On September 3, Labor Day, the Cards lost a doubleheader to the Pirates at the same time the Giants were winning two from the Dodgers. The Cards were now seven games out, with twenty-six to go. Frisch would later pick this day as the turning point in the season. "That was the end of the pennant boom, most everyone believed," he later told Sid Keener. "I never saw such a dejected bunch of athletes." So before the next game he held his team meeting an hour earlier than usual. "I burned them like they'd never been burned before. 'Are you fellows going to quit?' I shouted. 'It ain't over. If you fight to the finish, we won't be beaten.' 'We ain't givin' up, Frankie,' growled Dizzy. 'I'm pitchin' today and I'll show you we ain't beat.' "

Diz went out that afternoon and held the Dodgers to three hits as the Cards won, 2-1.

Baseball players are the most superstitious of athletes. There are countless stories of streaking hitters refusing to change underwear and pitchers on a roll following pointless routines because they seemed to corrolate with success.

So it was a breach of the highest etiquette when on Friday, September 14, Diz walked into the Giants' dugout at the Polo Grounds with a black cat in his arms. He aimed the feline's nose at Giant second baseman Hughie Critz and then began making mysterious hex signs.

" 'Cat, get Critz. Critz, get jinxed. Zmmmmm,' John Lardner of the New York *Post* reported Diz saying.

Critz vanished, and Lardner said Diz smiled. "That got him. This will get 'em all."

Diz then aimed the unlucky black cat up and down the dugout row before setting him loose in the bull pen. But the hex didn't work. The Dodgers won that night, 4-1, pushing the Cards to five and a half games back. But maybe Diz's hex wasn't designed to produce immediate results.

On September 7 and 8 an event had happened in Brooklyn that would play a major part in determining the pennant race. The Cardinals-Dodgers games were rained out. Since the two teams had no future meetings scheduled, the games normally would have been dropped. But the Phillies offered to move their September 21 meeting with the Dodgers to September 20 so the Dodgers could make up their games with the Cardinals, who also had an off day on the twenty-first.

The Giants agreed to the move, and the rest of the league

voted approval for the schedule switch. Harold Kaese of the Boston *Evening Transcript* wondered why the Giants would accept such a proposal: "The Giants motives in this matter are something to think about. Probably the New York front office thought its team was 'in' and to refuse the request would be considered 'small potatoes.' It was a generous gesture but may have an ironic ending. Can we guess the thoughts of the Giants players if they lose at least $3,000 each in World Series money because of the owners decision?"

The Giants' generosity was soon punished. On September 21 the Dodgers and the Cardinals went head-to-head at Ebbets Field in what would be a historic doubleheader. That the Cardinals won both, effectively gaining a full game on the Giants because of this scheduling quirk, was part of it. But the history was made on the field.

Eighteen thousand packed into Ebbets Field that afternoon to see the Deans versus the Dodgers. Diz would pitch the opener, Paul the nightcap.

Before the games Frisch held his usual clubhouse meeting to discuss how to pitch to the Dodgers. Years later Diz would tell the story of that meeting: "Frisch was giving us instructions, telling me how to pitch to Tony Cuccinello and Linus Frey and Sam Leslie and Ralph Boyle and all the other Dodgers and I give him an argument on everyone. I finally said, 'Let's stop this silly business, Frank. Don't you think it's kind of silly for an ordinary second baseman like you to be telling a great pitcher like me how to pitch to anybody?' Frank almost had a stroke. He told us to go out and pitch the way we wanted, he didn't care if we did get our ears pinned back."

That wouldn't be the case. Brooklyn would send fifty-eight men to the plate during the games; fifty-four of them would go back to the dugout frustrated, none crossing the plate. Diz shut out the Dodgers, 13-0, in the first game, giving up only three hits, the first one coming in the eighth. In the second game Paul entered the record books, shutting down the Dodgers, 3-0, and firing a no-hitter, the first in the National League since 1929. He allowed only one runner, a walk in the first.

After the games Dodger catcher Al Lopez told Tommy Holmes of the Brooklyn *Eagle*, "If there is such as thing as getting a kick out of losing, I got it today. I think we were all up there with our mouths open in admiration of the stuff those two were throwing."

Holmes reported left fielder Johnny Frederick chimed in, "I know I was. I'll swear that Paul struck me out with a fast ball that hopped a foot."

Despite being disparaged by Diz before the game, Frisch could claim some credit for the stunning victories. He didn't try to grab the spotlight that afternoon, but years later he admitted, "The big jughead didn't know I was calling all his pitches. I'd signal past him to Bill DeLancey, who'd give him the sign. I'd give it quickly so that the other side wouldn't catch on, or Dizzy either."

It would be the greatest day in the history of the Dean brothers, for not only did they enter the record books, they also made the history books. Paul's no-hitter put him in select company. He became only the fifth pitcher in the National League to throw a no-hitter since 1920 and the rabbit ball era. It was something his older, more famous brother would never accomplish.

And in recording his twenty-seventh win Dizzy broke the club record for wins in one season owned by the immortal Cy Young, who won twenty-six and lost sixteen in 1899.

But what earned the brothers a place in folklore was that the victory was Paul's eighteenth. Combined with Diz's twenty-seven, it meant the Deans had won forty-five games and made good Dizzy's boast that "Me 'n' Paul'll win forty-five games for the Cardinals this year."

Legend has it that after the games Diz complained, "If Paul'd told me he was gonna throw a no-hitter, why I'd a throwed one too." There is no evidence that Diz said that. No next-day game stories carry that quote, either in the New York or St. Louis papers.

Roy Stockton in the *Post-Dispatch* of September 22, 1934, quotes Diz as saying, "I didn't know that I had a no-hitter. I was way out in front and I was just coasting along. Boy if I had known that I was so near to a no-hitter I'd have given those Dodgers so much smoke and fancy curves that they wouldn't have even seen the ball."

J. P. Abramson of the New York *Herald-Tribune* reported a similar comment from Diz: "If someone only told me, we'd both had a no-hitter."

There is, however, evidence that Diz knew he was heading toward a no-hitter. The *Post-Dispatch* story said, "Manager Frisch however said he noticed that Dizzy was taking it easy and instructed catcher Virgil Davis to inform Dean that he had a chance to reach the goal of all pitchers."

There is one legend about the day that is true: that Diz predicted a no-hitter. Roscoe McGowen of the *New York Times* reported the next day, "The dizziest prophecy of all which was made good was voiced in the Cardinals' hotel yesterday morning, when the elder Dean told a St. Louis writer that 'Zachary and Benge will be pitching against one-hit Dean and no-hit Dean today.'"

Diz had missed by only a couple of hits.

In fact, Diz would never pitch a no-hitter.

He's not the only member of baseball's Hall of Fame to miss out on pitching's most thrilling achievement. Grover Cleveland Alexander, with 373 lifetime victories, never pitched one. Neither did Lefty Grove (lifetime 300-141) nor Rube Waddell (191-145).

Glenn Dickey in *The Great No-Hitters* believes that "to pitch a no-hitter a man needs both skill and luck. Some think the more important of the two is luck." Dickey blames Dizzy's sometimes laissez-faire pitching style for his not pitching a no-hitter. "He bore down only when he had to."

The final week of the 1934 baseball season was one of the most exciting in baseball history.

Most folks had already conceded the pennant to the Giants. After all, they were three games up as the season began its swan song. Not even the ever-optimistic Diz gave the Cardinals a chance. He'd told a sportswriter during a mid-September rain-out, "The Giants are in. There's no use kidding ourselves."

The sportswriters were already creating pitching matchups. St. Louis *Post-Dispatch* columnist John E. Wray wrote in his column of September 23, "Carl Hubbell, if the Giants win the pennant as expected, will carry a tremendous burden in the World Series."

But the schedule gave the Cards a break. After spending the first three weeks of September on the road, they would be at home for the final six games. And all six were against second-division clubs: two against the Pirates, then a season-ending four-game set against the cellar-dwelling Reds.

The last week would find the Giants at home too, playing first the Phillies, then their crosstown rivals, the Dodgers.

The Brooklyn club was finishing out a disappointing season. They would finish sixth, ten games under .500. But they had something to prove against the Giants. Before the season had begun, Giants manager Bill Terry had been giving sportswriters the lowdown on the upcoming season. As he ran down the list of contenders, he came to the Dodgers. "Brooklyn?" he asked sarcastically. "Are they still in the league?"

The final week began with the Giants losing to the Braves and the Reds-Cards contest being washed out. The Cards picked up a half game. They now trailed by two and a half with six to go.

The next day each club split a doubleheader. The Cards won the first when Diz came on in the ninth in relief of Jesse Haines and retired two men to preserve the win, 9-7. He also relieved in the second game, but his appearance was too late. The Cards lost, 4-3, and Paul was credited with the loss.

It was now Monday, six days left in the season. And the Cards were still trailing by two and a half games.

The Giants were breathing easy. Stanley Fry wrote in the New York *Post,* "The Giants are resting and preparing for the Tigers. Although the Cards are the best team in the National League right now, the Giants will play the Tigers because they cannot possibly blow the pennant now matter how hard they try."

On Monday the Cards beat the Cubs in Chicago, 3-1. With the Giants idle, that meant the Giants' once invincible lead was now down to two games.

In his autobiography Leo Durocher recalled the clubhouse meeting Frisch called on Tuesday to discuss the final games of the season. "[Diz said] I'll pitch today, and if I get in trouble Paul will relieve me. And he'll pitch tomorrow, and if he gets in trouble I'll relieve him. And I'll pitch the next day and Paul will pitch the day after that and I'll pitch the last one. Don't worry, we'll win five straight."

The Cards did beat the Pirates, Diz edging Larry French, 3-2, in a virtual replay of Diz's major-league debut nearly four years earlier. The Giants lost to the Phillies, and the lead was now down to one game with three to play for the Giants, five for the Cards. And in the important loss column, the two clubs were dead even.

It was a new season, and the Cards seemed to be in command.

But on Wednesday the Cards were shut out, 3-0, by the Pirates' Waite Hoyt. Paul Dean was the loser; Diz, who had start-ed only the day before, pitched three innings in relief. But the season wasn't lost. Not yet. The Giants lost to the Phillies. The lead was still one game. And the Cards had something the Giants didn't: a determined Dizzy Dean. It was only midweek, but already Dizzy had pitched on Friday, twice on Sunday, started on Tuesday, and tried valiantly to make a difference on Wednesday.

If the Giants were looking at the box scores and thinking Diz had to be giving out, they didn't remember Diz.

The Giants were idle on Thursday, so when the Cards beat the Reds, 8-5, it lifted them to within a half game of the lead. Diz rested.

But on Friday he returned to the hill. He went the distance against the Reds, limiting them to seven hits in a 4-0 win. It was his twenty-ninth victory of the season. But, more important, the Cards had caught the mighty Giants. After 152 games the two teams were dead even.

And the Cards were about to get some help. Dodger manager Casey Stengel, who hadn't forgotten how Terry had made fun of his club in the spring, had saved his two best pitchers, Van Lingle Mungo and Ray Benge, for the series with the Giants.

Out west it was as if the Cardinals had only two pitchers. The Dean brothers would each start one of the two remaining games. Paul went first, and with the pressure of 23,041 rabid Cardinal fans leaning forward on each pitch, he was masterful. He allowed eleven hits, but he scattered them so that the Reds managed only one run. The Cards won, 6-1. And when the Giants' score was posted on the scoreboard in the seventh, the crowd let out a cry that could be heard all the way to the Polo Grounds. The Dodgers, behind Mungo, had beaten the Giants, 5-1.

The Cardinals were in first place, the first time they had rested at the top of the league standings since June 5. There was one game to go. The worst that could happen now was a play-off. But Diz told his teammates in the dressing room, "Gimme a couple or three runs, there ain't gonna be any playoff."

The season now rested on the strong right shoulder of

Jerome Herman Dean. Diz had made it his personal quest to pitch the Cardinals into the World Series. He wanted the ball every day. And he nearly got it. He had pitched six times in the preceding nine days, winning three and saving another.

Some 37,402 fans poured into Sportsman's Park on Sunday. The Cardinals were going for a pennant, their first in three years. And if he could bring home the pennant, Diz in the process would notch his thirtieth victory, something that hadn't been accomplished in the National League since Grover Cleveland Alexander in the dead ball days of 1917. (Jim Bagby of Cleveland had won thirty-one in 1920.)

The Cards gave Diz his couple of runs early, and he headed into the top of the ninth leading 9-0. Then, suddenly, he seemed to relax and the first three Red hitters got on base. He bore down, striking out his old teammate Jim Bottomley. But with one out and two strikes on Ernie Lombardi, the crowd, for perhaps the first time ever, turned its collective attention away from Dizzy Dean and gazed out at the scoreboard in left field. The scoreboard boy had just posted a final from the Polo Grounds: Dodgers 8, Giants 5. The crowd began screaming.

Dizzy blazed a fastball past Lombardi, then coaxed a pop-out from Mark Koenig. The crowd was still screaming. The Cards had won the pennant! The Cards had won the pennant!

But a more appropriate cry might have been: "The Giants lose the pennant! The Giants lose the pennant!"

The next day Hugh Fullerton of the New York *American* summarized the season in one sentence: "In baseball history, the 1934 season probably will go down as the year in which Bill Terry asked if Brooklyn was still in the National League."

Riding the shoulders of the Dean brothers, the Cardinals had charged past the fading Giants. Diz had pitched seven times in the final ten days, Paul four. The team had been seven games back and thought dead in the race on September 4. But as the last light of September faded, they stood at the top of the standings, the champions of the National League.

In 1987 the *Sporting News* would name this the fifteenth most exciting pennant race in major-league history. For Dizzy Dean it ranked even higher. "This is the greatest thing that has ever happened to me!" he screamed over and over in the Cardinals' dressing room.

9

Dizzy Triumphant

It was a blue-gray sky that hung over Detroit the morning of October 3, 1934. NBC radio's Graham McNamee told his radio listeners, "Color is drab through the stands as it is through the sky."

At about 11:45 the sun broke through, giving fans of both teams hope that game one of the 1934 World Series might get underway on time. But that was not to be. Not because of the weather, but because of the jostling crowd trying to make its way inside Navin Field. The game was held up almost half an hour to allow the overflow crowd to pinch inside.

"I don't suppose there ever was a series that promised more color, pep and fight," McNamee commented to his radio colleagues Ford Bond and Tom Manning. "Opinion as to the outcome seems more even than I have seen it."

This was not the first time the World Series had been broadcast over radio, but it was the first time a sponsor had paid for exclusive rights. The Ford Motor Company—in large part because the hometown Tigers were in the Series—shelled out $100,000 for radio rights. The Associated Press calculated it would mean an extra $1,000 for each player on the winning team.

The starting pitchers for the first game were Dizzy Dean for the Cardinals and Alvin "General" Crowder for the Tigers. Diz's selection as opening-game pitcher was no surprise; after all, he had led the league in victories, strikeouts, shutouts, complete games, and winning percentage, and was second to Carl Hubbell in earned run average. In addition, Diz had been lobbying for the job since the season ended. "Dizzy has been hanging around Frisch's coat tails for the last three days saying, 'Frankie can I pitch?'" Manning quipped.

Sportswriter Grantland Rice wrote that Diz even asked him to intercede with the manager. "He asked me to fix it up with Frank Frisch so he could pitch the entire series."

Rice said he challenged Diz's confidence: "You can't possibly win four straight games."

"I know I can't," Dean answered. "But I can win four out of five."

In 1958, Diz told Frank Graham of the New York *Journal-American* another version of how he got the assignment after pitching the pennant-winning game only two days earlier. The team was on the train, heading for Detroit, when Diz wandered back to where Frisch was conferring with Sam Breadon and Branch Rickey: "They was settin' at a big round table with a big bowl of grapes and oranges and stuff on it and some of them had pencils and paper out and was figuring. 'Good evening, gentlemen,' I says. 'What seems to be troubling you?' 'Why,' Mr. Rickey says, 'we was just trying to pick the pitcher for the opening game.' 'Well, for God's sake!' I says. 'I got you this far! Who else is going to pitch the first game?' Frank says: 'You are.' And they put their pencils and papers away."

The shocker was Tiger manager Mickey Cochrane's decision

to bypass his two aces, Schoolboy Rowe, who had gone 24-8, and Tommy Bridges, who had a record of 22-11, for late-season pick-up Crowder. As early as September 22, when the Tigers seemed assured of the pennant, Cochrane had told reporters that Rowe would be his game-one starter. "I don't care who the other manager picks," he told the Associated Press. "It may be bad bridge, but it's good baseball to lead your ace and that's what I'm going to do…. Why, if we used any but our best against their best, we'd be in the position of conceding the game and the Tigers aren't conceding anybody anything."

Cochrane changed his mind, he said, because of Crowder's World Series experience. Crowder had started two games for the Senators in the '33 Series. And although he had been hit hard in those two games, it was against the bangers of New York, the Giants. The Cardinals were a team of slappers and scratchers, and Cochrane had confidence in Crowder's ability to finesse the scrappy Cards.

Although the Tigers had acquired him from the Senators for the waiver price, Crowder was no scrap-heap pickup. He had led the American League in victories in '32 and '33. The Senators had given up on him after he opened the '34 season 4-10. But he returned to form with the Tigers. After he arrived in Detroit in August, he won five games while losing only one. At thirty-five he was an experienced veteran, and the thirty-one-year-old Cochrane thought that might make the difference in a short series.

Diz had begun his preparation to pitch with a little mental exercise: the day before the game he called up Babe Ruth, who was in Detroit to watch the Series. Bill Corum of the New York *Evening Journal* reported the exchange went this way:

"Hello, is this Mr. Ruth?"

"Yes, this is Babe."

"Say, Mr. Ruth, this is Dizzy Dean. I just called up to say hello and to thank you for putting me on your All-American team this year. I sure was proud of that, and I don't know how to thank you enough, Mr. Ruth."

"Aw, that's all right, kid, you deserved to be there. What the hell, you deserved to be on there, kid."

"Well, thank you. I just wanted to say hello, Mr. Ruth, and thank you."

"That's all right, kid, I'll see you at the game."

"You mean you'll come in the clubhouse. Gee."

"No, I won't be in the clubhouse, but I'll see you on the field."

"That'll be swell, Mr. Ruth, but I wish you'd come in the clubhouse if you get a chance."

"I'll be seeing you, anyhow, kid, and though I'm an American Leaguer, good luck."

"Gee, Mr. Ruth, that's swell. I'll be seeing you out there."

That afternoon Diz and his teammates went over to get a look at Navin Field. They arrived while the Tigers were taking batting practice. Durocher remembered Diz walking onto the field in his street clothes, grabbing a bat, and jumping into the batting cage in front of Hank Greenberg, the Tiger slugger. "I'll show you how to hit the ball, Mo," Diz said to Greenberg, using a nickname ballplayers used for Jewish players—Mo, short for Moses. Durocher remembered Greenberg as being amused by the young hurler's antics. Diz hit a couple of long drives, then turned the cage back to Greenberg, who promptly launched one into the seats. "That's the way to hit the ball, Mo," Dean said, and headed into the clubhouse.

The first game began at 2:35, a half hour late. The Cardinals mounted a minor threat in the top of the first. Frisch was on second and Medwick on first when Collins lofted a lazy pop fly to center for the third out.

Detroit fans edged forward in their seats as Dizzy took the mound. The first batter was Joyner "Jo-Jo" White, the feisty son of Red Oak, Georgia. This was not the first meeting between Diz and Jo-Jo. They went back a long way, to Diz's Texas League days. White was the center fielder for the Beaumont Exporters in '31, Diz's only full year in the league. The Exporters and the Buffaloes had battled to a tie for the first-half championship that year, but the Buffs, behind Diz's pitching, won a five-game play-off. It was White whom Diz struck out in the ninth with the tying run on. They knew each other's strengths; they knew each other's weaknesses.

Diz, in his own words, "reared back and fogged one." It was a called strike.

"Dizzy Dean is wearing that big smile," said McNamee.

Then it was ball, ball, and ball. The third ball was inside, "and it drives Jo-Jo White away from the plate." Diz fogged another called strike past White before the center fielder nubbed a grounder Durocher's way. With one motion Durocher scooped it up and fired to Collins at first. One out.

As Diz prepared to face player-manager Cochrane, McNamee commented that Diz had "arms that extend down to his knees. Boy, he is a big fellow."

Cochrane grounded sharply to Durocher. Two out. Charlie Gehringer followed with a single, but Diz got out of the inning when Greenberg grounded out meekly to Frisch. The Cards jumped on Crowder in the top of the second, scoring twice, then adding another run in the top of the third. The Tigers pushed one across in the third but Diz got out of a jam—men on second and third—by striking out Greenberg. Medwick homered in the fifth to make it 4-1. Then the Cards put the game out of reach with four runs in the sixth. Diz began the rally by leading off with a double. The Tigers scored single runs in the sixth and eighth, but the Cards breezed, 8-3. In the eighth, with the Cards up, 8-2,

Greenberg creamed one of Dizzy's fastballs into the far reaches of the left-field stands.

Medwick would remember the towering home run in an interview in *The Redbirds*. "Bill DeLancey is giving the sign, and Diz refused to take it. Finally, Frisch called time. 'What's the matter?' he asked Diz at the mound. 'You won't take the sign, Diz? What's Greenberg's powers? Don't give him anything up high.' Frisch motioned. Diz went back to the mound, Frisch went back to second and DeLancey behind the plate. He kept giving the sign and Diz wouldn't take it. So DeLancey says, 'You throw it and I'll catch it.'" Greenberg proceeded to hit his homer. "As he's running around the bases, Diz is right with him. 'I'm going to strike you out three times after this,' he says. And he did it."

After the game Diz was asked about Cochrane's decision to go with his number-three pitcher. "Mickey used good gumption," he told the *Post-Dispatch*. "You see, he knew if I was at my best, nobody could beat me. So he saved Schoolboy Rowe for another game instead of puttin' him against me like I would have admired to have him done."

The media circus that would surround Diz for the next six months began in the clubhouse that afternoon. CBS radio had set up an intercontinental hookup so a player on the winning team could speak to Rear Admiral Richard Byrd and his exploration team in the Antarctic region. Diz, of course, was the person they wanted. "Hello Big Byrd down in Little America," Diz said, after announcer Eddie Bachelor explained that Diz would give the explorers the inside story of the game. "That game today, I want to say, was a hard-pitched game, although I want to say, I didn't have anything on my fast ball or my curve ball. That's why I had to work so hard…. I finally staggered through and won a ball game 8 to 3. I can pitch better than that. But it was a lousy, tick-flea-and-chigger-bit ball game. I think the Tigers are not as good a ball team as I had them figured out to be because I could take four National League teams baseball clubs and come over here this year and win the American League pennant with them."

Game two was a different story. Bill Hallahan opposed Schoolboy Rowe, and the Cards took a 2-1 lead into the ninth. But the Tigers scratched out a run on two singles and went on to win, 3-2, in twelve innings. Rowe went the distance, virtually untouched.

Except for the jockeying from the Cardinals bench.

"I tell you one time we really went to town was the 1934 World Series," Diz would later recall on radio. "We had a lot of fun with them Tigers. We called them the pussycats all through the series."

The Gas House Gang was notoriously tough on opponents when it came to verbal taunts. And in Detroit they had two ready-made targets. The day before the second game Rowe had paused a moment during a radio interview to insert a greeting to his wife: "How'm I doin', Edna?" Diz would remember, "I bet he wished many a time he'd never said that ... [He's] trying to pitch with Pat Crawford, our number one jockey, asking out loud how he was doing Edna."

The other target during the Series was Mickey Cochrane, who was injured slightly in the sixth game. The next afternoon the Detroit paper published a photo of Cochrane over the headline OUR STRICKEN LEADER. For the final game of the series, the Cardinal bench used that unfortunate caption when addressing Cochrane. "Mickey didn't show his nose anywhere without some jockey starting a cheer for 'Our Stricken Leader,'" said Diz.

The series returned to St. Louis for games three, four, and five with the teams knotted 1-1.

The Cards took a one-game advantage when Paul Dean out-pitched Tommy Bridges, 4-1, in game three. But the Tigers stormed back the next day, ripping up five Cardinal pitchers and tying the series again with a 10-4 win.

It was during this slugfest that perhaps the most famous non-pitching Dizzy Dean incident occurred. It was in the bottom of the fourth with the Tigers ahead, 4-2.

Ernie Orsatti and Leo Durocher were on, with no outs, when lumbering catcher Virgil "Spud" Davis, pinch hitting for pitcher Dazzy Vance, laced a single to right field, scoring Orsatti and sending Durocher to third. Like a flash, Dizzy Dean was out of the dugout, pinch running for Davis.

Diz always claimed he did it on his own. "Lots of people blame Frisch for sendin' in such a valuable star as me as a pinch runner, but I want to say right now, that's where they're all wrong. Frisch doesn't tell me to run for Davis. Since I'm such a fast runner and love to play the game, I just naturally jump off the bench to dash out and get in there."

Durocher, from his vantage point on third, in front of the Cards dugout, seconded Diz's version: "When I looked around, Diz, who fancied himself a great base runner, was pulling off his jacket and dashing onto the field to run for Davis. I assume that he put himself in because he had been doing it all year."

But in his autobiography Frisch indicated it was his choice to send Diz in: "I used Dizzy Dean as a pinch-runner and was criticized severely.... Diz was red-hot to run for [Davis]. Why not? He was a fine base runner."

Sportswriters' accounts at the time seem to confirm Frisch's account. Grantland Rice wrote, "The near tragedy of the wild and wooly afternoon came in the fourth inning when Frank Frisch took a momumental gamble by sending Dizzy Dean to run for Virgil Davis at first."

What happened next has been told and retold throughout baseball history. Pepper Martin hit a slow grounder to Tiger second baseman Charlie Gehringer, who flipped the ball to shortstop Billy Rogell for the force. But the determined Dizzy wasn't about to concede a double play. He went into second standing up, refusing, as is normal, to duck the relay to first. The relay throw hit Dizzy square on the forehead, and he collapsed on the ground. "The great Dizzy crumpled and fell like a marionette whose string had snapped," Rice wrote. Rice said the ball hit with such force that it caroomed thirty feet into the air and landed more than 100 feet away in short right field. "The blow that floored Dizzy would have knocked down two elephants. The wonder is that the entire top of his head was not shot away at such close range."

The crowd of 36,000 Cardinal fans sat stunned while medics rolled Diz onto a stretcher and carried him into the clubhouse, en route to St. John's Hospital.

Unbelievably, Dizzy wasn't seriously injured. Frisch reported that he regained consciousness in the clubhouse and, ever the team player, asked, "They didn't get Pepper at first, did they?"

Paul Dean, who was the first Cardinal on the scene, told his friend Wiley Thornton that Diz looked up from the ground and, ever the showman, said, "Make it look good, boys."

Diz was taken to the hospital for observation and X-rays.

In a story told by Diz and repeated by many others, the headline in the next day's paper supposedly read, X-RAYS OF DEAN'S HEAD SHOW NOTHING. But it's just that, a story. The fact is that no St. Louis newspaper ran such a headline.

The St. Louis *Star-Times* bannered: DIZZY KNOCKED OUT WHEN HIT BY BALL/CARDS PITCHING STAR SUFFERS CONCUSSION, CARRIED FROM FIELD. The *Post-Dispatch* headline was, DIZZY DEAN HIT ON HEAD; MAY PITCH TODAY. The headline in the *Globe-Democrat* was, EXAMINATION FAILS TO REVEAL ANY SKULL INJURY AFTER HE IS HIT BY THROWN BALL DURING GAME. The closest any newspaper came was the Detroit *Free Press,* which ran a headline on October 7 that read: THEY CAN'T HURT ME ON HEAD, SAYS DIZZY.

In fact, Diz pitched the next afternoon, doing a credible job, allowing three runs, only two of them earned, and striking out six. But Tommy Bridges was even stronger, taming the Cardinals on seven hits and striking out seven. The Tigers won, 3-1, and now the Cardinals were heading to Detroit trailing three games to two.

It was Paul's turn. It was a seesaw affair in game six, but the Cards scored the go-ahead run in the top of the seventh and Paul bore down, limiting the Tigers to three hits and no runs the rest of the way. The Cards had evened the series with their 4-3 victory.

John Carmichael of the Chicago *Daily News* described the scene in the Cardinal locker room afterward: "Kids out of school, a torrent rushing over a dam, madmen on the loose, that's how the Cardinals stormed into the dressing room. Uniforms were all but torn off, sweaty bodies engaged in bumping matches that threatened the permanency of the very walls."

Diz made a beeline for his little brother, who had now won two series games to Diz's one. "You can have anything I got," he screamed as he jumped on his brother and wrestled him to the floor. "Oh, baby, what a guy you are!—What a guy, what a pitcher!"

When sportswriters surrounded the rumpled Frankie Frisch, they had but one question: "Dean tomorrow?"

"Dean or Hallahan. I don't know yet," Frisch responded.

But not a soul in the locker room, not even Bill Hallahan, had any doubt who would be on the mound for the Cardinals in the seventh game.

In his autobiography Durocher indicates Frisch was wavering on his pitching choice right up until game time. Frisch and Durocher were going over the lineup card: "Frank ran down the eight regular positions, and when he got to the pitcher's spot he said, 'Let's have a meeting.' The first thing he did was to look at Diz. 'How do you feel?' Diz was indignant. 'You wouldn't think of pitching anybody else with the greatest pitcher in the world sitting here?'"

Frisch ignored the question and went on to go over the Tiger hitters. "Diz is lounging against his locker looking bored and half asleep and saying, 'Yeah ... yeah ... sure ...' Frank gets to ... Mickey Cochrane, their playing manager. He's telling Diz that you have to get the ball inside to him because Cochrane loves to line the outside pitch to left, but before he can finish Diz stands up and throws his scorecard down on the floor. 'What the hell you going over the hitters for? They're not going to get any runs off of me."

Diz then proceeded to launch an impromptu jam session of the Missouri Mudcats Band, a mock-hillbilly conglomeration that over the years would become synonymous with the Gas House Gang.

"I never heard so many four-letter words in my life as came streaming out of Frisch's mouth," Durocher recalled. "Frisch looks at Diz, who is doubled over with laughter, and [Frisch] yells, 'Hallahan is the pitcher!' "

Durocher recalled he was stunned at the choice: "I don't want Hallahan. I want Dean. I was still $6,000 in debt, which is just about what the winner's share is going to come to. The loser's share, I'm not interested in." Durocher tried every tactic he knew to get Frisch to change his mind, to no avail. So he went to Diz to convince him it was serious, that Frisch wasn't going to start him. The solution, Durocher said, was for Diz to apologize. So Diz sidled over to Frisch's locker. "Frankie-boy.... Let me tell you something. If you listen to me, Frank, I'll make you the greatest manager in the game."

That backhanded apology only made Frisch angrier.

As the team headed out, Durocher collared Frisch, insisting Diz would pitch great. It was Durocher's job to hand the lineup card to the umpire. "And when Frank didn't say anything, I whipped the card out, wrote J. Dean in the pitcher's spot and shoved it back in my pocket."

Diz would tell a different version of how he got the assignment. He would recount a conversation he had with Frisch after game six, when everyone had left the locker room. "Frisch and I are the last ones in the showers and he says to me: 'You are the pitcher tomorrow but don't tell nobody,'" Diz confided to Frank Graham in 1958. "'Whatever you do, don't tell Hallahan, because he thinks he's going to pitch.'"

Frisch didn't tell anyone either. "Frisch lets on Hallahan is going to pitch, and the next day, when I come up through the Tigers' dugout, which we have to do to get to ours, I set down, just for the fun, and all the Detroit players holler at me to get out and go where I belong. So I laugh and start across the field and they holler after me, 'It's too bad you ain't going to pitch today! We'd just love to get another crack at you!'"

Diz continued his gamesmanship as he headed across the field to the Cardinal dugout. "[Eldon] Auker is their pitcher and he starts throwin' that underhand ball to warm up and I walk over to him and stand there watchin' him and I says: 'You ain't going to try to get anybody out with that stuff, are you?' They was all jittery by that time and I know this don't do him any good and he curses me and I laugh and walk back and start to warm up. That's the first time anybody knows I am the pitcher."

Now the Tigers knew. Not that they shouldn't have suspected. Or dreaded. Roy Stockton in *The Saturday Evening Post* described Diz's last jab before heading into the dugout to await the start of the game. "He paused a moment at the Detroit dugout, where he spied Hank Greenberg. 'Hello, Mose,' said Dizzy. 'What makes you so white? Boy, you're a-shakin' like a leaf. I get it; you done hear that Old Diz was goin' to pitch. Well, you're right. It'll all be over in a few minutes. Old Diz is goin' to pitch, and he's goin' to pin your ears back.'"

* * *

In a 1970 book entitled *My Greatest Day in Baseball* Diz picked this as his greatest game. And it surely was.

The score was 0-0 when the Cardinals came to bat in the top of the third.

Durocher led off by popping out to center. Diz, who was next up, hit a high foul behind the plate, just barely reaching the front row of box seats. "Easily playable," Durocher would recall in his book twenty years later. "Should have been an out, except that Mickey Cochrane, a Hall of Fame catcher, the catcher picked on everybody's all-time All-Star team, didn't bother to go after it. The one time in his life probably that he so completely misjudged that kind of a foul ball."

On the next pitch, Diz looped a pop-up over third base. When left fielder Goose Goslin was slow charging the ball, Diz took off, running through first-base coach Buzzy Wares's stop sign.

No one in the partisan Tiger crowd expected the opposing pitcher to outrun Goslin's arm nor did they anticipate Hall of Fame second baseman Charlie Gehringer missing a tag.

But when the cloud of dust settled, Diz was standing on second and umpire Brick Owens was signaling safe.

The next batter, Pepper Martin, nubbed a checked-swing dribbler between first and the pitcher. Greenberg fielded it cleanly, but in the heat of the moment he hesitated, first appearing to want to throw to covering pitcher Auker, then thinking he could beat the fleet Martin, so he made a move toward first and ended up doing nothing. Diz wound up on third, laughing and shouting across the diamond to Greenberg, "Hey, Hank, don't forget to come in the clubhouse after the game and get your meal money. You are our most valuable player."

After Jack Rothrock walked, loading the bases, Frisch doubled, scoring all three men.

Diz would later say, "As I'm crossin' the plate, I yell at Mickey Cochrane, the Tigers' manager and catcher, 'You're beat now, Mickey.' "

Diz was right. The Cards would score four more in the third and Diz would get his second hit of the inning, tying a World Series record. By the time the Cards took the field again the score was 7-0 and the hometown crowd was silent.

The score was still 7-0 in the fifth when Greenberg, who had already struck out three times against Diz in the series, came to bat. Durocher recalled that Dizzy sidled over to Frisch and inquired, "Where did you say this fellow's strength was?" Frisch replied, "Just don't get the ball out and away from him." Dizzy promptly served up a high, outside fastball and Greenberg tattooed it back through the box and into center for a single. In Durocher's version Diz nodded to Frisch, "You're right, Frankie. He can hit the hell out of the ball if you get it out there." Another variation on the story has Frisch running over to the mound screaming, "What'd you do that for?" and Diz shrugging his shoulders and answering "I was beginning to think he couldn't hit nothin'."

By the time the Tigers came to bat in the bottom of the ninth, the Cards were leading 11-0 and the stands were emptying. But in later years Diz would recall looking out at the bull pen and seeing four Cardinal pitchers warming up. "So help me, I thought they must be gettin' ready for the 1935 season. Eleven-nothing I got 'em and that Billy Rogell on base and Hank Greenberg came up. I already struck him out twice, no trouble 'tall, and when he came up in that ninth I hollered over to the Tiger bench, I said: 'What, no pinch-hitter?' and Hank looked at me like he'd a liked to break one of them sticks over my head.... You know what that Frisch did? I put two fast balls right past the letters on that Greenberg's uniform and when he missed the second one I hadda laugh. I put my glove up to my face to keep from laughin' right in his face, he looked so funny, and before I could throw any more Frisch came out. He was mad. He said: 'Cut out the foolin', we got a lot at stake' and I just stood there and looked at him like he must be outta his mind … me leadin' 11-0 with one out in the last of the ninth. Just then Leo Durocher came in from short and he said: 'Aw, what the hell, Frank, let the guy have his fun. What's the matter with you?' Well you know what Frisch told me? Yeah … he said: 'You lose this guy and you're through.' Eleven-nothing…. I can't get over that yet. He was gonna pull me."

Diz struck out Greenberg, the third time in the day, and the ninth time in the series that Cardinal hurlers had fanned the Tigers' superstar.

Marv Owen then slapped a grounder to Durocher, who flipped to Frisch for the force on Rogell.

The Cardinals were champions of the world.

But for Diz it was a bittersweet day. Afterward in the clubhouse, as the jubilant players clowned around, posing in pith helmets and twisting the tails on rubber tiger toys, Frisch would corner Diz.

"Anybody with your stuff should have won 40 games this year instead of a measly 30," he told the shocked winning pitcher. "You loaf, that's the trouble. Thirty games! You ought to be 'shamed of yourself."

10

Barnstorming

The World Series ended October 10. And already the offers were piled so deep that Diz couldn't even sift through them. He tried to get sportswriter Roy Stockton to handle all the requests, but Stockton turned him down. Stockton would later write that it would have been a full-time job.

The first offer Diz accepted was from a Muscatine, Iowa, promoter named Ray Doan. Doan, who had a baseball school, was an old friend, a veteran at arranging barnstorming tours: a handful of major leaguers would travel around playing exhibition games, often against teams from the Negro Leagues. This series of games, called the Dizzy and Daffy Tour, teamed Diz and Paul with local pickup players, ex-big leaguers, semipros, whoever was available, in games against a number of Negro National and American League teams.

Diz and Paul flew that next night to Oklahoma City to begin a series against the Kansas City Monarchs. The Monarchs won the first game, a shortened contest, 4-2. Newt Allen, one of the Negro League players, told John Holway in *Voices of the Great Black Baseball Leagues,* "We had so many people the grandstand wouldn't hold them. The ball game quit in the fifth inning—had to, people were all out in the outfield, and every inning they would press closer to try to see Dizzy. We had to stop the ball game, but the people were satisfied, they got to see Dizzy and Paul pitch."

Many Negro League veterans have praised Diz for his willingness to play against black teams at a time when many major leaguers made it clear they wouldn't play in the big leagues if black players were allowed in. Hilton Smith, a pitcher with the Monarchs, told Holway about a barnstorming game in which a white player spiked a black second baseman who was looking the other way. "Big fellows like Dizzy Dean and all those guys wouldn't have a fellow on there that felt that way. Some fellows never played exhibition ball games against us. They felt that way, and they wouldn't play."

But Diz did play against the black teams and seemed to enjoy himself mightily.

An October '34 affair against the New York Black Yankees in a New Jersey stadium was typical of the approach Diz took to barnstorming. He started the game in right field. In the fourth he went in to pitch, and Paul replaced him in right. Diz pitched the middle three innings but seemed as interested in impressing the crowd as his opponents. When the home-plate umpire changed a call after Diz's team was already in the dugout, Diz came out, feigning indignation, and led the crowd in a chorus of boos.

In the next inning Dizzy picked a runner off first base only to have the base umpire's call overruled by the plate umpire, who made a show of running out to first to make the call change. Dizzy got that sly grin on his face and yelled, "Go back to your position; you're silly enough there!"

The Deans lost to the Black Yankees, 6-0, that night, but the important score came from the box office, a record 15,000 paying customers.

The two-week barnstorming tour was marred by an incident that occurred during the last game, a night contest in Pittsburgh on October 24. The Deans were playing the Pittsburgh Crawfords of the Negro National League and were leading 3-1 in the last of the fifth when the trouble started. Vic Harris, center fielder for the Crawfords, beat out a bunt, then raced to second when catcher George Susce's throw was wide.

A newspaper account at the time reported: "Dizzy raced in from center field, where he [had] retired after pitching two innings, pointing out to Umpire James Ahearn that Harris didn't touch first base. The umpire called the runner out. Harris walked straight in from second, picked up a mask, and is alleged to have cracked Ahearn on the head. That started the firing with men on both teams 'mixing up' and the spectators vaulting into the park to join in the rumpus. A squad of bluecoats charged onto the field and restored peace." The Crawfords went on to win, 4-3.

The next day, October 25, Diz and Paul were in New York, preparing for their Broadway stage debut. The *New York Times* reported that their salaries were the largest ever paid baseball players for theater appearances. Dizzy and Paul were to play for one week at the Roxy Theatre as part of the regular vaudeville show. They would appear for six minutes during each show, reciting prepared dialogue and, with any luck, eliciting a few laughs. "This will be the only New York stage engagement the Deans will make," the *Times* announced with a straight face.

The boys were supposed to pose for publicity photos with the chorus girls the day before the show, but Diz balked: "Lands' sakes, man, I can't do that. It ... well, it's undignified. What I mean is maybe my boss, Sam Breadon, wouldn't like it."

But it wasn't *that* boss Diz was concerned about. He relented and posed, but as he left, he insisted his agent accompany him home: "I want you to explain this to the Missus, she's likely to get very sore. She don't mind my being an actor, but she don't allow for no dancing with show gals."

The show opened that Friday to unusual reviews. Most newspapers left it to the sports staff to cover the event.

Tom Meany wrote in the New York *World-Telegram,* "There is a remarkable similarity between the Brothers Dean before the footlights and the Brothers Dean on the pitching mound. In each case the Deans rely on brute strength rather than mental agility."

The show was standard vaudeville: a setup followed by a punchline. Diz and Paul were aided by radio announcer Ford Bond. They stood in front of a backdrop with a dugout painted on it.

"Who's your favorite radio broadcaster?" Bond would ask.

"Schoolboy Rowe," Diz would reply, a dig at Rowe's famous "How'm I doin', Edna?" radio remark.

For his exit line, Diz shaded his eyes with his hand, peered out into the audience, and asked, "Is Hank Greenberg in the house? I sure would like to strike him out once more."

Paul then closed the show by asking, "How'm I doin', Edna?"

Meany concluded that the brothers' stage show lacked any subtlety. "The Deans make no more effort to fool the audience than they do to deceive a batter. The family slogan remains, 'Plow it through there!'"

From their Broadway run the brothers Dean headed over to Brooklyn to star in a Warner Brothers short called *Dizzy and Daffy.* It was filmed at Erasmus Field, a high school stadium, and barely kept the brothers occupied. New York *Sun* reporter Edward T. Murphy reported they spent most of the time passing balls between themselves, awaiting the latest order from the director. Paul, in particular, was having a fine time between shots, impersonating various big-league pitchers. Diz ended the session, warning Paul, "You'd better cut out those imitations before you try to copy Freddie Fitzsimmons and fall off the platform." Diz amused himself trying to hit a cop stationed in the outfield with fungoes. As for the plot of the now forgotten short, Paul told the reporter, "I will not know what it is all about until I do see it."

Then, at last, it was back home for the winter. "And we're gonna make ourselves scarce," Diz told a reporter.

If Diz had had a great year on the diamond, he was having an even better one in the marketplace. Everyone, it seemed, wanted Diz's mug or autograph or just his nickname on their product.

The St. Louis National Base Ball Club had paid Jerome H. Dean the sum of $8,500 for his services during the baseball season of 1934. After the season merchants, merchandisers, promoters, entrepreneurs, broadcasters, and furniture store owners paid him almost three times that much for endorsing their products, appearing on their shows, performing in exhibition games, or just showing up at an opening to say a big "Howdy, folks."

Cashing in didn't begin with Joe Montana smiling into the camera in the Super Bowl locker room and announcing, "I'm going to Disney World." Baseball players had been earning extra money for years by marketing themselves on the side. In 1934 Babe Ruth made $39,000, $4,000 more than the Yankees were paying him for his baseball feats, just for doing a thrice-weekly radio show for Quaker Oats.

It was in 1934 that Diz began learning the valuable lessons of marketing. Frankie Frisch had given him his first lesson during the Dean brothers' famous midseason walkout. As Frisch later explained it, he told Diz, "Without his baseball background, his value in other fields immediately would have diminished. If he had been J. H. Dean, clerk in a citrus exchange, no manufacturing company would have paid him $15,000 a year for endorsing a product."

Frisch didn't just pluck the $15,000 figure out of the air. That was the sum the advertising firm of Young & Rubicam, Inc., was paying Diz annually to endorse a breakfast cereal. And that was just the beginning.

His earnings outside baseball became a matter of public record when his agent, St. Louis Browns general manager Bill DeWitt, later sued to recover his agent's commission on Diz's earnings. DeWitt asked for one third of all Diz's outside earnings between May 29, 1933, and November 1934 and 10 percent of his outside earnings in November and December 1934. DeWitt's original agreement with Diz for one-third commission was considered exploitative by Commissioner Kenesaw Mountain Landis and slashed to the standard 10 percent in November 1934.

DeWitt listed Diz's outside earnings from May '33 to November '34 as:

- Ray L. Doan, $7,000 (barnstorming baseball tour)
- General Foods, $500 (advertisement)
- Christy Walsh News Syndicate, $728.34 (syndicated World Series column)
- General Mills, $300 (Grape Nuts cereal advertisement)
- M. Hohner, Inc., $250 (endorsing a harmonica)
- Fanchon and Marco, $1,625 (vaudeville appearance at Roxy Theatre)
- Artagraph Pictures Company, $2,250 (appearance in movie short *Dizzy and Daffy*)
- Caradine Hat Company, $500 (use of name on hat)
- Nunn-Bush Shoe Company, $100 (radio commercial)
- Western Tablet and Slate Company, $500 (use of name on children's writing tablet)

The total came to $13,753.34.

And that was only the beginning of Diz's outside earnings. DeWitt claimed Diz also owed him 10 percent on these earnings: A. Cohen and Sons, $233.29; Barr Rubber Products Company, $187.60; Young & Rubicam, Inc., $15,000; J. C. Ayling, $67; Rice-Stix Dry Goods Company, $2,089.52; Marx & Haas Clothing Company, $538.60; M. D. Dreyfach, $885.60; W. C. Schneir, $19.36; Hall Brothers, Greeting Cards, $16.57; Nok-Out BB Company, $250; Beech-Nut Tobacco Company, $250; Kate Smith Broadcast, $600; Sidney Weil, $100; Al Jolson Broadcast, $450; Ray L. Doan, $3,358; Jack Rothrock, $2,574; J. G. T. Spink, Sporting News Publishing Company, $100; Dick Slack, Slack Furniture Company (for 1934), $1,450; Dick Slack, Slack Furniture Company (for 1935), $5,000; A. G. Spalding & Brothers, $4,260.71; and Young & Rubicam, Inc. (second year), $15,000.

That totaled up to $53,158.59.

In the eighteen or so months that DeWitt served as his agent, Diz had earned $66,911.93 *off* the diamond.

During that same time he had earned a mere $21,389 for playing baseball ($7,500, 1933 salary; $8,500, 1934 salary; and $5,389, World Series share).

Diz's name was everywhere that winter: there was the Dizzy Dean watch and the Dizzy Dean pants, the Dizzy Dean baseball uniform and the Dizzy Dean kite, the Dizzy and Daffy table baseball game and the Dizzy and Daffy sweatshirts. Diz's face was staring out from Camel cigarette ads, his voice was heard on Nunn-Bush shoe commercials.

The second marketing lesson Diz learned in '34 was: Protect your own. And he did. Before the winter was out he and Paul were in court against a pair of firms for using their nicknames without permission. They went to court to block Elmer H. Phillips, a New York manufacturer, from gaining a trademark for his Dizzee and Daffee sport shirts. And they battled Arthur Redner, a Battle Creek, Michigan, candy manufacturer who had the temerity to apply for a trademark on his "Dizzy and Daffy Bar, Dean of the Candy Bars."

Neither firm had a contract with the Dean brothers for the use of their names. In his deposition Diz noted, "Everybody knows us as Dizzy and Daffy. A lot of people in this country that know us don't even know what our real names are." The brothers won this match too, the patent office declining to grant trademarks to the offending companies.

In 1934 Diz had earned in the neighborhood of $70,000. But when Branch Rickey called him in Bradenton that winter to talk about his contract for 1935, Diz announced he was broke and that he needed to sign soon in order to get the $2,500 first payment from his cereal advertising contract.

Not even the normally sympathetic sportswriters believed this one. Wrote Roy Stockton: "It is, at least, unreasonable to believe that he had squandered half of $19,182 within a period of four to six weeks."

The truth is, he probably had.

11

"The White-Haired Boy of the Over-Flowing Mississippi"

When hot-stove leaguers, those baseball fanatics who spend the winter warming their hands around a hot stove and discussing baseball, talk about legendary baseball teams, two groups are always mentioned: the New York Yankees' Murderers' Row and the Gas House Gang.

The Yankees of Ruth, Gehrig, and Lazzeri would win pennants in 1926, 1927, 1928, and 1932 and world championships in those last three years.

But for the Gas House Gang the 1934 season would be the high-water mark. There would be no more pennants, no more world championships. They would slip steadily in the standings through the end of the decade. And by 1939 the only survivors of that great season still left in St. Louis would be Joe Medwick and Pepper Martin.

But the fact is that the Cards of the Gas House Gang actually improved in 1935. They won one more game than they had won in the pennant-winning season of '34. The team batting average declined slightly, from .288 to .284, but they scored more runs, 829 in '35 to 799 in '34. And the pitching staff's ERA dropped significantly, from 3.69 to 3.54.

And, if anything, Diz had a better season in '35 than in '34. He won two fewer games, twenty-eight (actually only one fewer if you consider one of his '34 wins was tainted), but he still led the league in that category. In fact, he led the league in five positive categories: games won, games started, complete games, innings pitched, and strikeouts. He'd also led the league in five categories in '34.

But one event made it all a disappointing season for Diz. For the first time in his career he saw the home fans turn against him. During his first three seasons they had listened with amusement at his boasts, chuckled as he denigrated his teammates, even shrugged off his numerous holdouts and strikes.

But on June 11 Cardinal fans actually booed the Great One. And some even threw lemons.

It was a new experience and Diz cried, openly, on the field.

Diz began the '35 campaign the fair-haired boy of the overflowing Mississippi. If he strutted before, his walk now rivaled a peacock's. The major focus of his derision was the once mighty Giants, who had folded up like a cheap lawn chair in the '34 pennant chase. Before one spring exhibition against the Giants, he strolled over to the New Yorkers' dugout and calmly asked if anyone could cash a check for $5,300. That just happened to be the winner's share from the last World Series, and the Giants didn't receive him with good humor.

Diz was so full of himself that during the season when the Cardinals were in Boston to play the Braves he took his catcher,

Bill DeLancey, aside after the clubhouse meeting and suggested, "Bill, let's see how we can get by today without no signs and without pitching no curves. I'll just fog that fast one in there, mixing in a change-up once in a while, and we'll see how we get along." The Braves were a hapless bunch—they would lose 115 games in '35—and Diz had no trouble mowing them down. "[They] didn't know what was going on. There wasn't nary a sign all day and we played that game in about an hour and a half and we shut 'em out without even throwing a curve ball."

But life would not be as simple in 1935 as it had been just a year earlier. In spring training everywhere Diz went he was beseeched by autograph hounds and worse. "Everyone else seemed to be trying to sell me something or give me something when they weren't asking me to make personal appearances at all sorts of things. And if I hadn't called a halt on it I'd have gone nutty."

It was Pat Dean and Cardinal officials who decided to limit access to Diz. And when the season began Pat even traveled with the team to screen Diz's callers. She didn't mind, she said.

Diz would later recall during a radio show the first exhibition game of spring training. Because camp had just opened, the pitchers weren't putting anything on the ball. The Cards were scrimmaging the Columbus farm club at Avon Park in Bradenton, where the fences were deep. Diz was pitching, "lobbing the ball, having fun seeing the kids hit. [Centerfielder] Terry Moore was really having a workout chasing them to right center and then to left center. Finally after retrieving one of them long ones, instead of throwing the ball in, Terry just carried it. He walked all the way into second base and then to the mound. He handed me the ball and said, 'Hey Diz, please walk a couple of them guys, will you, till I get my wind back.'"

As spring wore on, the pitchers got their game arms. In another game the Cards were playing the Phillies, who were in the process of converting Bucky Walters from a third baseman to a pitcher. Walters was struggling to learn control, using opposing teams as guinea pigs while he did. Diz faced Walters in one game. He recalled, "He walked two men, hit one and then cleared the bases with two wild pitches. The batters wasn't digging in when Bucky was pitching. When I went to bat, he liked to took off the peak of my cap with the first one. Then by some chance he got two strikes on me. I was glad to see the next one come outside. I'd had enough of hitting against Walters by that time. When the umpire said 'Ball two' I said 'Ball two, nothing, that ball was right in there and I am out.'"

The Gas House Gang broke camp all ready to roll over the rest of the National League. On paper the Cardinals seemed a good bet to repeat. All eight regulars were back. And when rookie Terry Moore had such a strong spring that he actually beat out Orsatti for the center-field job, the Cards looked stronger than in '34.

In the season opener, April 16, against the Cubs in Wrigley Field, Diz took a first-inning smash by Freddie Lindstrom on the shin and had to leave the game. Diz didn't return to action until April 21 at Forbes Field, when he beat the Pirates, 6-1, on five hits.

But early on the team couldn't seem to get in gear. Frisch was bothered by a bad leg that would eventually limit him to 104 games, only 88 of them as the starter, at second. The Cardinals rumbled out of the gate, settling into fourth place early on.

On May 7, in a game against the hapless Boston Braves, Diz faced Babe Ruth for the first time in a league game. They had met before in spring training, but this was the first time it meant something.

The Babe was on his last legs. He would retire before the month was up. But Diz was still leary of the legendary hitter. "Babe was watching me pretty closely while I was warming up before the game," he told reporters. "He had that old eagle eye of his on every move I made, so I figured that if I didn't steal the show he would. I wasn't giving him anything to hit when he first came to bat. But after I hit my homer and we collected a six-run lead, I felt I could take a chance on pitching to him and I did get quite a kick out of slipping my fast one past him on his second time up for a third strike."

Diz also attempted to enter the world of sports journalism in 1935, signing up to write "Poppin' Off," a column for the *Post-Dispatch*. In half-grammatical prose actually penned by Roy Stockton, who took Diz's native Arkansas speech patterns and turned them into a mishmash of grammatical errors, illiteracies, and, especially, "ain't's," Diz ventured opinions on everything from the Cardinals' fortunes to trades over in the other league.

This column from May 23, 1935, is typical of Diz's style:

"Washington gets a good pitcher in Buck Newsom and it's about time he starts winning, but without usin' no sledge on my good friend Buck I do want to say that Rogers Hornsby must have used a big bottle of clory-form, if he gets more'n forty grand from out Foxy Grandpa Griff's pocket for a pitcher with only two arms. But Hornsby can take care of hisself and he won't be in Mr. Harridge's basement very long.

"Speaking about Mr. Harridge, he and Mr. Ford Frick was right when they says this should ought to be a good season. Me and the Cardinals has drawed good crowds so far. We had 41,000 at the Polo Grounds, 31,000 at Boston, Philly's biggest crowd in years of 16,000 and we made Pittsburgh use their right grandstand for the first time since 1927, with a mob of 28,000.

"It's color that does it. We showed the Phils some color the other day and did they get mad? But the trouble was we get mad too and we lose a ball game, but when the big chips are down watch us when we puts all our shoulders to the grindstone and steps on the gas. They ain't never paid off in May yet."

* * *

The team was beginning to show some life in early June and had climbed into second place when the incident that tore the team apart and ended Diz's honeymoon with his fans happened. It was the June 5 game in Pittsburgh. In the bottom of the third inning, with Diz on the mound, the Cardinals committed two errors, allowing the Pirates to score four unearned runs. The *Post-Dispatch* reported, "The sensational Cardinal pitcher got it into his head that he was not being properly supported in the field. In the fifth, it is alleged that he merely lobbed the ball over the plate, with the result that the Bucs scored four more runs." Roy Stockton called it "one of the most unusual and disgraceful exhibitions of childish temper that the writer has ever seen on a baseball diamond."

There's a dispute about what happened next. One report had Diz accusing his teammates of loafing. Diz told reporters after the game that the incident was instigated by an accusation against him: "When I got back to the bench after the fourth inning I was yelling at Umpire Rigler. Medwick says to me 'Lay offa Rigler and bear down in there.' I looked at Medwick and said, 'Whatta you mean, bear down? I'll punch you on your Hungarian beezer.' "

There's no disputing what happened after that because it happened in full view of the crowd. Diz started toward Medwick, his brother Paul trailing behind him. Medwick grabbed a bat off the ground and shouted, "Keep coming, brothers Dean. Come on, both of you. I'll separate you real good."

The other players jumped between them before blows could be struck, but the feud had begun. Later in the game Medwick hit a grand slam that went out of Schenley Park. When he finished his home run trot, he headed for the cooler, filled up with water, and spit it on Diz's shoes. "See if you can hold that lead, gutless," Medwick spewed. Again players had to separate them.

Dizzy was removed for a pinch hitter in the seventh. In the clubhouse after the game, Frisch read Diz the riot act, warning that if he ever acted that way again—tossing up marshmallow pitches—it would cost him $5,000 and an indefinite suspension.

The next day Diz was still fuming. He felt Frisch had unjustly taken sides: "[He] gets on me, bawls me out about bearing down and says he'll fine me $10,000. I told him to go ahead and fine me. After the game in the clubhouse Frisch gave me another bawling out. I waited until he was all through. Then I told him something. I said, 'Listen, Frank, you can say what you want, but if you can thank anybody for the job you have as manager you can thank me, and you know it.' Can you imagine anybody telling you he's going to fine you $10,000? ... You know what I think? They're trying to get me in bad so they can take away a big chunk of the money my contract calls for. That's what they're trying to do."

Word of the fracas reached St. Louis ahead of the team. And when Diz took the mound on Tuesday, June 11, the next home game, to face the Cubs, lemons came raining out onto the field. Dan Daniel of the New York *World-Telegram* reported the scene this way: "When the fans hurled the yellow citrus fruit at Dizzy he actually cried. Then he got a new hold on himself and pitched his best game of the year, giving the Cubs only six hits and two runs, while the Cardinals ran riot with twenty-one blows and thirteen tallies. The fans here say Frankie Frisch did a fine thing. After it was all over and the lemon hurlers had been converted into cheering maniacs Frisch welcomed Dizzy in front of the dugout and before the 15,000 onlookers shook Dean's hand. It was a gesture of forgiveness, and its effect was instantaneous and contagious. Those on the inside here say that if Sam Breadon has entertained any idea of trading or selling Dizzy, Sunday's developments dissipated that chance. Once more is the elder Dean the hero of the St. Louis fans, the white-haired boy of the overflowing Mississippi."

As a gesture of goodwill, Diz went to Frisch with a plan for overtaking the Cubs. "Listen, Frank, I want to ask you some-thing. Could you see your way clear to let me pitch every third day? I figure I won't lose more than three games the rest of the year. I'd like to do what I can to put the club up. Maybe we can make up some lost ground."

Frisch declined the offer. "Diz, if you give me your best every fourth day, that's all I want or expect."

But the damage had been done. Branch Rickey would admit three years later that he began shopping Diz around in '35.

Shortly before the All-Star Game Diz got in trouble again over an exhibition game. This time it was in St. Paul, Minnesota. Diz didn't sleep through the stop, but he hadn't wanted to go and he made his displeasure known, pouting on the bench and refusing even to take a bow in front of the dugout when he was intro-duced. The next day the Twin Cities papers lambasted him. Diz responded, "I am a pitcher and not a movie star. I would have been glad to pitch an inning in St. Paul if Frisch had asked me." The papers had neglected to mention that Diz stood outside the dugout after the game signing autograph after autograph.

Diz was asked to pitch one inning in the All-Star Game at Cleve-land. He came on in relief in the eighth. The St. Paul incident had taken place only a few days before, and when his name was announced, the fans released a volley of boos. Bill Walker, Hal Schumacher, and Paul Derringer had preceded him on the mound, and by the time he appeared, the game was lost to the American League, 4-1. He allowed a double to Al Simmons and a walk to Jimmie Foxx, but then worked out of the jam. After three attempts, the National League had still failed to win an All-Star Game.

The first week in August the Cardinals began a winning streak that would land them in first by the end of the month. The Gas

House Gang was back on top, where they thought they belonged. Before a home doubleheader against the Dodgers, Diz and Pepper began debating the question of who was the best wrestler. Even though Diz was scheduled to start the first game, he and Pepper decided to see who was best, and they began grappling on the clubhouse concrete floor. Durocher would later recall, "When they got through, Dizzy had hurt his arm and Martin had scraped a piece off his nose and had a cut above his eye, where he had struck a wire locker during the bout. Dizzy pitched and won his game, sore arm and all."

But the Cards had made their move too soon. On September 4, as the pennant race began in earnest, the Cubs started an incredible twenty-one-game winning streak. On September 10 they moved into a tie for first with the Cards, and by September 26 they had a four-game lead.

"Every day we'd look for the Cubs to crack ... to lose a game or two," moaned Pepper Martin. "But they kept winning.... They have improved one thousand percent within two months."

Still, the Gas House Gang had a chance because a fortunate turn in the schedule had the two teams ending the season playing each other in St. Louis for four games—and for the pennant.

The opening game was washed out and rescheduled the next day as part of a doubleheader. Frisch announced that the Deans would pitch the twin bill, Diz in the opener, Paul in the nightcap, despite the fact that Paul had pitched nine innings two days earlier and that together the two had pitched in seventeen of the last twenty games. Paul had asked for the assignment, and if Frisch had learned one thing about the Dean boys it was that you could never underestimate their durability.

This was baseball at its finest: the top two teams head-to-head, the defending champions trying to return to the World

Series, the upstarts on a nineteen-game winning streak.

"Yah, they're good, those Cubs," crowed Diz, "but ol' Diz will stop them."

Cub manager Jolly Cholly Grimm shot back, "We'll clinch the pennant tomorrow with Lee."

Lee was Big Bill Lee, a former Cardinal farm hand and one-time teammate of Diz's at St. Joseph. In '34 Branch Rickey had to make a choice between rookie pitchers and elected to keep Paul Dean, selling Lee to the Cubs. After a lackluster rookie season in '34, Lee had found his control and was on his way to winning twenty. Only one thing stood between him and that magic number: Diz. Diz was going on four days' rest, more than he had had all month. He had a personal goal too. If he won, it would be his twenty-ninth, and no doubt the Cardinals would need him in one of the remaining two games with the league leaders. With three days left in the season, Diz still had a chance to duplicate the '34 season and win thirty.

It was thirty degrees in St. Louis that day, but 9,000 fans turned out for the game of the year. The Cards took a 2-0 lead in the bottom of the first on two singles, a walk, and errors by Cubs second baseman Billy Herman and third baseman Stan Hack.

Diz had been in this spot many times before—an early lead in an important game—and the Associated Press reported he had "a smirk of invincibility on his lips."

He mowed down the Cubs in the second, but they tied the score in the third, then took a one-run lead in the fourth.

It was enough, as Lee held the Cards to four hits the rest of the way. By the time the dust had cleared, the Cubs had tapped Diz for fifteen hits, including a home run by Stan Hack that land-ed on top of the right-field pavilion. The final score was 6-2, but the Cardinals' season was over. Frisch didn't even bother to start Paul in the second game.

What had happened to Diz? After the game Cub center fielder Freddie Lindstrom explained, "His fastball didn't have a thing on it. He's one tired-ball pitcher."

The Cardinals had nothing to be ashamed of. They were the victims of one of baseball's all-time great streaks. Only one other team had ever won that many games in a row; the '16 Giants had a twenty-six-game winning streak. But the Cubs' streak was more remarkable because almost half the twenty-one wins, eleven, were on the road. The Giants' streak had been accomplished exclusively in the friendly confines of the Polo Grounds.

The Chicago team ended up winning 100 games; the Cardinals wound up in second, four games back. It was a bitter defeat for the Gas House Gang, who had hoped to establish their claim as a dynasty.

After the Cubs pennant-clinching victory, Diz visited the conquerors in the dressing room, even offering Cub pitchers tips on how to pitch to Hank Greenberg and the other Tigers; Detroit had just clinched in the American League.

Diz finished 1935 with a record of 28-12. He was the stopper of the staff, starting thirty-six games and completing twenty-nine of them. He needed relief help but seven times the entire season, about once a month.

Brother Paul didn't do so bad for the season either, again winning nineteen. That gave the Dean brothers a total of forty-seven wins, more than the forty-five Diz had forecast for them the previous season. Over two years the firm of Dean & Dean had won ninety-six games, one more than half the games the Cardinals won in that two-year span.

Once again there was no resting for the Dean brothers. They set out on a transcontinental barnstorming campaign as soon as the season ended. The Dizzy Dean All-Stars, featuring brother Paul, Cub pitcher Larry French, Cardinal rookie pitcher Mike Ryba, retired A's first baseman Joe Hauser, and retired Cub slugger Hack Wilson, toured with a team of Negro League all-stars that included Webster McDonald, Cool Papa Bell, Ted Page, Boojum Wilson, Jerry Benjamin, Josh Gibson, Buck Leonard, and Satchel Paige. According to Ted Page, the Negro team won seven of the nine.

The teams played in major- and minor-league stadiums alike. A crowd of 30,000 turned out in Pittsburgh; 18,000 watched in Los Angeles' Wrigley Field. But crowds in Chattanooga and New Orleans were so small that Diz walked out instead of playing.

It was nonetheless a profitable tour. A Los Angeles newspaper reporter wrote that Diz was paid $3,000 for the two exhibition games he pitched October 27 and 31. He performed a feat in the October 27 game against an all-star minor-league team that belongs in the record books.

A Los Angeles newspaper reported, "Dizzy pitched three innings for the minor leaguers and then hurled the final six for the major leaguers, who won 12 to 4. Dean was charged both with a defeat because he was behind 2 to 0, when he shifted from the minors' to the big leaguers' cause, and credited with victory, because Newt Kimball, the major leaguers' opening hurler, didn't pitch the required four and two-thirds innings for him to get the win."

Diz didn't take that exhibition too seriously, but local reporters noted he pitched hard four days later in the Halloween game against Satchel Paige and the Royal Giants. "He pitched seven innings and retired with the team in front, 3 to 2. However, the colored club got to Kimball for two runs to take the lead in the eighth, only to have Dean's cohorts pull the game out of the fire with a pair in the final round." The final score was 5-4. Paige pitched only four innings, but during that time he struck out seven and allowed two hits.

Paul left the tour because of his wife's illness. Diz carried on until the end, stopped off briefly at St. Louis for a visit with Rickey, and, only half kidding, mentioned he had been thinking about asking for a three-year contract.

Branch Rickey spent a very restless winter because of that remark.

12

The Last Good Year

The Cardinals were a changed team in 1936. Three fourths of the infield had turned over, leaving Durocher as the only holdover from the championship season of '34. Johnny Mize, a bear of a man out of the hills of north Georgia, had beaten out Ripper Collins for the starting first-base slot. Manager Frisch, now thirty-eight and suffering from leg pains, frequently benched himself in favor of rookie Stu Martin at second. Charley Gelbert, fully recovered from his hunting injury, reclaimed an infield position, taking over at third, allowing Pepper Martin to move back to the outfield. Martin took over in right for Rothrock, who retired. Terry Moore's rookie success (.287 in '35) convinced Ernie Orsatti it was time to pursue his lifelong dream of acting, and he too retired.

Even the catching position was changed. Bill DeLancey, who had platooned there with Spud Davis in '34 and '35, was out of baseball, suffering from tuberculosis. His spot was filled by rookie Ambrose "Bruisie" Ogrodowski. The starting lineup frequently included four regulars who weren't with the team the previous season.

It was a considerable change for a team only a season removed from a world championship, a team that had actually improved on its '34 record in '35. But if some of the bricks had changed, the mortar was still the same. Durocher was still the team spark plug and the anchor of the infield. Frisch was still the guiding hand on the bench. Dizzy was still the ace of the pitching staff. And Pepper Martin, whom Diz often referred to as the heart and soul of the Gas House Gang, was still batting third, even if his glove was now in the outfield.

Diz's contract negotiations—always a three-ring circus—were the craziest ever in '36. Branch Rickey had written Diz a letter during the winter warning, *Do not arrogate to yourself some of the prerogatives of the management.* Diz showed the letter around to sportswriters, chuckling over the language. He didn't know what those big words meant but he knew one thing, they must mean he was important to the team, and he upped his price from $27,500 to $40,000.

He ended up signing for less than half his demand. A lot less: $12,500.

Dizzy Dean and Opening Day were rapidly becoming synonymous in St. Louis. The Cardinals opened the season, as usual, playing the Cubs, and Diz was on the mound. And, as usual, his jinx club battered him, scoring nine runs in the first six innings and sending Diz to an early shower. The Cubs ended up winning 12-7.

Diz blamed his defeat on bad luck, but he didn't claim it had anything to do with his old nemesis team. He said he pitched so poorly because he was without his lucky rabbit's foot. A week earlier the team had played an exhibition game at Springfield, Missouri, and Diz had sent his suit—with the lucky talisman in the pocket—to the local cleaners. It wasn't until the morning of the season opener that he discovered the cleaners had neglected to return the lucky charm. It was too late to do anything about it, so he took the mound unprotected, so to speak. Diz's squawk reached back to Springfield, where the cleaner located the rabbit's foot and returned it in time for Diz's second start.

And, magically, Diz's luck returned, and he won his second outing of the season, a tough game with the Reds, 8-7. The Cards headed into the bottom of the ninth trailing 7-3 when his team-mates rallied for five runs, climaxed by Medwick's two-run single. Diz watched the fireworks from the end of the bench; he'd already been removed for a pinch hitter. But he still received credit for the win.

Frisch would later recall in his autobiography how the game made him think that perhaps, at last, Diz was growing up: "I tried to impress on him the fact that many a close game could be salvaged by a capable pitcher, if he'd continued to bear down, even in the face of discouraging breaks. And after the second game of the 1936 season ... he took hold of my arm going through the runway on our way to the clubhouse. 'Frank,' he asked, 'did I act all right?' He knew he had, and it was quite a satisfaction to him, but the boy in him wanted that pat on the back."

In 1936 playing baseball for the Cardinals was fun again. They would lead the league almost the entire season. Diz didn't strike during the '36 season, but he still found time to become involved in a lot of high jinks.

When the Dodgers were in town in late June, Diz and Pepper Martin decided it was too hot to play ball. Teammate Don Gutteridge remembers, "They dragged an old blanket out of the dugout and sat in the field. Him and Pepper got out peace pipes and started smoking them." News photographers had a field day and wirephotos of the stunt appeared in papers around the country.

Diz made the papers for something other than pitching on July 23 when he refused to board the team train to Cincinnati. Wife Pat delayed the train while Diz debated with Cardinal club officials about his "earache," which, Roy Stockton reported, "He says he has and which Dr. Robert Hyland, club physician, says he hasn't."

"I'm not going to Cincinnati," Diz insisted to reporters. "My ear pains me too much. I don't care what Doc Hyland says, I have got an earache."

Diz may have had an earache, but he also had cold feet. He knew a Cincinnati deputy sheriff was waiting to serve him with papers claiming he hadn't paid for a suit he purchased the previous season. Diz won the argument but later lost the suit, *lawsuit,* and paid for the clothes suit.

The most notorious event of '36 occurred during an eastern swing. Diz, Pepper, and reserve infielder Heinie Schuble were bored staying in Philadelphia's staid Bellevue-Stratford Hotel. Diz would later tell his radio audience about that incident, an evening of high jinks that would become emblematic of the Gas House Gang spirit: "It was an off day in Phillie and while we was window shopping Pepper sees some overalls and striped caps to match. He says he has an idea and before we know it we all got overalls and one of them caps. When we get back to the hotel, we change into them overalls and caps. Pepper borrows a hammer and a yardstick and says, 'I think we'll have some fun.' We went into the dining room where some kind of meeting was being held. I think it was about child welfare. Well, Pepper had them move a couple of tables. He measured a space on the wall and said that pictures got to come down. Then he starts hammering on the stove and the Chinese cook like to have a fit. Then we get back in the dining room and gets into an argument about what's should be moved. Pepper holds up his hand next to his big snoozle and that's my cue. I haul off and hit his hand with the palm of my hand and it looks like I scored a clean knockout. The youth welfare speaker quit his speechmaking and them that was eating their desserts jump to their feet to see the fight among us carpenters.

"About that time somebody recognizes Pepper and says, 'Them is Cardinal ballplayers.' They take us up to the head table and insist we tell them about the ballclub and baseball. Then we spied a gentleman over at the end of the head table we didn't know was there."

It was their manager, Frankie Frisch. "He said he had just two words for us: 'I am mortified.' Them overalls and caps went into the trunks for good."

It was during the fun-filled '36 season that fame would also come to Pepper Martin's famous Missouri Mudcats Band. Diz would later recall that the band grew out of Oklahoma-born Martin's fascination with country music: "There was days we couldn't get him [Pepper] to the clubhouse in St. Louis because Martin would have hillbillies draped all over the benches and trunks."

The band became a fact of Gas House Gang life after "Pepper got himself a guitar and found out which hand to use here and there. I don't know whether you'd call it music but it sure gave Pepper a big thrill. So we organized a little band on the ball club."

The band's membership would ebb and flow with the changing Cardinal roster, but the two constants were Pepper banging the washboard and Diz crooning—what else?—"The Wabash Cannonball."

It was in '36 that Branch Rickey ordered the band disbanded. "Uncle Branch noticed that whenever the Cardinals arrived in a town there was more in the paper about the Mudcats than there was about baseball," Diz later said. "Baseball writers were quoting Pepper about 'Wabash Cannonball,' 'Coming Around the Mountain' and 'Willie, My Toes Are Cold' and wasn't paying no attention to the pennant race. So Rickey issued orders. The jug and the washboard was thrown away. No more public appearance or even rehearsals for the Mudcats."

Diz and Pepper were a pair in '36. In a game against the

177

Giants, when Pepper had a rare start at third, Bill Terry smacked a single back through the box off Diz. After the ball was returned to the infield Pepper nonchalantly strolled over to the mound. "He put up his hand so nobody else could hear it and says, 'Jerome, I don't think you're playing Terry deep enough.'"

The Phillies were having a dreadful season in '36—they would end up losing 100 games—so when the Cards arrived in town for a series in September, the players didn't expect a large crowd in the Baker Bowl. Only a couple of hundred folks showed up, and as the game progressed and the Phils fell further and further behind, even those folks began leaving. Diz would later recall, "We noticed one crowd in the right field stands and they stayed inning after inning. Not one of them left. I got curious. I said, 'I'm going to the bullpen to warm up and find out why they are staying.' 'How come [you're still here] with us leading 17-2?' [I asked.] 'We'd like to go home. We're like everyone else but we can't. You see we're the grounds crew.'"

Even manager Frisch joined in the fun in '36. One day the Cards were in Boston playing the Braves and all the close plays seemed to be going against the visitors. After the third or fourth close one, Frisch, on his way back to the dugout, stopped for a chat with plate umpire Larry Goetz. Diz would recall the conversation going like this:

"It's a nice day, isn't it, Lawrence? By the way, do you have a couple of cigars in your pocket?"

Goetz eyed the Cardinal skipper suspiciously, suspecting a setup. But because Frisch was normally a pleasant fellow, he replied, "Why would I have cigars in my pocket?"

"Because, Lawrence, you look so much like a cigar store Indian today."

Goetz's face flushed, and he chased Frisch off the field and out of the game.

* * *

In 1936 even the umpires got in on the fun. Diz would later tell about an encounter that season with Cy Pfirman. It was a close game with the Giants, and Diz was on first base with a walk when Frisch laced a single to right: "I rounded second, tore for third and me and the cloud of dust and the ball all arrived at third at the same time. I thought I'd made it but umpire Pfirman called me out. But before I could get up and squawk, he brushed the dust off my shoulders and said, 'Diz, that was a great piece of base running and Frisch couldn't have run no faster. And that slide, Ty Cobb couldn't have done no better. But Dizzy, Ott made a great throw on the play and you're out.' I didn't have the heart to say no more to Pfirman. On the way to the dugout I passed Bill Klem who was working at the plate and I said, 'Bill, did you see that play?' Bill said, 'Yes, Jerome, I seen it.' I started telling Bill I was safe and [Travis] Jackson hadn't tagged me and I beat the throw when Bill broke in and said, 'Jerome, remember me? I'm Bill Klem behind the plate. If you want to get on somebody, talk to Mr. Pfirman.' ... No sir, I couldn't say nothing to Cy. You know he was so nice to me if I'd a had a quarter in my pocket I'd a tipped him."

Baseball was so much fun for the Gas House Gang in '36 because they were playing well. The team seized first place in April and, except for a few days in late June and a few days in late July, led the league. But the gang—and Diz in particular—faded in September and finished in a tie with the Cubs for second, five games back of Bill Terry's Giants.

Diz was 22-9 as September began but struggled to finish 24-13, winning only two and losing four during the last month.

Baseball for the Gas House Gang, and for Diz, would never be this much fun again.

Diz's numbers in 1936 were similar to his numbers in '34 and

'35. There was no discernible slipping. He didn't win as many games, and his ERA was up a bit, from 3.04 to 3.17. But he continued his workhorse ways, leading the league in games pitched, complete games, and innings pitched. And with 195 strikeouts he had five more than in '35, although he finished second in the league to Van Lingle Mungo, who had a career year and fanned 238, fifty-four more than he had ever struck out before in one season and more than a hundred over the number he would strike out the next season.

But all was not right with the Dean brothers. Paul had fallen to 5-5. His arm had gone lame in midseason, and his career was effectively over. Paul had won forty-three games his first three seasons; he would win only seven more.

It was the end of the Me 'n' Paul circus that had entertained the nation almost daily for three years. And it was near the end of the line for the sad-faced Paul, a young man who was so clearly out of place in the media limelight his brother loved so much. Diz had always claimed Paul was the better pitcher, and he may have been right. Paul had won nineteen games in the big leagues at age twenty-one; at a comparable age Diz was still pitching in the bushes. At age twenty-two Paul was 19-12; at twenty-two Diz was a rookie struggling to finish 18-15.

Both averaged six strikeouts per nine innings in their first two seasons. But Paul had a much superior strikeout-to-walk ratio, a measure of control that Branch Rickey charted. Diz averaged 2.3 strikeouts per walk his first two years; Paul 2.7.

1934 was gone forever.

13

The Toe

It is the most famous arm trouble in baseball history, and with the possible exception of Goliath's trouble with little David's arm, perhaps in all history. Dizzy said his sore arm happened this way: "In the ['37] All-Star game ... Earl Averill of the Cleveland Indians, who is a very murderous hitter, is the batter. He lines the ball back at me like a shot out'n a cannon, and it cracks me on the left foot. That night I don't sleep much, and the next morning my foot is all swoll up to twicet its normal size. X-rays show my big toe is busted.... I want to get back in there to help [the team], and on July 20th, no less than two weeks after the All-Star game, I'm startin' a game in Boston with splints on my foot, and a shoe two sizes too big for me.... Bein' a righthander I come down with all my weight on my left leg, and every pitch is killin' me. Pain is stabbin' clean up to my hip. Because of this, I change my natural style, and don't follow through with my body on the delivery, so's I won't have to tromp down on my hurt foot. Instead I cut a fast one loose just throwin' with my arm. As the ball left my hand, there was a loud crack in my shoulder, and my arm went numb down to my fingers. Nobody knowed it then, but Ol' Diz's great arm was never goin' to be the same agin after that one pitch."

This has been the accepted story for half a century: Diz came back too soon from a broken toe, altered his pitching style, strained his arm, and ended his career.

There's no doubt that pitching with an unnatural motion hurt Diz's arm. And if Diz says he heard a pop in his arm while throwing, then he probably suffered some sort of immediate damage in that July 20 game. But the facts about Diz's famous sore arm are a little more complex.

Roy Stockton notes in his book *The Gas House Gang, and a Couple of Other Guys,* "There were rumors in the spring of 1937 that he, finally, really, had a sore arm. Everybody wondered and anything Dizzy said didn't help, because of people knowing him so well."

And an Associated Press story published the day *before* the All-Star Game quotes Diz as saying, "My arm ain't just right, but I'll give 'em the best I got."

Paul doubted the broken toe story. Paul's friend Wiley Thornton wrote, "Paul has never believed that Dizzy's arm trouble resulted from the broken toe in the 1937 All-Star Game. All writers agree that it did but I'll accept Paul's conviction since they always confided to each other."

Pitcher Mike Ryba, who played with Diz on the '35, '36, and '37 Cardinals, would later tell reporters, "Dean didn't take care of his arm when he was young.... He was careless. He'd dash into the showers after pitching a hard game in hot weather and dash right out. He never took time to cool out and he wouldn't allow the trainer to touch him. 'I've got the kind of arm that will last a lifetime,' he would say. And with that he'd jump into his car, still sweating heavily, and off he would go at a 60-mile-an-hour gait."

The broken toe was probably the straw that broke the camel's back. After all Diz had been the hardest-working pitcher in the major leagues for the previous five years. And he was a workhorse in the minors the two years before that. Add in the barnstorming innings, as casual as they may have been, and the spring training innings, and you have a picture of a pitcher with the stamina of a Clydesdale.

Diz led the league in innings pitched three of his first five years, finishing second one of the other years and third the other. He pitched 1,531 innings those five years, the highest total in the majors. His closest rival was Carl Hubbell, who threw 1,512 innings in that time frame. No one in the American League was even close.

The difference between Diz and King Carl was that Hubbell was twenty-nine when the stretch began in 1932, Diz only twenty-two. Hubbell didn't even reach the big leagues until he was twenty-five.

Bill James, the premier student of baseball statistics, believes, "Most pitchers who throw a lot of pitches before they are 25 have arm trouble the rest of their careers." We don't know how many innings Diz threw while in the army, but he pitched 311 innings in 1930 with two minor-league teams and in one game with the Cards. The next season he pitched 304 innings for Houston in the Texas League.

From the time he pitched his first professional game at age twenty until his arm trouble, he was averaging 306 innings a year. Joe "Iron Man" McGinnity, a pitcher from an earlier era who earned his nickname by winning five games in six days in 1900, averaged only 374 innings in one particularly hard seven-year stretch, 1899 to 1905. But McGinnity threw underhanded. Diz was a straight overhand fastballer, and by 1937 all that work had begun to take its toll.

Diz's '37 season got off on the wrong foot, a different kind of wrong foot. In April he was the instigator in a well-publicized spring-training hotel brawl between the Cardinals and two sportswriters.

It happened on the afternoon of April 3. Diz and his teammates, still in uniform, were returning to the Tampa Terrace Hotel after an exhibition game with the Reds. Reports said that Diz and Pat were entering a hotel elevator when Pat inquired of her husband, "Isn't that Mr. Miley standing there?"

Mr. Miley was Jack Miley of the New York *Daily News*, who had written a column critical of the Cards and Diz in particular, claiming that the team lacked punch and Dizzy appeared to be an ordinary pitcher based on his earned run average. The story also insinuated that Pat Dean was the real boss of the Dean household.

Miley reported that he and Chicago *Times* columnist Irv Kupcinet were walking into the hotel lobby when Diz approached him and said, "I wish you would not write those things about me.... I don't want a $120-a-week man writing about me. I don't want you ever to mention my name again."

Miley said he responded, "That's fine! I don't like to write about bush leaguers anyway. What are you going to do about it?"

What Diz did was take a poke at the sportswriter, which Miley described as "a lady-like left hook." It was only a grazing blow, but before Miley could respond he was swarmed by what seemed like the entire Cardinals squad, led by brother Paul. "They all swung. Some of them had bats, others had spiked shoes and a few had only their fists."

Miley said one reached around Diz and landed a right on Miley's eye. Then another "reached over, tapped me with a pair of spikes on the skull. 'How do you like them, chum?' he said."

The fight was over as quickly as it had begun, the only legacy of the melee a broken sand urn and a few overturned potted plants and chairs. Cardinal coach Mike Gonzales was able to quiet the mob.

Afterward Diz was uncharacteristically reticent. "Maybe I hit him; maybe I didn't. I ain't quite sure. Maybe I just threw a curve."

One team member who wasn't reticent about the incident was Frisch. He read the riot act to his team, at one point asking Diz, "Haven't you any better sense than to risk your pitching arm in taking a sock at a sports writer?"

For Diz and the Cards the run-in was over and done. But not for Miley. An hour later Miley said he called Diz's room and "invited [him] back down to have the thing done right, but he declined the invitation."

The next day, in his column, he wrote, "If the Cards haven't any more punch than they showed in that little impromptu battle with me and Kupcinet, they'll finish the season in the International League."

They wouldn't finish that far back, but it would be the Cards' worst season since the pre–Gas House Gang days.

Once again the Cardinals opened the season on a roll, and by the second week they were 7-3 and leading the league. Diz began his season with five straight victories. In those games he allowed only three earned runs. It wasn't until May 14 that he lost his first game. The Pirates got to him early, scoring four runs in three innings in a game they would win, 14-4.

After the fast start the Cards settled into a comfortable gait, and by the All-Star break they were 37-30, six games back. Diz too slowed down. After his sizzling 5-0 start, he was 7-7 the rest of the way to the break. Something was wrong, even if the signs weren't that obvious.

Diz was named to start the All-Star Game—he was the only Cardinal representative—but it was apparent he didn't want to go. When the team finished up the first half of the season with a series in Chicago, Diz took the train back to St. Louis with his teammates instead of heading to Washington for the game.

Diz would later say it was club president Sam Breadon who talked him into going to the All-Star Game, agreeing to fly with him to D.C. Diz finally arrived in the nation's capital by plane late the night before the game. He told reporters he had never had any intention of passing up the All-Star major-league game. "Aw, that's just a lot of talk. I'm just a Boy Scout, anyway, here to do my good deed," he said, referring to the thousands of Scouts who were in town that week for their annual jamboree. Diz said he was in good shape and all set to pitch "three fast innings" on behalf of the National League team.

In the game Diz pitched like a man who didn't want to be there. In the third inning, facing Yankee Joe DiMaggio, he shook off catcher Gabby Hartnett's call for a curveball, instead trying to fog one through the middle. DiMaggio spanked a single past Diz's ear into center. Lou Gehrig parked Diz's second pitch onto the right-field roof, foul by inches. Diz worked Gehrig to a full count, then, again disregarding Hartnett's curve sign, tried to blaze one down the middle. "Gehrig hit one a country mile over the right field wall," Diz said afterward. "Lou guessed right on that one. He guessed I would throw him a fast ball with a count 3 and 2 and I sure did."

The American League was ahead, 2-0. Earl Averill, the Cleveland center fielder, was the next batter. A career .318 hitter, on this day Averill would make his most famous out. "Boy, I'll never forget him," Diz would later tell radio listeners. "He hits one back to me like a mile and … it hits me right on the left foot. I grab the ball and throws Averill out at first but, boy, that line drive was Mr. Trouble."

Actually, according to inning-by-inning summaries, it was Billy Herman who picked up the carom and threw out Averill.

The American League went on to win, 8-3, with Diz absorbing the loss. In the dressing room afterward, Diz took full responsibility for the mistakes. "I shook Hartnett off twice and was belted each time.... The National League should have won with the three runs we made if the pitching had been up to snuff. ... Those guys were lucky stiffs."

The first reports on the toe were that it was merely sore. And that diagnosis was still being propagated as late as July 18, when Diz told reporters he expected to be out another ten days. "It's so swollen I can't get my shoe on." He said he didn't plan to pitch before the Cards returned home July 27, if then.

But the next day he boarded a train and met the team in Boston. He would later say, "I walked into the clubhouse and first thing Frisch ast me is could I pitch. The toe was stickin' outa my shoe with a splint on it, but when somebody asts me will I pitch, I can never say no."

Frisch's account of Diz's return was at odds with Diz's. In his autobiography, he recalled, "[Diz] grew impatient recuperating at home and insisted on joining the ball club, which was on the road. We were in Boston when he reported back for action and it was my judgment that Dizzy ought to wait several more days, possibly weeks, before trying to pitch in a ball game. I explained this to Diz, but he laughed off my caution. 'There ain't nothing wrong with Old Diz,' he insisted. 'You don't think a little old broken toe is going to keep me out of action.'"

Frisch acknowledged that he and Cardinal management had often been accused of sending Diz back into action too soon, but argued, "If he pitched too soon it was because he insisted on pitching. And if you think imposing your will and what you consider your superior wisdom on Dizzy Dean is an easy task, you don't know that man Dean."

So Diz pitched that day. A week and a half later, Diz pitched eighteen innings in an 8-6 victory at Cincinnati. It was his thirteenth and last victory of the season. It would also be his last victory as a Cardinal.

* * *

By mid-September, Diz's record was a mere 13-10. He was only 8-10 since his blazing start. Even more telling, he had struck out only eighteen batters since the All-Star break. It was apparent Diz no longer had it, so Branch Rickey asked him to stop by his office for a chat. Diz, playful as always, entered carrying a pistol, one he had spotted in the team safe. "Now just what do you want to say to me?" he bellowed.

Rickey laughed, but he had a serious topic he wanted to discuss. He suggested Diz retire for a year to give his arm some time to heal. Rickey later told reporters he thought a year off would help Diz, otherwise, "I would be the last person in the world to want him to go on the voluntarily retired list." Diz agreed the request was reasonable but insisted his arm would be all right soon. He predicted he'd be back in '38 and win thirty games.

14

The Trade

Branch Rickey was easily the most inventive executive baseball has ever known. He created, out of thin air, the farm system, conceived the idea of a spring-training complex where major and minor leaguers could train together, and encouraged the development of such gadgets as the batting cage, the batting helmet, and the pitching machine.

His most lasting action would be the breaking of baseball's color line, in 1947. But his most famous action prior to that was a trade he made on April 16, 1938.

One of Rickey's maxims was: It's better to trade a player a year too early than a year too late. But in this case, Rickey was a year too late.

Had he traded Diz in the spring of '37, with Diz coming off a 24-13 season, he could probably have landed two or three regulars, a pitcher, and maybe a couple of bench warmers. By the time he swapped him to the Cubs on the eve of the 1938 season, he could wangle only three little-known players and a hunk of cash.

It had been obvious all during spring training in 1938 that Diz was a broken-down pitcher. He had pitched well against the

189

Yankees in one spring game, but against even minor-league competition he was rocked hard. Still, it was a shock when on April 16 Sam Breadon made the announcement to a stunned Cardinal clubhouse. Only minutes earlier the Gas House Gang had been celebrating a Medwick homer that gave the Cards victory in their annual "city series" with the Browns. One clubhouse wag joked, "The Mudcats won't have any more competition from Dizzy." But that lame joke was the only lighter note in the suddenly silent dressing room. Diz made the rounds, shaking hands, saying good-byes, before huddling with Cub vice president Clarence "Pants" Rowland. It was even a banner headline across the top of the *New York Times* sports section, stealing thunder from a Max Schmeling boxing match: DIZZY DEAN TRADED TO CUBS; SCHMELING STOPS DUDAS.

In a deal that Rickey had been working on for three weeks, the Cards sent their onetime ace to the Cubs for pitchers Curt "Coonskin" Davis and Clyde "Hardrock" Shoun, journeyman outfielder Tuck Stainback, and $185,000.

"Jeez, $185,000.... If I'd a had a good arm wonder what I'd a brought," Diz would later quip. The newspapers reported it was the second biggest money deal to that time. In '34 the Red Sox had paid $250,000 to pry Joe Cronin away from the Senators. And it far surpassed the most famous sale in baseball history, the $125,000 the Yankees paid Boston for Babe Ruth in 1920. Cubs owner Phil Wrigley said the total deal was worth $270,000; the Cubs valued the three players at $85,000.

Neither club benefited much on the field from this swap. Diz would win one important game for the Cubs but only sixteen games total.

Shoun would have a mediocre 25-23 record with the Cardinals over five seasons. Davis's record would be a bit better, 34-28, with a twenty-two-victory campaign in '39 that landed him a spot on the All-Star team. Stainback would play in only six games, never even managing a hit.

But the trade would help both clubs in other ways. The $185,000 covered the Cards' entire season payroll. And Diz helped the Cubs fill the seats at Wrigley Field.

The Associated Press hinted that the trade was the Cards' way of dealing with their "problem child." But that wasn't it at all. Rickey was convinced Diz's career was over, and he was up-front with the Cubs about Diz, never insinuating that he was the same pitcher who'd won thirty games four years earlier. The Cubs knew they were getting damaged goods.

Rowland later told Joe Williams of the New York *World-Telegram* that he knew Diz had a bad arm when he bought him. "It was no secret. Even Sam Breadon warned me, but we still thought we could get some good games out of him, bad arm and all, so we went through with the deal."

But all this was not common knowledge at the time of the trade. Cub manager Charley Grimm, on hearing the news of Diz's acquisition, gushed, "I'm tickled to death we got him. I know he'll help us." Diz's partner in mirth, Pepper Martin, moaned, "There goes our pennant and World Series money."

In fact, the condition of Dizzy's arm that spring was pretty much a mystery. After all, Diz had only had a bad second half in '37. Many pitchers came back from a bad season. Even Martin, Diz's best friend on the Cardinals, was uncertain: "Well, he's been sort of in and out so far. He hasn't been pitching his fastball." The shrewdest comment on the trade came from Giants manager Bill Terry: "I do not believe that Branch Rickey would get rid of the pitcher Dean was two years ago. If he were still a man who could win twenty to thirty games, I think he would have stayed with the Cardinals. Rickey must know that he is through as a great pitcher and has got what he can for him."

Still, the Cubs had hopes. Maybe, just maybe, the arm would come back. So they inserted him into the starting rotation with Big Bill Lee, Clay Bryant, Tex Carleton, and Larry French. In his first outing on April 20, he held Cincinnati to two runs and eight hits in six innings and was the winning pitcher.

When the Cardinals arrived in Chicago four days later to take on the Cubs, there was more at stake than the lead in the National League. There was already a full-fledged feud between Diz and his former teammates. He had angered them by telling Chicago sportswriters that he didn't start the 1937 brawl with sportswriters Miley and Kupcinet, that it was started by Joe Medwick.

It didn't take long for the story to get back to Medwick, who responded, "He's right in one respect. He wasn't in the fight after fists started to fly. He usually does a crawfish act about that time. Dizzy was retreating when I arrived. He needed protection when I got there and I gave it to him. We didn't even know Dizzy was fighting baseball writers.... Dizzy Dean likes to start trouble, but he can't take it.... If he ever throws at anybody, it will be some little guy, and then he will hide behind Hartnett [Cubs' catcher] and cry that he didn't do anything."

Diz countered, "That Medwick is dumb ... saying when I dust off anybody, it's always a little guy?... that I run from a fight. Say, if that guy would show any sort of hustle at all, the Cards would have a helluva lot better ball club than they got now."

On the afternoon of the twenty-fourth, in front of a crowd of 34,520, Diz made it seem as if Branch Rickey had made a mistake. Diz shut out the Cardinals, 5-0, on four hits.

As he walked off the field after beating his old mates, he told autograph hounds, "Just twenty-eight more wins to go."

He wouldn't win that many the rest of his career.

Medwick's charge—that Diz ran from a fight—was not a new one. It had haunted him since he beaned the little Brooklyn

catcher Clyde Sukeforth in 1932, and there was some validity to
the charge. His most famous fights were with much smaller men:
the 155-pound Sukeforth, the 5′10″ Jimmy Ripple. Since his bat-
tles in the minor leagues with Vic Shiell and Al Todd, both burly
brawlers, the 6′3″ Diz had aimed his most famous beanballs at
men a head shorter.

Don Gutteridge, a Cardinals infielder from '36 till '40,
remembers, "I used to say to Diz, 'I have been in five or six fights
with you and have yet to see you throw a punch or get hit.'" But
Gutteridge says his teammates didn't mind. "We would protect
Dizzy. He was our star. In that one game with the Giants he
threw a pitch at Jim Ripple's head. I could tell there was going to
be a fight. Our third base coach said, 'Let's go, there is going to
be a brawl.' Me, Johnny Mize and Leo Durocher protected
Dizzy. I got a black eye and Dizzy didn't get a scratch."

But the charge of cowardice ignores a few facts. Diz scuffled
with the larger Paul Derringer in the Cincinnati outfield in '35.
He was charging the muscular Medwick in the Cardinals dugout
in '36, and it was Medwick, not Diz, who grabbed a bat. Irv
Kupcinet, of the '37 hotel brawl, was a former college football
star.

The truth is much simpler: Diz just preferred bawling to
brawling. He learned that lesson from Al Todd in '31, when Todd
felled him before he knew what hit him.

Diz's early outings in '38 were misleading. The fastball was gone
and so was the arm.

In the Polo Grounds Mel Ott hit one of Diz's fastballs into
the right-field stands. After the game the Cubs were on the train
pulling out of Penn station, heading back to Chicago, when rookie pitcher Vance Page sat down next to Diz. Years later Diz would
recall the conversation. "[Page asks] 'Dizzy, whatever become of
your fastball?' I says, 'Sonny, you'll probably find it still bouncing

around them upper right field seats at the Polo Grounds.' "

While Diz's old club was heading downhill—they were out of the race by August—his new ball club was full of spunk. They battled the Pirates to the wire. And on September 27 manager Gabby Hartnett, who had replaced Charley Grimm in July, called on his twenty-eight-year-old warhorse in the most important game of the season. The Cubs and Bucs were going head-to-head in a season-ending series. The Pirates had a one-game lead, but the Cubs were surging; they had won seven in a row.

With his arm strength sapped, Diz turned to a new pitch, a change of pace that he called his "nothing ball." Using only two speeds, slow and slower, he managed to hold the Pirates to one run; meanwhile his teammates scored twice. Diz was up, 2-1, with the pennant on the line.

In the top of the ninth Hartnett went to the mound for a little pep talk with his pitcher. Diz would later recall the conference. "[Gabby says], 'Diz, try to throw this one a little harder.' And I says, 'Gabby, I'm throwing twice as hard as I've ever thrown in my life.' Gabby looks at me funny. I says, 'The only trouble is I throw hard enough but I can't throw fast enough no more.' "

Even with his nothing ball Diz managed to hold on and win the game. He contributed seven wins to the Cubs' total of eighty-nine, the lowest win total by a National League champion since 1926, when the Cards won with an 89-65 record. He finished 7-1, but his record was deceiving. He started only ten games, pitched only seventy-four innings for the season, struck out a mere twenty-two batters. These were not the kind of numbers he was used to.

But he was heading to the World Series, while his old mates in St. Louis were heading to their winter homes.

The Cubs were facing the Yankees, a team that in the thirties didn't need to rebuild. Gone from the Murderers' Row of the twenties were Babe Ruth, Earle Combs, and Tony Lazzeri, replaced by Joe DiMaggio, Tommy Henrich, and Joe Gordon.

Frankie Crosetti, Lou Gehrig, and Lefty Gomez were still around to remind the Cubs of a World Series six years earlier, the '32 classic when the Cubs had also faced the Yankees. In that one the Yankees had steamrollered the Chicago club in four straight.

In game one at Wrigley Field Red Ruffing limited the Cubs to one run, and the Yankees won, 3-1.

To head off a repeat of '32 Hartnett sent Diz to the mound to start game two. With no fastball to set up his curve, Diz was pitching on courage alone. And going into the top of the eighth, he had held the powerful Yankees to five hits and two runs and the Cubs were up, 3-2. "[Then] Crosetti come up and hit one in the seats and beat me 4-3. I was taken out. Fans in the Chicago ballpark stood up and cheered. Connie Mack was the first man I saw in the clubhouse. 'Son, you pitched a great ball game out there with what you had on the ball.'"

The Yankees went on to finish off the Cubs in four straight.

If Diz didn't make much of a contribution on the mound that season, he was still an asset to the Chicago club. He pulled folks into the park. And fellow pitcher Clay Bryant says he kept his teammates loose: "When we were on the road and someone would be reading the newspaper, he would light it, just take a match and catch it on fire. Nobody could read the paper. He would also do a lot of 'hot footing.' He'd stick a match between the cleats and light it when we were in the dugout. And in the dugout he would take a big mouthful of chewing tobacco and spit it on the back of your jersey. But no one got mad because they knew he didn't mean anything. He was just kidding. Everybody loved Dizzy."

The Cubs' 1939 press guide optimistically noted that Diz's ailing shoulder was "reported to be in splendid shape. Expects to triple 1938 win record in coming season."

There was no way Diz was going to win twenty-one in '39. In

fact, he wouldn't even pitch in twenty-one games. He finished 6-4 with a good ERA, 3.36, but his most telling statistic was in the K column. He struck out only twenty-seven batters. He was lost in the shuffle as the Cubs slipped to fourth.

During the winter of 1940 Cubs trainer Andy Lotshaw suggested that Diz become a southpaw. It was an outrageous proposal, but Diz considered it for a while. He even talked about making it as an outfielder. After all, he was a .223 lifetime hitter—not bad for a pitcher—going into the '40 season. In the end he rejected both ideas and elected to go to spring training and try to regain his fastball.

After a couple of years of relative tranquillity, Diz got in trouble during the spring-training season of '40. This time it wasn't the mischievous Diz of old, the impetuous kid. This time it was a vicious, unwarranted act of desperation.

The problem began with an April 8 exhibition game in Fort Smith, Arkansas, only a hoot and a holler from Diz's home in Lucas. It was Diz's first appearance of the spring, and he accused Hartnett of sending him out to pitch expecting "I would get my brains beat out in two or three innings." Actually, Hartnett was following an established practice of featuring players in exhibition games played in their home areas. Diz knew that; the Cardinals had played exhibition games in Fort Smith precisely for that reason.

But 1940 was different from 1932. Diz was the bottom man on the staff. He'd had no work in game situations, and probably it was he, not Hartnett, who thought he would get his brains beat out.

Instead he rose to the situation, pitching five innings against the St. Louis Browns, limiting them to two singles and no runs. But when Diz asked to finish the game, Hartnett declined. Other pitchers needed work too.

It all might have passed except that the next night, in Topeka,

Diz was caught sneaking back on the train after curfew and was fined $100. A humorous sidelight to the affair was Diz's excuse for missing curfew. He claimed he had been 139 miles away in Wichita, at the home of his preacher uncle, Bland Dean, discoursing on the virtues of chocolate milkshakes as contrasted with hard stuff. Uncle Bland would later deny—in the most indignant terms—that his nephew had visited the Dean parsonage.

When Hartnett refused to rescind the fine, Diz went on a tirade, unleashing all the pent-up frustrations of a spring spent on the bench. He blasted Hartnett, calling him Tomato Face, Pickle-puss, and a few names that newspapers weren't allowed to print. He claimed, "Hartnett has been on me ever since I reported March 17," and accused the manager of refusing to allow him to visit his father in Dallas and—most heartless of all—refusing his request to visit his mother's grave in Lucas.

Diz hadn't pitched a fit like this since he ripped up his uniforms in '34. Not only did he verbally abuse Hartnett and vow never to play for him again, he also tattled on some of his teammates and promised to do more tattling as soon as he could talk to Cub owner Phil Wrigley. He even threatened to organize his own barnstorming team, claiming he could make more in three weeks than the $10,000 the Cubs would be paying him for the season.

It was an unbelievable overreaction to a $100 fine, but Diz was supremely frustrated. After two years of rehabilitation his arm showed no signs of regaining its old form. He jumped the club in Topeka, zigzagging from relative to relative until Pat finally got hold of him.

Once Pat interceded, things were settled. She told the club Diz would pay the fine. "Hartnett was absolutely right in fining Diz," she told reporters. "He's going to take the fine and take it gracefully. Diz did wrong in staying out, and then just got mad and blew up. He shouldn't have done it. Dizzy realized he made a mistake. He just got mad because Gabby fined him in front of all the players and baseball writers. If he had done it in the usual way, a note in the box, this wouldn't have happened. We want the season to open next week under pleasant circumstances. As soon as all this is forgotten, the better off it will be."

Diz was uncharacteristically silent.

But he showed up in uniform at the April 14 city series game with the White Sox and heard boo birds from both sides of the stadium.

Diz opened the '40 season in the Cubs' starting rotation, but he had no success. Hartnett was patient, giving him five starts—Diz was bombed in four—before pulling him from the rotation.

Diz decided to experiment with a sidearm delivery and in early June asked to be sent to the Tulsa Oilers of the Texas League to work on this new pitching style. His first start, June 9 against Fort Worth, was a success. He limited the Panthers to six hits and Diz's tutor, Oilers coach Dutch Ruether, proclaimed it a "splendid exhibition." Just as important, 7,000 fans jammed the Tulsa park to see the onetime ace.

Five days later, against his old team, the Houston Buffs, Diz was routed. But he came back two nights later to limit the Buffs to three runs and four hits in eight innings; he even struck out seven.

On July 18 the New York *World-Telegram*'s Tom Meany declared Diz finished. "The chances of Dizzy Dean pitching in the majors again are slim," he wrote in his widely read column. "A poll of Texas League players, managers and officials was almost unanimous. Dean remains a minority of one. He thinks he can make it. No one else does. Dean's effort to develop a sidearm delivery has produced nothing. When Diz throws three-quarters, he looks his old self, loose and limber, with the important exception that there is little on the ball."

Meany noted that observers around the league said the fastest ball Diz had thrown in the Texas League was a duster that dropped young Dallas catcher Al Weiland. "Weiland, who popped up the first time he faced Dean, yelled at Diz, 'Go warm up, you broken down old-timer.' Dean came back, 'Listen, you fresh busher, I'm giving you your bread and butter with these crowds.' When Weiland next came to bat, Dean cut loose with one under Al's chin and there were no further exchanges of repartee."

Diz was not about to give up and, shortly after Meany's column was published, he began a run of strong performances. During the next month he pitched seven times and had only one bad outing—on August 2 San Antonio hitters tagged him for ten hits and five runs in five innings. During the stretch he twice went eleven innings and even had a string of twenty-eight consecutive scoreless innings.

Former Cub coach Roy Johnson, now manager of the Oilers, for one, was impressed. He said Diz looked better with the Oilers than at any time since his purchase from St. Louis two years earlier: "His arm doesn't hurt anymore, he can go nine innings and he wants to work."

Johnson promised to start Diz every third day. But he didn't get a chance to deliver on the promise.

On August 28 the call came: the Cubs were recalling Jerome Herman Dean from Tulsa of the Texas League. Gabby Hartnett told reporters he hoped to have Diz ready to pitch in the Cincinnati series opening in Chicago September 7.

Johnson was happy for his charge: "That's swell. Dean won't disappoint them. He is 50 per cent better than when he came back to the Texas League. He's trim, hard and far under the weight at which he reported to the Cubs back in the Spring."

But behind the happy news was a serious warning: This would be Diz's final chance with the Cubs. "There won't be any more experimenting with Dean," said Hartnett. "If we can pitch him, we'll keep him. If he can't pitch I'm not even sure he'll be with us at camp next spring."

Diz started four games in September and was hit hard in three of them. His success with Tulsa was purely minor-league success. The Cubs sent him home early, hoping that a winter of rest might restore his once dazzling fastball.

Diz pitched only once the first month of the '41 season and was knocked out by the Pirates in one inning. His ERA going into May was 18.00, and it looked like the end of the line. Soon the Cubs would have to make a decision whether to keep Diz or go with a fireballing young right-hander named Paul Erickson.

Diz made the decision for them. On May 14, 1941, one day before clubs had to reduce their rosters to twenty-five, he sat down and wrote a letter to Cubs general manager Jim Gallagher:

> After giving my arm a thorough trial during training and since the season opened, I feel as though I can be of no benefit to the club as a pitcher this year—and for this reason, I am asking to be placed on the voluntary retired list for the remainder of the season. As you know I have tried everything I know about to get my arm in shape and this is a step I deeply regret having to take. The only hope I have is that maybe complete rest of the arm for a while will do something for it. I sincerely and gratefully appreciate the many kindnesses the Chicago National League club has extended me since I have been a member of the organization. And I only hope that some day, some way, I may be able to repay in part, at least the debt I owe it.

He hinted that maybe after a year's layoff he could make a comeback, but he knew the truth: with that letter Dizzy Dean was giving up forever his career as a baseball pitcher.

Gallagher wrote Diz back, "Your petition to be placed on the voluntary retired list is rejected. Come down town tomorrow and we'll sign a contract as coach."

An elated Diz told reporters, "Boy, has this club ever been good to me!"

But Gallagher's move was more than sentimental. "Diz's too valuable to wind up in the minors. He'll be of great value helping young pitchers."

The balance of Diz's player contract, about $9,000, would be put into an annuity. For the rest of the season he would work for a coach's pay, about half what he was used to.

It was over. There would be no more boasts about beating some bunch of clowns, no more predictions about thirty wins in a season, no more holdouts or walkouts or strikes. Dizzy Dean's pitching career was over.

Hearst Newspapers' sports cartoonist Burris Jenkins paid tribute to Diz in rhyme:

GUNGA DEAN

You may talk of pitching kings
Rube's or Matty's famous wings
Before the hand of time forgot to blot it;
But when the fight gets busy
You will talk of guys like Dizzy,
And you'll lick the bloomin' boots of him that's got it.

Now in St. Lou's sunny clime
Where he used to spend his time
With the toughest fightin' crew you ever seen
Of all that screwy crew
The screwiest I knew
Was that cock-eyed lead-off pitcher Dizzy Dean.

OL' DIZ

It was Dean! Dean! Dean!
You big-mouthed hunk of ivory, Dizzy Dean!
Why aren't you in condition
For tomorrow's exhibition?
Don't you know you're just a cog in the machine?

The Uniform he'd wear
He'd scarcely know or care—
It could be the House of David if you chose—
For the only thing he knew
As he fogged his fast one through
Was to mow opposing batters down in rows.

When they'd sit all day somewheres
In them hotel lobby chairs
While the rain was washing out their game of ball,
You could always hear him gabbin'
How he's overlooked—or crabbin'

Because they wouldn't let him pitch them all!

It was Dean! Dean! Dean!
You moron, where the mischief have you been?
We must beat that bunch of Terry's
Or we'll fine you fifty berries
For not obeying orders, Dizzy Dean!

You would brag and blow and spout
Till the final man was out
For you didn't know what meek or modest mean
Nothing to this game atall—
Throw the ball to me and Paul—
Then chalk up forty wins for Dean and Dean!

202

THE TRADE

With your chawin' in your cheek
You might pitch three games a week
Or they might not find you anywhere around;
But for all your crazy ways
You could make your fire-ball blaze
In a crucial game when all the chips were down.

It was Dean! Dean! Dean!
With the batters bouncing horsehide off the screen—
When the hits began to score
You could hear the bleachers roar
"Hi! Take that cousin out for Dizzy Dean!"

I shan't forget the night
When we dropped behind the fight
With a homer where a goose egg shoulda been.
When things was at their worst
The face that we spied first
Was that good old grinnin' wind-bag, Dizzy Dean!

It was Dean! Dean! Dean!
They're crackin' up the Cardinal machine,
They are breakin' like a reed,
They have blown a five run lead
For Gawd's sake, stop the slaughter, Dizzy Dean!

Well, you fanned each batter twice
And you put the game on ice
Though they scratched an infield bunt just in between
At the end I heard you grunt
How'd I let them get that bunt
"I didn't have my stuff!" said Dizzy Dean.

So we'll meet him later on
When we all are dead and gone
Where it's double-headers daily, 1:15.
He'll be out there on the moun'
Rarin' back and bearin' down,
And we'll get a win in Hell from Dizzy Dean!

Dean! Dean! Dean!
You long-legged noisey fog-horn, Dizzy Dean.
Though they've fined you and they've played you
By the living Gawd that made you
YOU'RE A BETTER MAN THAN THEY WERE, DIZZY
    DEAN!

But it was left to Diz's old St. Louis buddy Roy Stockton to pay Diz the highest tribute in writing of his retirement: "Baseball is mourning the passing of Dizzy Dean from the major league scene, and it does well to mourn. There will never be another Dizzy. They broke the mold when he was born. There will be other great pitchers but no Dizzy Dean."

That same day, 800 miles away, the Giants were making cuts to bring their roster down to twenty-five. On the Giants' list of waivers was another familiar name from the heyday of the Gas House Gang, another broken-down pitcher trying in vain to make a comeback: Paul Dean.

15

Turn Your Radio On

Dizzy Dean and radio were meant for each other. That it took almost a month for anyone to figure that out is, in retrospect, difficult to believe. But that's how long Diz served as a Cub coach. And then came the call from St. Louis. They wanted him back, to announce the ball games on radio. Diz had been gone from St. Louis for three years, but he was still the biggest name in town. Since the unpopular trade that sent him to Chicago, the Cards had finished sixth, second, and third. No pennants. No World Series. The last flag hoisted at Sportsman's Park had been lifted by Diz and his Gas House Gang teammates.

So on July 6, 1941, at the conclusion of a doubleheader in Pittsburgh between the Cubs and the Pirates, Diz took off his uniform for the last time—or so he thought anyway—and left the dugout to embark on a new career. He would still be pitching, only now it would be pitching a product, Griesedieck Brothers Brewery's Falstaff Beer, while he broadcast the Cardinals and Browns games on radio.

Maybe his arm would no longer fog 'em in there, but it was just fine for draping around a shoulder or slapping on a back. In addition to broadcasting he would work as a goodwill ambassador for Falstaff Beer.

"I think I am going to like radio," Diz told Chicago sportswriters as he prepared to leave. "The experience I have had on several occasions has been enjoyable, yet I must say I am leaving baseball with deep regret. The game has been very good to me and I feel I am obligated to it."

Helping to ease Diz's deep regret was a familiar motivating force in his life: money. As a coach he was paid about $5,000 a year. His new salary with Falstaff would bring him $25,000 for the period from mid-1941 and the end of 1943, a raise back to his 1941 playing salary of $10,000 a year.

His first duty for Falstaff was to host a reception at the All-Star Game in Detroit. When players checked into their rooms at the hotel they found cards that read: "Jerome H. (Dizzy) Dean, who in the future will do his broadcasting over the radio, invites you to drop in for a chat. Parlor H. 9th Floor, Book-Cadillac Hotel, 6 to 9 p.m. Monday July 7."

Baseball was not the broadcasting attraction in the forties that it is today. Paul Enright, who was program director of WTMV in East St. Louis during the forties when the station broadcast Cardinals and Browns games, says the big stations in St. Louis didn't even want baseball games and that his small station across the river in Illinois ended up with baseball almost by default.

"None of the other stations would think of programming it because you couldn't program it. You didn't know how long it would last. It would go into their other programs. You couldn't run into your other programs or they'd cancel." And that cancellation would mean lost revenue.

Because baseball was such a poor money-maker, few stations would even incur the costs of broadcasting away games: leasing phone lines, sending announcers to distant cities, putting them up in hotels, and paying for their meals.

That meant Diz would broadcast only Cardinals and Browns home games. And these broadcasts would be divided between two stations. WEW, a daytime-only AM station, would broadcast afternoon games; Enright's WTMV, a tiny 250-watt station, would take over for evening contests.

Later in the forties the games were shared by WTMV and WIL. Enright recalls the ball clubs wanted to use only one radio outlet: "They tried to switch it to WIL exclusively but the best they could do was keep it on both. All they were selling was beer. It wasn't worth it to WIL if they had to split it so they didn't keep it long."

WTMV stuck with baseball throughout the decade. "We were a little peanut whistle station," says Enright. "At that time we were going in for sports. All we did was sports and hillbilly music. Nobody wanted to carry baseball at that time. There were about ten or twelve stations in the market, so we figured that was the best thing to go for. We started carrying the Cardinals and Browns, just the home games. We were getting a good audience on the Cardinals but poor with the Browns. They never seemed to attract much audience. The papers would use the line for the Browns: 'less than 500 attended.'"

Diz was one of a staff of sportscasters at the station. Enright recalls, "We had seven or eight sports announcers on that little station. Dizzy was hired to do color with Johnny O'Hara. At that time we weren't paying him much. We were paying Harry Caray about sixty-five dollars a week. None of them made much."

Diz's first radio broadcast was on July 10, 1941, over WTMV. It was the lowly Browns versus the mighty Yankees, with Joe DiMaggio in the midst of his landmark fifty-six-game hitting streak. "I never will forget the first game I broadcast," Diz would later recall. "Joe DiMaggio is havin' his fine hittin' streak and there is a big crowd. They introduce me at home plate and everybody cheers to welcome me back to St. Louis. Our broadcastin' booth is way up on top of the second deck, and I am scared to death as I climb up there. I know now how a prisoner feels when walkin' to his death, because every step I take toward that booth is just like me goin' to my doom. It's funny how a little ol' thing like a mikerphone can put such fear into the hearts of growed up men and women. DiMaggio hits in his 49th straight game, in the '49th State,' as they call the St. Louis area. And I'm glad when the game is called because of rain after the sixth inning, because I would rather have been pitchin' to Gehrig, Ruth and Hornsby in their prime with the bases full than to be talkin' into that mike."

But Diz got over his stage fright rather quickly. He took to broadcasting as naturally as he had once taken to pitching. He told John Carmichael of the Chicago *Daily News,* "You can see more mistakes sittin' up here than playin' on that field. That's an honest-to-goodness fact. I never thought of that before, but you can see all kinds of things that the fans have always seen and crab about and you think they're nuts. Well they ain't."

In no time Diz had built up quite a following. In August a local ratings survey showed the games he was broadcasting attracted 80 percent of the listening audience. Of course, it helped his ratings that his first three broadcasts were the forty-ninth, fiftieth, and fifty-first games in DiMaggio's fifty-six-game streak.

The mail regarding his broadcasts was also large, running more than a thousand letters a month. Not all of it, however, was fan mail. Some letters were the early rumblings of concern among language purists who wanted Diz and his "them Cardinals" and "ain't that right, Johnny" phrases off the airwaves. But that wouldn't come to a head for another five years.

* * *

One thing Diz accomplished immediately on radio was to bring the language of the ballplayer into fans' homes. Players had been referring to an easy pop fly as a "can of corn" for years; Diz brought that terminology into everyday use. He educated listeners on such inside phrases as *"frozen rope," "Texas Leaguer,"* and, his favorite, *"blue darter."*

And to this sports lingo he added a few creations of his own. He turned the adjective "nonchalant" into a verb, describing a casual catch as "nonchalanting." He also invented new past participle forms for such standard baseball verbs as "slide" and "throw," turning them into "slud" and "throwed."

The New York *World-Telegram*'s Joe Williams would later claim he had been sitting next to Diz in the St. Louis press box the day Diz invented his most famous word, "slud."

When a Brooklyn runner beat the throw to a base, Williams said he distinctly heard Diz say, "He slud in and was safe." During a commercial break, Williams said to Diz, "Never heard you use that one before." Diz's response was, "Oh, that, well, that's just what the boy did, he slud." Williams said he realized he was present at the creation of a new word, so he asked Diz to spell "slud" for him. Diz's spelling: S-l-o-o-d.

Diz's descriptive phrases and grammatical inventions were fun, but the most appealing thing about a Dizzy Dean broadcast was Diz's approach. For him the game was just that, a game. And if the game got boring, he was as bored with it as the average listener. So he did what he had to do to keep himself interested. And in the process, he became an entertainer. The broadcast became more than just the Cardinals' game or the Browns' game (especially more than just a Browns game), it became Dizzy Dean's game. After all, listeners had their choice of more than one station to hear the game.

Dizzy Dean was the first announcer to become bigger than

the game he was covering. It was just an extension of his on-field career, when he became bigger than the matchup, causing the Cardinals to advertise games as "Dizzy Dean vs. Giants" rather than "Cardinals vs. Giants."

Thirty years later an announcer named Howard Cosell would startle television viewers into paying attention to the game announcers, in the process causing them to realize how incompetent some were. In the early forties Diz jump-started the radio sportscasting business that way. Even when he was calling the lowly Browns contests, he would draw an audience simply by what Cosell would later label "telling it like it is."

It was Diz's nature, not his style. He'd never held back from telling the truth, even if it meant offending his teammates. As early as 1934 he was disparaging the other members of the Cardinals pitching staff in front of them.

Paul Gallico of the New York *Daily News* reported interviewing Diz while he was playing poker with fellow pitchers Jesse Haines and Tex Carleton in September '34:

> [Dizzy] was asked what he thought of Frankie Frisch. He said, "I think Frisch is the most wonderful manager in the world."
>
> The reporter asked, "Why, Diz?"
>
> "Because," replied Dizzy, "he's the only man who could keep a club in a pennant fight with only two pitchers."
>
> "Who are the two pitchers, Dizzy?"
>
> "Me and Paul."
>
> Three other Cardinal pitchers were standing beside him when he made this earnest statement.

So when he climbed into the broadcast booth, he had no inhibitions, no protectionist feelings, about members of the brotherhood. If a player made a mental error, Diz pointed it out.

And if the club made a mistake in a trade, Diz would voice his opinion of the matter.

Murray Robinson of the New York *Daily News*, in a 1950 column, credited Diz with being the first honest announcer: "Broadcasting the games of the loutish Browns in St. Louis, Dizzy set two records. He was the only commentator to call a bonehead a bonehead and he fractured more English than Mrs. Malaprop."

No tape recordings of Diz's radio broadcasts survive. But in 1946 and again in 1947 the *Sporting News* published a transcription of a complete Diz broadcast to give its national audience a feel for Diz's unique broadcasting style, which was then heard only in St. Louis.

The second transcription, from an April 27, 1947, doubleheader between the Browns and the White Sox, demonstrates how unremarkable much of Diz's sportscasting was. During an average afternoon, he might utter 3,000 words on the radio, of which only a hundred were memorable. But it was those few notorious remarks that made people want to listen to Diz. He was like the proverbial loose cannon on a ship's deck. No one knew at any moment what he might say. And in a live medium that was both dangerous and exciting.

Diz's colleague on WIL that day was his longtime radio partner, Johnny O'Hara, who opened the broadcast and then introduced Diz to the radio audience as "the pitching ace who thrilled you out there on the mound, the one and only Dizzy Dean."

Announcer teams worked differently in those years. There was no designated color man and designated play-by-play man. The two announcers traded off innings, rarely interrupting the other's call.

Dizzy began his inning of play-by-play with a fairly mundane description of the first inning:

"Yes, this is the first double-header of the year between the White Sox and our Browns ... Floyd Baker is the first batter ... Muncrief warms up ... there's the pitch ... he's out on a grounder to Berardino. Now good ole Loo-oo-oo-k Appling is up."

The *Sporting News* used the unique "Loo-oo-oo-k" spelling of Luke to demonstrate how Diz stretched the one-syllable name to unrecognizable length. Diz and Appling were old friends, and Diz would continue that funny pronunciation throughout his television broadcasting years.

Referring to O'Hara's replay of the broadcast of ceremonies at Yankee Stadium honoring Babe Ruth, held earlier that day, Diz remarked, "Yep, it was great listening to that Babe Ruth broadcast and here is hoping the Babe lives a long time for the young kids comin' up."

Then, without missing a beat, it was back to the game: "There's the windup and a pitch ... he swings ... it drops out there and Walt Judnich picks it up ... that's a single for Loo-oo-oo-k Appling ... Now Philley is up ... he has his right foot 'way in the bucket—it looks like ... he has No. 9 on his uniform."

A Diz broadcast was like that: an exercise in nonsequiturs. Diz would describe the positioning of the fielders: "Judnich's playin' this feller over in right field, about two or three steps ... Ball one."

Then, suddenly, he was off on something else: "Talkin' to Johnny O'Hara and Luke Appling before the game ... they say they're both the same age ... Johnny says they're 41 ... guess he's right at that."

Diz would interrupt his play-by-play call for chance observations about the players: "Strike one ... strike two. Appling lumbers back to first ... That is the laziest lookin' player to be a great player I ever saw."

And there was nothing neutral about Diz's play-by-play. He

was an unabashed homer, and understandably so. Who else would be listening to a Browns game but a Browns fan? "The Browns are now at bat ... there's Bob Dillinger at bat an' Lopat's on the mound, smoothing it out, lookin' around at his infield and out-field ... Last time he pitched—I believe it was in Detroit—they hit five home runs offa him an' we wanna hit five home runs offa him here ... Mike Tresh was hurt yesterday slidin' into third ... noth-in' broke ... leeglemints torn, we hear ... so Dickey is ketchin'."

"Leeglemints." That was vintage Diz, a mangling of what was then a fairly technical medical term, "ligaments."

Here's how the rest of that inning went:

"Ball one ... ball two ... ball three. Johnny, keep yer head out of the grandstand ... yer always lookin' for pretty bonnets ... Strike one ... strike two ... Earle Combs is a-coachin' over thar at third and Freddie Hofmann at first ... Boy, after comin' back to St. Louis after that road trip to Detroit, an' seein' this sunshine, Johnny, you won't know how to act ... Whaddaya mean it was cold this mornin'? ... you wuz dreamin'—it wasn't cold. Hey, hey—Dillinger hit one to center—he's agonna try for second—no—he made it a single ... That looked like Johnny O'Hara—26 years ago—runnin' down thar ... Zeke Zarilla's up now ... He bunts the ball, but Kolloway at first comes in an' takes the pop fly ... one man out. Vern Stephens is the next batter in there ... Wind's a blowin' into right field ... Lopat gets the signal ... Throws to first; put nothin' on it—just a bluff—and Dillinger gets back ... Ball one ... Gotta nice crowd out here today.

"C'mon, Vern, getta holda one—I wanna see ya tear loose ... Foul, strike one ... right into the upper deck here, to our right ... Lopat, with a new baseball, gets another signal ... He throws and Stephens hits it right through the pitcher's mound for a hit ... hey, hey ... it gets away from the center fielder an' Dillinger scores easy ... an' Stephens goes to second ... I believe it'll be a two-base hit, because the ball took a bad hop when Philley came charging in at it. Yep, it's a two-bagger.

"Fred Hofmann's bending over down there ... Will he make it—whoops—don't think so ... Yep, he did ... Boy, when he bends over, he scares me to death ... I'm afraid he won't make it ... There's the pitch to Heath an' Heath hits it to left; Taft Wright takes it ... two out and the next batter is Jerry Witte. Brownies lead, one to nothin' ... They're gonna walk Witte purposely ... Ball one, outside ... there's ball two; lotta people are wonderin' why they're walkin' Witte ... Well, here's the reason why ... Jerry's a righthand hitter; Lopat's a lefthand pitcher ... Lefthand pitchers has lots of trouble sometimes with righthand batters an' the next batter is Walt Judnich, a lefthand hitter ... Come on, Walt, hit one!

"Ball one ... strike one ... swing and missed ... Johnny, jerk the caps offa few of those bottles of Falstaff and we'll sip up some o' those suds ... With your teeth? ... What teeth? ... Too expensive tryin' to open bottles that away ... haw, haw, haw ... Strike two; there's a curve, way inside.

"Lopat has his signal, stretches and throws ... The runners was movin' but Judnich foul-tipped it an' the runners had to go back to their respectable bases ... Crispi says they're not respectable when you cain't git to 'em ... haw ... Boy. Look what Cincinnati did to Pittsburgh ... four runs in the last of the first ... Here's the pitch—ball three ... On the next pitch, Witte an' Stephens'll be movin' ... a two-base hit would score both runners ... there's the pitch and it's foul ... Oh boy, it was just foul; both umpires called it foul, but Freddie Hofmann, putting on the ole decoy act, yelled 'Go on; go for two!' but back they came.

"Here comes the pitch ... he swung on it, a high inside pitch, striking out, retiring the side ... One run, two hits, two left."

That was just one inning.

Diz's play-by-play was riddled with howdy-do's and asides to

Room Service: The St. Charles Hotel, one of Diz's many crash pads when he was playing for the St. Joseph (Missouri) Saints in 1930.

Dizzy and Happy: Diz lunches with A. B. "Happy" Chandler in happier times, circa 1936. Chandler would later become baseball commissioner and call Diz on the carpet for betting on games he was broadcasting. (Courtesy of Hillreich & Bradsby Collection, Photographic Archives, University of Louisville)

The Brothers Dean: The most successful brother pitching act of the thirties. This photo was taken during the 1934 World Series. (Courtesy National Baseball Library, Cooperstown, NY)

Bubblegum Cards: Diz was depicted on only a handful of baseball cards during his career. This card was issued by the Goudey Card Company of Boston in 1934, and was Diz's second bubblegum card. A Goudey Puzzle Back was issued in 1935.

Ol' Number 17: Diz's Cardinal uniform on display at the Dizzy Dean Museum in Jackson, Mississippi.

Diz and Satch: Diz poses with Negro Leagues star Satchel Paige before a barnstorming game at Louisville, Kentucky's Parkway Field. Diz and Satchel locked up in many a pitching duel, but because of the "color line" their matches were only for pride, not a pennant. (Courtesy R. G. Potter Collection, Photographic Archives, University of Louisville)

The Game of the Week: Dizzy poses with future Hall of Famers Stan Musial and George Kell before a "Game of the Week" broadcast at Sportsman's Park in St. Louis in 1958. (Courtesy Hillreich & Bradsby Collection, Photographic Archives, University of Louisville)

Dizzy's Hall of Fame: The Dizzy Dean Museum is not a major tourist attraction in Jackson, Mississippi. In fact, a Jackson city councilman told *USA Today* that the only thing deader than the Dizzy Dean Museum was Dizzy Dean.

Deanash: The Bond, Mississippi, house where Diz and Pat lived from 1958 until their deaths: his in 1974, hers in 1981. It is now a children's home.

Salesman Dean: A candid photo of Diz on the road promoting Holiday Rambler brand motor homes in 1972. (Photograph courtesy of David Coleman)

his partner. But if you look closely, you'll notice that he worked much information into his call. It was sunny, the wind was blowing to right field. The Reds had taken a four-run lead over the Pirates in their game. There's even a rudimentary explanation of the right-left advantage in platoon baseball.

And in the first inning he even managed to get in one of his trademark lines: "The runners had to go back to their respectable bases." He even made fun of his mixing up "respective" and "respectable," demonstrating that what may have begun as a funny mistake years earlier was now an intentional malaprop.

In the course of the afternoon's broadcast, Diz would acknowledge his wife in the stands ("Strike one, foul into the upper deck ... it bounced into the stands ... Who got it, Johnny? ... A blonde ... You don't mean my wife, do ya? ... She's a brunette, boy ... Say, I gotta be careful; she's lookin' right up here at me"), make a joke at her expense, which she couldn't hear ("Dillinger's the next batter ... One strike ... Lopat gets all set ... Yes, Johnny, I see my big fat wife sittin' down in the box ... oh, that woman gettin' big"), and complain about his empty stomach ("Johnny, when's the Falstaff an' food comin' down? I'm gettin' kinda hungry here ... Ten minutes? ... Guess I can take it").

He would yell words of encouragement to Browns players on the field. During O'Hara's fourth-inning stint, the *Sporting News* reported Diz could be heard in the background yelling, "Hey Jerry Witte, hit one, boy!"

And he'd even make a few silly conjectures. "Now he steps off the mound and Muncrief an' Moss is gonna have a little meeting out there in the middle of the diamond to see if they're gonna have a nice cold bottle of Falstaff an' a nice steak after the game ... We used to do that ... The ketcher'd walk out to me an' say: 'Have ya decided where we're gonna eat after the game?' ... I'd say: 'We've got a game on,' but he'd say: 'Whatcha worryin' about—everything's under control.' ... haw, haw, haw."

But even his silliness had a weight to it. Those who never played big-league ball wondered what the pitcher and catcher talked about during a conference on the mound. Diz knew, he'd been there, and even if what he said sounded ridiculous, it also sounded plausible.

Diz might brag that he didn't keep a scorecard because he "never fooled with them statics [statistics]." But he knew more about "statics" and strategy than he let on. In this game he noted, "Next batter is Michaels an' it looks like they might walk him purposely ... Ball two, ball three ... there's ball four ... They do that to set up a double play, but you might say: They're aputtin' the winnin' run on first' ... But they play the percentages."

In 1947 the Browns were in the midst of their worst season in a decade, a last-place finish that saw them wind up behind the notorious Washington Senators, the team hailed as "first in war, first in peace and last in the American League." So they needed all of Diz's considerable selling abilities.

Part of Diz's job, a big part, was selling seats and selling beer, and he let neither of his patrons down: "Come on in, Johnny, for the eighth innin' ... an' all the folks they's a lotsa seats still, available out here," he said during the first game of the doubleheader.

In the top of the ninth, he rooted, "Come on, Denny ... One ball an' one strike ... Ball two ... Runners all over the sacks—first, second an' third ... Let me enjoy my hamburger an' Falstaff after this, Denny."

He seemed never to let an inning go by without mentioning Falstaff, but not with an obvious commercial pitch. Diz's plugs were believable. The fan at home would hear Diz talking about the heat and how he needed a Falstaff to quench his thirst and soon Falstaff sales were skyrocketing.

(For the complete transcription of this game, see Appendix B, page 297.)

* * *

Dizzy Dean was a competent announcer. He was not a teacher in the Tim McCarver or Joe Morgan mold. What strategy he mentioned was basic. He didn't detail the position of each pitch for his home audience, although he told them Judnich struck out on a high-inside pitch. But he kept things moving, kept things enlivened. Today's announcers focus on statistics and strategy. But this was another era and Diz focused instead on stories.

He was often maligned for what his critics considered mangled pronunciations but what were in actuality just southern, particularly southern hill country, patterns of speech. When he called Mort Cooper "Cupper," he was just using the pronunciation favored by the Coopers of west Tennessee and Arkansas. Newspapers tried to capture his pronunciations on a few words: "ketcher" for "catcher," "umparr" for "umpire." But on close examination there really isn't much difference in the spellings. What the papers were doing was casting a hillbilly net over Diz.

And when they made fun of his pronunciations, Diz, ever the clown, played along. Rather than attempt to pronounce the last name of White Sox shortstop Chico Carrasquel, Diz just called him "that hitter with the three K's in his name." And when it came to Cubs pitcher Ed Hanyzewski, Diz said he wouldn't even try: "I liked to have broken my jaw tryin' to pronounce that one. But I said his name by just holdin' my nose and sneezing."

Folks outside Dixie might have had some trouble understanding his slurred speech—"movin'," "runnin'"—and his country accent—"cain't" for "can't," "over thar" for "over there," "chancet" for "chance," "oncet" for "once." But he wasn't broadcasting for those folks, not yet anyway. He was broadcasting for Missouri. And in the forties, that was part of Dixie.

And mostly he was just entertaining. And selling.

As Diz progressed, so did the media's perception of his broadcasting skills. In 1942, he was called "baseball's announcer with the worst diction." But two years later the *Sporting News* named him Announcer of the Year.

That same season Judge Landis removed him from the all–St. Louis World Series, dubbing his diction "unfit for a national broadcaster." Diz replied: "How can that commissar say I ain't eligible to broadcast? I ain't never met anybody that didn't know what ain't means."

In the fifties and sixties Diz's television broadcasts would give him national attention, but it was his decade in local radio that gave him his reputation. People who had never heard a Dizzy Dean broadcast during the forties could tell you stories about things Diz had supposedly said on the radio.

Perhaps the best known came from the war years, which Diz sat out with a perforated eardrum. The government was heavy-handed in its regulation of broadcasting and forbid radio announcers to make any mention of the weather. During one extended rain delay, Diz talked and talked and—yes—was about talked out, mentioning everything except why the game was delayed, when he decided to let his listeners in on the secret: "Folks, I can't tell you why this game is being held up but if you just stick you head out the window you can soon find out."

Another rain delay caused him to exclaim, "I can't tell you the weather we're havin', but what the players are wipin' off their faces ain't sweat."

And when nature prevailed while he was on the air, Diz took it in stride. Once during a game, he belched with gusto into the mike. "Oh, excuse me, folks," he cackled. And then, to Johnny O'Hara, "You know, Johnny, it's very impolite to belch, especially over the mike, unless you excuse yourself. I done belched and I done excused myself, so let's go, everything is hunky dory."

His natural curiosity was his greatest asset and also one that frequently got him in trouble. Once he interrupted his game call to ponder a commotion in the stands. He told his listeners there was a bunch of people crowded around some fat lady. An advertising agency man in the booth whispered to Diz that the woman was royalty. "I've just been informed that that fat lady is the Queen of the Netherlands," Diz said.

Diz was just being himself in a time when folks were used to pretentious announcers with end-of-the-world voices reading self-important commentaries. They heard Edward R. Murrow's dramatic war reports that always began: "This is London." And then they'd hear Diz hiccup and cackle with delight. He never took himself seriously. He was the hillbilly who sneaked into the opera house. And radio listeners in St. Louis just lapped it up. Diz's radio popularity was just instantaneous.

In the winter of '42 Republic studios offered him $75,000 to star—à la Roy Rogers of Cincinnati—in four B westerns. But he demurred: "I just don't want any part of Hollywood. I'd have to do a lot of readin' to play in pictures. Besides there's no baseball connected with it." He knew people associated him with baseball, not cowboys.

Diz's confrontation with language purists had been building for a decade, almost from the time he gave his first interview. It was heightened during the '35 season when he began "authorin'" (Diz's word) his St. Louis *Post-Dispatch* column, "Poppin' Off."

"Branch Rickey don't make many mistakes ..." began one column. Another described Pittsburgh's pennant chances this way: "It looks like they're gonna be in this here 1935 race all the way." And in still another he gently chided league president Ford Frick for fining him for fighting: "That ain't gonna stop me."

It was these "ain't's" that produced Diz's first run-in with the English teachers of America.

The story has varied in its retelling, but it usually goes like this: An English teacher complained to Cardinal management about Diz's abuse of the language. When sportswriters covering the team got wind of the complaint, they asked Diz about it. "A lot of folks that ain't saying 'ain't' ain't eating," he is supposed to have replied.

Agnes Schuble, wife of Cardinal Heinie Schuble, vouches for the veracity of the story. She says she can't remember exactly who had complained about Diz, but she remembers his impudent retort.

There's no evidence, no contemporaneous newspaper clipping, that proves Diz ever actually made the statement. In fact, on a 1948 NBC radio show Diz would attribute the quote to his "good friend Will Rogers."

Diz's mangling of the language immediately became a national joke. Poet Ogden Nash even composed an ode to Dizzy's syntax problems:

> D is for Dean,
> The grammatical Diz,
> When they asked, Who's tops?
> Said correctly, I is.

When he moved from the mound to the radio broadcast booth in 1941, the Diz stories continued. An oft-told tale from his radio years concerns an English teacher who chastened him for using the word "irregardless" on the air. The teacher is supposed to have cornered Diz and asked, "Don't you know the King's English?" And Diz is supposed to have answered, "Yup, and so's the queen."

Another story has it he was accused of not knowing syntax, to which he replied, "Are they taxing that, too?" Good stories, but they are just that, stories.

It was during the summer of '46 that his use of the King's English became part of a national debate. It began on July 22, when nationally syndicated columnist Leonard Lyons reported that a group of schoolteachers in St. Louis had filed a complaint with the Federal Communications Commission, the governmental body overseeing the radio industry.

According to Lyons, the English Teachers' Association of Missouri complained to the FCC that Diz's broadcasts of Cardinals and Browns games were having a bad influence on their pupils' grammar and syntax.

Lyons' column brought a quick response. Diz's fans flooded his radio stations, WTMV and WIL, with more than 150 telegrams and letters supporting Diz.

The St. Louis *Globe-Democrat* weighed in with an editorial headlined THE CASE OF PURE ENGLISH VS. DIZZY DEAN:

Mr. Dean does present something of a problem. Since he quit the pitcher's box to become a baseball commentator on the air, he has maintained his status as a dizzy individual which he won on the mound. It need not be argued here that the dizziness which permits him to earn a five-figure salary after he retired as a player, is a quality more to be respected than laughed at. Dizzy is dizzy in name only; he's crazy like a fox.

To listen to the broadcast of a game with Dizzy at the microphone is a pleasant interlude. It is a melange of grammatical errors, vaudeville, observations of his "hongriness" and his yearning for a helping of fried chicken, plus a routine calling of strikes and balls and a scientific analysis of the game as it is being played or should be played. It is fun and information rolled into one.

But the question remains, how damaging is Dizzy's murder of the King's English to the youths of St. Louis and its environs? We do not share the apprehension of the teachers. Exposure to shattered syntax as perpetrated by Dizzy may encourage a certain degree of laxity among his young hearers—and adults as well—but their interest is in the game, not in the linguistic precision of the broadcast. The imperfections of his speech may be remembered and copied, but we doubt it.

All this is respectfully referred to the FCC if it considers the case of Pure English vs. Dizzy Dean. We frankly hope Dizzy wins the verdict. We can imagine nothing more painful than Mr. Dean attempting to speak according to the book. And besides he can sing "The Wabash Cannonball," which is something else for youngsters to learn. We've heard him—between innings. Such talent should not be circumscribed by stodgy school teachers or dull government agents, whatever may be its influence on the youths of America.

Even the lofty *Saturday Review of Literature* took Diz's side. Editor Norman Cousins wrote a signed two-page editorial in the August 3 issue:

> Right off the bat we've got our money on Dizzy Dean to win his fight with the English teachers who are trying to throw him off the air as a play-by-play baseball announcer....
>
> Never before in history have man and machine been so perfectly wedded to each other as Diz and his microphone.... Radio listeners, too, became inordinately fond of Diz; he sounded like a combination of Bob Burns, Red Barber, and the kid next door. They liked his language—some of it authentic baseballese, but most of it just plain Dizzy Dean.... They knew just what Dizzy meant when he said that the batter was a-sendin' a tall can o'corn out into center, or when the runner couldn't get his tail out of the way of a hit-and-run play. All the customers loved it, that is, except the English teachers....
>
> The editors of *The Saturday Review* take their stand with Dizzy. Anyone—young or old—who is interested enough in baseball to tune in on Dizzy's broadcasts has already heard just as bad or worse treatment of the American language from his general contact with the sport.... Abuse of English is the standard occupational disease of the national pastime—a disease which, if cured, would do irreparable damage to the patient. Not a small part of the vigor of the American language comes from our sports; and we are sure we can count on

Henry Mencken to join with us in a holy crusade to put Dizzy back on the air should the Missouri teachers succeed in their efforts at grammatical decontamination of the baseball broadcasts.

Anyway our private hunch is that the teachers won't get to first base.

Diz himself seemed uncharacteristically unperturbed by the brouhaha. The Associated Press reported he told his WIL listeners: "All I got to say is that I always regretted I never got beyond third grade. But when I was a kid, me and Paul and Pa had to chop cotton for a living and I didn't have no chance to get much schooling. But education is a great thing and my advice to kids is to get as much of it as they can."

In the end all the verbal potshots were for naught; the debate was moot. No group had complained to the FCC. Ila Maude Kite, secretary of the English Teachers' Association of Missouri, told the *Sporting News* that Lyons was in error: "The complaint was not made through me and it would have been if it were an official complaint. If a complaint was made, it must have come from an individual teacher."

The discussion was over, for a time, but it was revived again in the fifties, when Diz became a baseball announcer for the CBS network. By now exasperated language teachers accepted defeat and began to use Diz as an example to their students, a bad example.

Anyone who ever listened to Diz on radio or saw his television broadcasts knows he stretched grammatical rules to their limit. And like many people with little education, he misused words, confusing a similar-sounding word for the one he intended: "respectable" for "respective," "confidentially" for "confidently," "hit" for "it." But there has always been a suspicion among Diz followers that maybe Diz exaggerated his grammatical shortcomings for publicity purposes.

Infielder Johnny Vergez, who played with and against Diz in the thirties, says, "When he was in public, he would put on a little, say 'slud' and things like that. In private he talked, well it wasn't perfect English, but it was understandable."

Cardinal Don Gutteridge agrees: "I think Dizzy put on a lot with his talk. He wasn't book smart. But he did it for publicity."

Agnes Schuble says she knew Diz and Pat well, and she is sure Diz exaggerated for effect: "I think he partially faked it [the way he talked]. He played it up, sold himself. I used to tell my husband to be more like Dizzy. Sell yourself, I'd say."

And sales were the bottom line on Diz's diction. Paul Enright, who was at WTMV during much of Diz's term there, says, "The grammar complaints didn't bother the station. It was good publicity really. I sometimes thought our biggest audience was the schoolteachers and they just tuned in to complain about his language. Our general manager was always writing them, telling them we were trying to teach him, to give him a chance."

Everything seemed to be going great for Diz in his new career. Then, in the winter of 1947, Cardinal owner Sam Breadon dropped a bombshell on Diz. Breadon had decided to allow only one radio station to carry the broadcasts of the Cardinals. Breadon chose the announcing team of Harry Caray and Gabby Street as the official voices of the Cardinals.

Diz and his longtime partner, Johnny O'Hara, were left with the crumbs of the city baseball scene, the Browns, who would finish the season dead last in the American League.

When the Cardinals went with Caray and Street, the papers blamed it on Breadon. Chicago *Sun* columnist Jack Clarke denounced Breadon's callous disregard of his onetime pitching ace: "All who cherish the inalienable rights of free speech and abhor censorship, as well as students of Elizabethan English, view with dismay Sam Breadon's decision to let Diz go. Blessed with the gifts of tongues, Dean proved to be an extraordinarily popular announcer. When Dean did not have at his disposal a word suitable for the occasion, he simply invented one."

But Enright says it was Oscar Zanner, who handled advertising, who made the choice. And his decision had nothing to do with Diz's style. "What bothered Zanner was we [WTMV] had to make money any way we could and on Sunday we had about eight colored quartets on right before the game." The brewery didn't want its baseball games run immediately after black music programs.

But the Browns didn't mind having Diz as their announcer. "Our radio surveys showed Dean has the largest baseball following in St. Louis," Browns general manager Bill DeWitt told reporters. "We're happy to offer Dizzy the opportunity to continue his contacts with his large local following."

Whatever the real story, Diz certainly took it personally. He frequently lashed out at Breadon on Browns broadcasts. And the *Sun*'s Clarke reported that Diz described Breadon to him as "a shameless skinflint, so tight he even sends paper towels to the laundry and schemes to save further money by requiring the players to hitchhike between cities."

But it wasn't just Breadon who was feeling Diz's stings that season. Diz could no longer ignore the miserable team the Browns were sending onto the field in front of him. Shirley Povich, columnist for the Washington *Post,* caught up with Diz during the summer of 1947 and gave readers of his column a slice of Diz's ability to "tell it like it is," two decades before Howard Cosell would make the phrase famous:

Jerome Herman Dean, who in public life is Dizzy Dean, retired pitcher and unretiring broadcaster of the Browns' games, had a word for it yesterday when Jeff Heath took a third strike with his bat on his shoulder.

"Awful," was Dizzy's microphone message to his St. Louis listeners.

He didn't let go at that, though. Dean's radio fans get the full treatment when Dizzy is broadcasting, such as his apologies for his grammatical mistakes. "Never went fur in school," he says. "Didn't get out of the third grade, you know didn't want to pass my father."

He was broadcasting yesterday from a box in the second tier behind third base in Griffith Stadium, and pelting third base Umpire Bill Summers with peanuts when his full attention to the game wasn't needed.

"Them guys what take third strikes don't deserve no sympathy," Dean was broadcasting. "I always said if they're close enough to call, they're close enough to swing at. 'Course that's the pitcher's point of view, and I'm for the pitchers."

He talked about the ball game, the weather, the beer he advertises, and himself. "Too hot in Washington today," he told the St. Louis fans, "and Johnny O'Hara and me wish we wuz there with you, guzzling some of that old Falstaff which goes so smooth on these hot days."

The team of Dean and O'Hara, which travels with the Browns to do the "live" play-by-play broadcasts, is a study in contrasts. The meticulous O'Hara, a smooth-tongued grammarian who alternates with Dean, is given to smart polysyllables and is the perfect foil for Dizzy, who makes no scholarly claims for himself. "All you fans which ain't got college degrees can listen to me," he said, "and O'Hara can have the others."

When Stan Spence singled in the opening inning, O'Hara recalled how Spence for years had been fattening his average against St.Louis pitching, and commented, "It would be nice to see Washington dispense with Spence, right Dizzy?" Whereupon Dean leaned into the mike and said, "I don't know what that word 'dispense' means, but I'm in favor of it if it means we git him."

Diz took out his '47-season frustrations by knocking everything from the Browns' players to the peanut vendors. "The peanuts vendors is going through the stands. They is not doing so good because there is more of them than there is of customers."

"Boy, I'd have me a picnic if I was playing today," he said on a day when Browns hitters were mired in futility.

Povich also overheard him berating Browns management: "Never could understand why they let Tom Ferrick get away to Washington at the waiver price, or sold Chuck Stevens, a good first baseman, back to Toledo. They'd both look pretty good with the Browns now. Ferrick's the best relief pitcher in the business, and Stevens can outfield anybody on first base in this league."

Browns pitchers would hear about Diz's condescending comments from their wives, and near the end of the '47 season they challenged him to back up his boast that he "could beat nine out of ten who calls themselves pitchers today."

He pulled the largest jersey the Browns had over his oversized frame (he now weighed almost 260 pounds), and in an appearance that was as much box-office hype as it was answering a challenge, he started the final game of the '47 season against the White Sox.

It was not a game of any import. The Sox were situated snugly in sixth place, twenty-seven games back of the league-leading Yankees. The Browns were even further back, hopelessly mired in last, no matter what Diz did.

What he did was account himself admirably both on the field and at the box office. He allowed only four hits, and no runs, in a three-inning stint that ended when he strained a leg muscle sliding in the bottom of the third. And despite the fact that the Browns were thirty-eight games out of first—and five games out of seventh—a crowd of 15,916, one of the largest of the season, turned out.

Afterward he told reporters, "I think I still could pitch well enough to win up here but I don't intend to try it. I have a contract as a radio announcer and I intend to stick to that job."

The money wasn't right either. He was signed to a contract that paid him only one dollar for his pitching.

By this time Diz was earning $20,000 a year as the Browns' broadcaster and he and Johnny O'Hara were no longer restricted to broadcasting only home games. They were traveling with the team, sending back the call from distant American League outposts. In 1948 Diz was in the second year of a five-year contract that would pay him a total of $100,000.

That's when NBC and Johnson's Wax decided to let the rest of the country in on Diz's dizzy radio style. Diz signed to do a series of fifteen-minute radio shows during the second half of the 1948 season. Diz would spin yarns, advise Little Leaguers, analyze the current season, and trade digs with his colleague Frank Ashen. Diz didn't even have to travel to New York to do the broadcast. It was sent out from the studios of KSD in St. Louis.

Diz made his network radio debut Saturday afternoon, July 3, 1948. The show, transmitted by NBC radio, was called simply "Dizzy Dean." Anyone who ever thought Diz was illiterate need only listen to tapes of these shows to understand the error of his ways. It's obvious he is reading from a script. Frequently, he mangles a good story by missing a word, rendering the anecdote meaningless.

The show was sponsored in toto by Johnson's Wax and Johnson's Carnu, "the wax-fortified auto polish that cleans and polishes your car in one easy application.... Rub it on, wipe it off, that's all you do with Carnu."

Between stories about current players and tales about his hardscrabble childhood, Diz would offer advice to young boys who hoped to grow up and become big-league ballplayers. Sometimes it was advice he should have taken himself. On one show, he advised, "Don't pitch too much. Do a lot of running and get your legs in shape. And always get 3 or 4 days rest. And another thing. Never throw curves. I'm talking about boys 14, 15. The curves will come later. The third is warming up properly. You must have 15 minutes of warming up before starting."

There was a mailbag segment that featured letters with a suspiciously scripted sound to them. "Dear Dizzy. I heard you the other night and you used some mighty fancy words. Remember, if you ever get an education, you're ruined."

It added up to little and at the end of the season, Johnson's Carnu elected not to renew the show.

Diz barely noticed. He went back to his regular announcing schedule on the Browns' games. As the '48 season came to an end, things were going swell for Diz. But they were about to turn sour.

16

The Gambler

On September 7, 1948, with his radio popularity at a peak, Diz was called to baseball commissioner Albert B. "Happy" Chandler's office on official business.

Diz and wife Pat cooled their heels for two hours and forty minutes in the anteroom of the Cincinnati office suite, waiting for the commissioner to return from eating lunch. It was a short meeting, and when the Deans emerged neither had anything to say about the goings-on. "Gentlemen, we will have no statement," Pat told sportswriters as she and Diz hurried out of the office.

Acme Telephoto reported that when asked why he had been summoned there, the normally loquacious Diz smiled and said, "Just a friendly visit."

Chandler's executive secretary Walter Mulbry announced, "Mr. Dean's silence following the conference is of his own choice and was not suggested by the commissioner." Of course, that wasn't true. Nor was Diz's "friendly visit" explanation. The commissioner had suggested the Deans remain mum on the meeting. And the friendly little meeting was on a deadly serious topic.

But neither side was commenting. And with the English-teacher complaint still fresh in their minds, the members of the sporting press speculated that Diz's latest run-in with a commissioner concerned something Diz had said on one of his broadcasts.

It wasn't even close. Like Ty Cobb before him, and Pete Rose after, Diz had been called on the commissioner's carpet for betting. In his autobiography, *Heroes, Plain Folks, and Skunks,* Chandler says the first thing he asked Diz at the meeting was, "You like to broadcast the games?"

Diz answered in the affirmative, and Chandler quickly followed with another question: "Can you broadcast them if you don't see them?"

A puzzled Dizzy mumbled that he couldn't, and Chandler launched into his lecture: "You're sending bets by the clubhouse boy to the saloon on the corner. You're broadcasting the game and you're betting on the game. Make your choice. Quit betting or I'm taking you out of the broadcast booth."

Chandler says Diz didn't hesitate: he'd quit betting. And Pat chimed in, "I'll see that he does."

Before he left the office Diz wanted to know what Chandler was going to tell the assembled reporters. Chandler told him, "I'm not going to say anything. It's nobody's business. If I were you, I'd not say anything."

Diz followed the commissioner's advice, and the betting matter stayed a secret, for a while anyway. But the problem didn't go away. Perhaps Diz stayed away from the bookies for a long time. In all probability, he didn't. He just shielded his activities from the commissioner's eyes.

His gambling problem exploded into the public light again in 1970 when he was named an unindicted co-conspirator in a Detroit gaming probe. A chastened Diz faced reporters, his eyes red, his voice quivering, and told them he hadn't been booking bets; he'd only placed a few for a friend with a bookie of his acquaintance.

"I became involved in this thing ... through a friend who asked me to make wagers for him. And I did, as a favor. He told me that he enjoyed wagering and I was told there was no harm in it. I tried to keep him from wagering. His family knows that. Later on I was told it was the wrong thing to do and I stopped it long before this thing broke seven or eight weeks ago. I also want to say I never received one dime for it, not one penny. I have nothing to do with big-time gambling, never did and never will."

Diz closed his press conference with a story about a letter he had received from a little boy named David: "He told me how his daddy enjoyed watching me pitch when he was a youngster and how he admired me. And he wrote in closing that he hoped I wasn't involved too much in this gambling. Well, David, I want to say to you, son, I've done a few foolish things in my life and I hope that you never do."

When it came to gambling, Diz did many foolish things. Hundreds of thousands of people in this country gamble. Few ever get dragged through the mud over it. Diz was caught in the web twice. That should give some indication of how heavily involved he was during his lifetime.

Was Diz himself a gambler? Yes. From the moment his name began popping up in newspapers in the early thirties, there were frequent mentions of his bets on this and that and his winnings at the track.

Did Diz have a gambling problem? From this distance it's impossible to say.

It is possible to say that he bet on baseball and he even bet on the game while he was a player. He admitted as much.

He told the Chicago *Daily News*'s John Carmichael a story

about one bet he made during a baseball game. Diz didn't say when, but a little research reveals it was May 5, 1937, in Boston.

"Remember seein' a big fat guy around with me a lot? Well, he was Johnny Perkins and he worked in a night club around St. Louis and he made this trip with us. He made us a bet I wouldn't strike out Vince DiMaggio the first time he came up. I did and when I went back to the bench I made motions to Perk I'd double the bet the next time. I struck him out again, and I put everything back on a third bet and I fanned him three straight times. Then Perkins wanted to make it all or nothin' so I took 'im and when DiMag came up again he lifted a pop foul back of the plate. I thought [catcher Brusie] Ogrodowski was gonna catch it and I ran and hollered: 'Let it go, let it go.' He couldn't get the ball anyway, as it turned out, 'cause it hit the screen, but I'd a bumped him sure as hell if he'd got under it. I wanted to win that bet. I struck DiMaggio out next pitch ... four straight times."

In that game DiMaggio struck out swinging in the second and fourth innings and on called strikes in the seventh and the ninth. And the Cardinals won the game, 13-1.

The story of Diz's in-game betting was published in the next day's *Post-Dispatch*. Reporter W. J. McGoogan noted,

[Diz] bet on the length of his drives in batting practice and wagered that he would do some good at bat during the game. Finally he found a fish who offered to bet him 10 cents each time that he went to the plate that he would not advance a runner, either himself or somebody else. And when he was 50 cents ahead with two sacrifices, a single and a double, late in the game, his foe wagered double or nothing that he could not strike out Vince DiMaggio for the fourth time.

"Listen," shouted Dizzy, "if that guy gets a hit off me, there'll be a dead Maggio."

And after he had fanned Vince three straight times he bore down on the kid in the ninth inning as though the game depended on it. He struck him out after Vince had hit two fouls.

"If he had popped one up in the air I would have chased Ogie [Ogrodowski] away from it," declared Diz later. "I wanted to strike him out."

And he did. Now he is the proud possessor of something like a dollar more than he had yesterday.

In 1937, not yet two decades removed from the Black Sox scandal, shouldn't someone have questioned the propriety of a nightclub comedian traveling with a ball club and betting with the players on the outcome of game situations? But no one did. Probably Diz's bets that day were nothing more than innocent soda-pop bets. But it was not investigated nor commented on by the commissioner, Kenesaw Mountain Landis, who had been hired to get gamblers out of the clubhouses.

Diz's Cub teammate Clay Bryant says Landis knew about Diz's betting on horses but didn't do anything about it: "Dizzy was always betting on the horses but Commissioner Landis was real good about letting it go. At the time we were not supposed to bet on horses but Dizzy never paid much mind to that. [Commissioner Landis] would have stepped in if it got out of hand. But he was real good to Dizzy."

Diz's gambling was not checked. And it would get out of hand when Happy Chandler became commissioner a decade later.

The Dizzy Dean story, from its beginning, is littered with talk of bets and betting, gamblers and horseplayers. Many of Diz's bets are the wagers of innocent youth, standard ballplayer fare like penny poker. But others were for substantial sums of money.

Diz won a widely reported $190 bet from Babe Ruth during a golf tournament for baseball players in Sarasota in February 1936. Diz shot an eighty-five, not nearly good enough to win, but when he sank a long putt on the last green he jumped in the air and exclaimed, "Hot damn, did you see that one. I'm as far off from that cup as second base but I kissed it in. Wait'll Babe Ruth hears about it."

The reason Diz was so anxious for Ruth to hear about the putt was it meant Diz had won $190: "He fixed me up playing level yesterday and was so cocky today he bet me nearly two hundred dollars he'd come closer to a 75 than I would to a 95." Ruth finished with an eighty-seven, meaning Diz was also closer to 75 than the Babe.

During that same spring training Diz had a run-in with Sarasota golf pro George Jacobus over an eighty-dollar bet. The pro had bet that Diz couldn't break eighty-four. When Diz shot seventy-seven, the pro refused to pay, pleading a technicality, saying Diz played the shorter women's tees. Pat took greater offense at the pro's insolence than Diz did, entering his pro shop, asking for a fifty-dollar bag and thirty dollars' worth of clubs and balls, and walking out without paying.

This was at a time when the average American worker didn't bring home $50 a week; $190 and $80 were very large bets.

And Diz would bet on anything: golf or gin rummy, pinochle or poker, horses or dogs. In his July 1, 1935, "Poppin' Off" column in the *Post-Dispatch,* he thanked a helpful police officer in Cincinnati, who escorted Diz's taxi from the local dog track to the hotel "so I'd beat the 12 o'clock order." On June 11, 1936, photographers caught Diz at the horse track. He dodged them, saying, "If my horse wins, you boys can shoot me all day." His pick, Limit, won the first race at 7 to 1 odds, and Diz posed for photos all afternoon. Later in 1936 Diz even bought a racehorse.

It was a Texas-bred thoroughbred that Pat renamed Kizzy D, her nickname for Diz.

Why did he do it? Durocher would later comment, "Diz is one of those fellows who will play you any game for any amount of money, and beat you."

I think that's it, pure and simple. Diz liked to win. He could never have taken money from gamblers to throw a game. That wasn't why he gambled. He just wanted another piece of action, another chance to win.

Paul Enright, who was at WTMV when Diz was caught broadcasting and betting on the same games, says he doubts it ever occurred to Diz that the commissioner would frown on his betting on games: "Diz wouldn't have done it knowing he was doing wrong."

And when Diz was caught with his hand in the cookie jar in 1970, he immediately agreed to cooperate with authorities in the case, not that he had any choice.

That case was closed three and a half years later, when the accused bookmakers pled guilty and received a one-year probation. One of the accused, Frank C. Duvic, told the court that he had taken wagers from Dizzy at a Biloxi club. Duvic said he knew Dizzy was not placing the bets for himself but for a Lansing, Michigan, millionaire, Howard Sober, who phoned them to Dean from Michigan. He said Diz would come in every Monday to settle the gambling account. And Duvic assured the court that as far as he knew he had never taken a bet for Diz himself.

It's hard to believe Diz didn't throw a few of his own dollars into the pot. But Duvic made his statement under oath and could have received a much more severe sentence than simple probation had he given testimony that the FBI knew to be untrue.

Diz's latest gambling run-in didn't end his wagering ways. Up until a couple of weeks before his death he was still winning bets on the golf courses of south Mississippi, playing the local gentry just close enough to keep them coming back. His Mississippi buddy Charles Mathis says, "He just knew how to win."

What it all comes down to is this: Dizzy Dean had a gambling habit. But it wasn't because he needed the money. He just needed to win.

17

Things Folks
Ain't Seeing

Diz would give different reasons for abandoning radio for the
fledgling television medium. He told one reporter he was tired of
"talkin' about things that folks ain't seein'." To another he laid
the blame on the inept Browns: he was tired of being associated
with a loser.

The fact was Diz was not exactly on top of the world broadcasting Browns games over a little peanut-whistle station in St.
Louis. Television was an opportunity: an opportunity to get in on
the ground floor of a blossoming new technology, an opportunity to conquer New York but—most important—an opportunity
to get back in the national spotlight and make some money.

The opportunity came during one of Diz's many Las Vegas
golf outings. He was playing with Yankee co-owner Dan Topping
when Topping was struck with an idea, an idea whose seed Diz
had probably planted: why not add the knowledgeable, loquacious Diz to the Yankees' television broadcasting team? Why not

238

indeed, except that that team, with Mel Allen and Curt Gowdy, was already full. No problem; Topping would make Diz the designated interviewer. He would conduct pregame and postgame interviews with Yankee stars over New York station WABD, the DuMont network station, during home games, adding his two cents' worth during play-by-play every second game, and scout college players when the team was on the road.

Diz would tell *The Saturday Evening Post* that all the pieces of the television contract came together so quickly that he had to hustle to get to New York in time for his first game. He said he even had to cancel an appearance before a Southern Methodist University speech class to discuss the Dizzian topic "Radio Announcing I Have Did." Actually, Diz's hiring was announced April 4, during spring training, and he didn't begin telecasting until April 16, when the Yankees played the Dodgers in an exhibition game.

Yankee manager Casey Stengel is supposed to have cut rookie outfielder Clarence Wotowicz at Diz's behest so Diz wouldn't have to wangle the Polish name on his hillbilly tongue. Diz did have a long history of mangling the names of Polish players.

Johnny O'Hara often told the tale of the time he and Diz were doing a Reds game on radio: "Ted Kluszewski was on third and Diz kept calling him 'Kluziwskir.' A guy named Wyrostek was on second, and another guy named Filipowicz was on first. I could see Diz was sweating, hoping nobody'd get a hit and he wouldn't have to call all those names." It was then that a Reds batter laced a line drive toward left center field, a sure double and a cinch to drive in all three runners. "There's a long drive," Dean is supposed to have screamed, then, in a flash of brilliance, adding, "Yep, it's a long drive and here's Johnny O'Hara to tell you all about it."

It's a great story, but it ignores the fact that the only year it could have happened, the only year all three of those players were on the Reds' roster, was 1948 and Steve Filipowicz didn't score a run all season.

It's just as unlikely that Stengel would cut Clarence Wotowicz in 1950 and tell Diz, as it is alleged, "When I heard you were going to do our games, I knew I couldn't keep him. Now, look our lineup over carefully and anybody you can't pronounce, I'll trade." It's more likely that Wotowicz wasn't good enough to make a Yankee outfield that included Joe DiMaggio, Hank Bauer, Gene Woodling, Cliff Mapes, and Jackie Jensen. Mickey Mantle couldn't even make the Yankees that spring! (He spent the '50 season in Joplin.)

In fact, Diz arrived in New York ahead of the season and, wearing what would become his trademark ten-gallon hat, did a round of newspaper interviews, promoting the upcoming season and the broadcasts. He was his usual self on the interviewee end. But a few days later, when he had to turn the tables, he had problems. Understandably. Interviewing was not something Diz had had any experience doing, and his first was a lulu. He was assigned to interview the master of double-talk, Yankee manager Casey Stengel.

Diz's opening was as ingratiating and as inane as any fledgling jock reporter has made since: "Mr. Stengel, I'm a stranger around these parts and I'd appreciate it if you'd sort of give me a hand in this here interview."

That gave the legendary double-talk artist a chance to take over, and he did:

"Sure, son. I can see where you'd feel like a stranger in Yankee Stadium after all your years in the National League."

"You ain't just a-woofin', Mr. Stengel."

"Well, boy, you ought to begin this interview by asking me how my ball club is shaping up. And I ought to answer you by saying we got pretty good infielding and pretty good outfielding and pretty good reserves and we got fair pitching and pretty fair hitting. And then, son, you ought to ask where I figure we'll finish in the race. And I ought to answer you that ..."

On that first broadcast Diz is supposed to have told viewers, "The score is nothin' to nothin' and nobody's winning."

On the whole Diz was a better match with TV than radio. Keeping a tight watch on the game was not his specialty and with TV he didn't need to. He recognized this crucial difference early on and, according to one newspaper account, explained his TV philosophy to those early viewers this way: "Only difference between television and radio is they ain't so much to talk about in television. If a batter is taking his stance at the plate, all you got to do is name him. They ain't no point in saying he is taking his stance at the plate. All you folks can see he is doing that. And, for an example, say that Rizzuto has got forked out while trying to steal second. If you got your eyes on your set, you seen him tagged out or seen the umpire signal. So they ain't no use for me to say much except to commentate, maybe, why Rizzuto's taken such a chance and tried to steal second."

His style was an instant sensation in Manhattan. Hugh Bradley of the New York *Post* wrote, "New York's newest video inspiration is a gent named Dizzy Dean. He has been doing his stuff in our town only three weeks, yet already he has the wrestlers writhing jealously and he is causing the maidenly mayhemers of the Roller Derby to spill new buckets of blood in order to compete with Dizzy."

To Frank Conniff of the *World-Telegram*, Diz was "the next big rage of television. He'll be the video's delight in a matter of weeks.... His homespun wise-cracks were refreshing after overlong exposure to the slick patter of the comedians. His technical understanding of the game contrasted sharply with the hit-or-miss guesses of some commentators. And the mispronunciation of names that brought protests from Missouri teachers when he broadcast over a St. Louis station were so amusing that here in

241

broad-minded New York his style may even be recommended to pupils as an example of the suppleness of our language."

And if New Yorkers couldn't understand the suppleness of Diz's language, Diz told Murray Robinson of the *World-Telegram and Sun* it would make matters even: "Because I never could make out what folks around here was sayin', either." Robinson had heard rumors Diz was boning up on diction, even taking lessons, to prepare for his New York debut. Diz denied it: "Ain't nothing to it. I'm gonna talk the way I always talked. Maybe I won't learn the fans no English but I'm gonna learn them a lot of baseball." Diz also expressed his disdain for the heavy makeup generally used by performers on early TV broadcasts: "I ain't gonna paint and powder up like some other fellers on television."

Even the *New York Times* liked Diz. TV critic Jack Gould wrote, "Legend had it that Dizzy was a cross between a dope and a clown who murdered the English language and turned a ball game into a vaudeville show. It's not so: the Diz is good.... Many of his amusing observations convey real information and lend an authoritative touch to his commentary. And when it comes to using back-country expressions, the Diz has it all over Red Barber. Incidentally Dizzy also knows his television: he doesn't talk too much."

In some ways the New York writers were blinded to Diz's shortcomings by his unique style. But the fact is his early TV work was rough, a fact recognized by the *World-Telegram*'s Joe Williams: "I regret to state that Dean is not yet altogether at home in television—a new medium for him—and the decision to force the commercials and such onerous details as particulars of the out-of-town games on him slows up his natural artistry and eloquence. The Yankees have given him a stooge, what he needs is a straight man. At one stage following a sweaty hand-to-hand grapple with an awkwardly worded commercial, Ole Diz grumbled: 'I don't see why I have to read all them commercials. Why don't they just let me tell 'em to drink the beer.'"

And it wasn't just his problems with commercials. Diz didn't know how to conduct an interview and wasn't really interested in learning. He was forty years old with nine seasons of radio announcing under his expanding belt. His problem with interviews was that the spotlight swung away from him. Soon he was grousing, "This here interviewing ain't in my contract, Mr. Topping. This ain't no job you give me. It's a sentence."

So at the end of the season he was let out of his contract—by mutual agreement. There were rumors Diz's departure was initiated on the golf course, that he had set up Topping and some of his corporate friends once too often. It's a possibility that was a contributing factor. Diz's golf hustling was legendary. Leo Durocher and others have even suggested Diz could have made a living on the links. Charles Mathis says, "Diz wouldn't beat you but one stroke so you'd come back again."

But the main reason Diz and the Yankees parted company was that Joe DiMaggio, whose name was synonymous with Yankee baseball, had decided to retire after the '51 season. Topping wanted DiMaggio to do the postgame television show.

And Diz didn't care. He soon signed to do Mutual Radio's "Game of the Day."

After the '50 season "Me 'n' Paul" were reunited in a business venture. They took over operations of the Lubbock (Texas) Hubbers baseball team in the Class C West Texas–New Mexico League. Paul would run the team; Diz would be his not-so-silent partner. The Dean brothers leased the team for five years, at $12,000 a year, with a down payment of $24,000. Where did the Dean boys get $24,000?

From Hollywood.

* * *

It's not surprising that a Hollywood studio decided to make a Dizzy Dean movie; the Dizzy Dean story was ripe for big-screen treatment. It had all the elements: a rags-to-riches plot, a well-known lead character, a love triangle (Diz, Pat, and baseball), and much opportunity for humor and exaggeration.

Twentieth Century-Fox began work on a Dizzy Dean movie in 1950. Getting Diz's permission was no problem. Money? Fame? Where did he sign? He was paid $50,000. "They're going to give me fifty thousand smackers just for living," he bragged. Pat decreed that the money come in five annual installments, for tax purposes.

Brother Paul was the hang-up. Paul Dean was reluctant to sign over use of his name and story. *The Saturday Evening Post* reported that Paul told Fox producer Jules Schermer, "I ain't signing you Hollywood fellows the right to make no fool out of me."

So Diz and Pat put on a full-court press. Pat Dean pointed out that $15,000 was a lot of money just for signing his name. Still Paul balked. It was left to Diz to bring his baby brother in line. The *Post* said Diz told him, "They ain't aiming to make no fool out of you. You ought to be proud they want to make a picture story about a couple of sockwads like me and you. And you can buy a good farm with the money they'll give you."

Diz also agreed to fork over $5,000 of his largess.

Paul signed.

Fox contract player Dan Dailey was lined up to portray Diz. Dailey, a lanky song-and-dance man who had starred in such Fox musical extravaganzas as *Mother Wore Tights, Give My Regards to Broadway,* and *My Blue Heaven,* was athletic, if not exactly baseball-wise. To help in that area Fox hired former Browns catcher lke Danning, who spent six weeks teaching Dailey the rudiments of the game.

It helped. *The Saturday Review*'s critic, for one, noted that

"Dailey easily outshines, with his playing ability, former major leaguers like Jimmy Stewart, Gary Cooper and William Bendix. By this I mean that Mr. Dailey looks considerably less spavined than the portrayers of Monte Stratton, Lou Gehrig, and Babe Ruth, and even good enough to have lasted two-and-one-third innings in a department-store-league game. This represents a wholesome improvement over the usual style of ball playing in movies, and it's all to Dan Dailey's (and the cameraman's) credit that he manages so well."

Joanne Dru, a popular leading lady and former model, would play Pat, and Richard Crenna, who had been a radio actor as a teenager, was signed to make his screen debut as Paul.

Fox assigned Canadian newcomer Harmon Jones the task of directing. It was only his second film. The script about Jerome Herman Dean was by another Herman, Herman Mankiewicz, a Hollywood heavyweight who a decade earlier had penned the Lou Gehrig film biography *The Pride of the Yankees*. Diz's movie was even titled *The Pride of St. Louis,* an attempt to capture a little of the magic of the earlier acclaimed baseball film.

Diz feigned nonchalance toward a movie about his life, but he still managed to sneak an advance plug for the film into a 1951 *Saturday Evening Post* profile of him.

Francis X. Tolbert described the scene at Plaza Barbershop, "Dean's favorite Dallas indoor loafing spot."

Diz was playing checkers with his barber-pal Claude Carpenter when a customer asked which studio was going to make the movie.

"Dogged if I know," replied Dean. "I didn't pay no heed to the name of the company on the letter."

"Who's going to take your part, Diz?"

"Some fellow name of Danny Something. I forget his last name."

A few days later, Producer Jules Schermer and Writer Guy Trosper, of Twentieth Century-Fox, were in Dallas. And they told Dean that it had been planned at first to cast actor Dan Dailey in the title role, only Dailey had come down with a nervous breakdown and might not be available when shooting started.

Dizzy translated this news to his friends at the barbershop. "After this Danny fellow found out he was going to have to take my part he went nuts."

The Pride of St. Louis had its world premiere Easter week 1952, four days before the Cardinals' home opener, at the Missouri Theater, a 3,500-seat house in downtown St. Louis. Diz was in attendance, along with Dan Dailey, Joanne Dru, and two other Fox stars on publicity tour, John Ireland and Constance Smith. Paul was not there. The ads for the film ballyhooed, correctly, "There just ain't ... never wuz ... and never will be anybody else like him!"

Variety reported the film "naturally clicked on its launching in St. Louis." It grossed $17,000 its first week. Still, that was good enough for only second place on the St. Louis box-office chart. *Singin' in the Rain* opened the same day at the smaller Loews Theater and chalked up $23,000 in weekly business.

Ticket prices at the Missouri were sixty and seventy-five cents, so *The Pride of St. Louis* drew about 25,000 paying customers its first week. Of course, two decades earlier that many people would have paid to see Diz on any given afternoon.

Dizzy may have gotten the idea that the film wasn't going to score as solidly as he had in his playing days when the studio-sponsored Dizzy Dean Day, scheduled for Sunday at Sportsman's Park, was rained out.

In its second week the film made $16,000, a very small slip. But when it moved to the Ambassador for its third week, it played on a double bill with the Monogram western *Rodeo* and earned what *Variety* called a "disappointing $8,000."

In the week after Easter it opened in cities around the country. Box-office results were mixed and seemed to follow no pattern. In Cincinnati, another National League city, the movie opened with what *Variety* termed an "okay $10,000." But in another National League city, Pittsburgh, it did a "stout $7,000."

In Chicago it played a double bill with a live act—the Ink Spots—and did a "mild $35,000." But Portland, Oregon's theater did a "powerful $15,000." And in Louisville it registered a "strong $4,500."

For the week of April 23, 1952, it was the number-ten movie in the country on the *Variety* box-office grosses chart. The next week it jumped to number five. Then it fell back to seven for two consecutive weeks before falling off the chart. The movie, like a washed-up pinch runner, didn't have any legs. It also had extremely strong competition. It opened against *Singin' in the Rain* and the eventual Oscar winner for Best Picture, *The Greatest Show on Earth,* in many cities. And soon it was playing against another future classic, *High Noon.* By the time the pennant races and the weather were heating up, *The Pride of St. Louis* had vanished from the screen.

The critics were kind if not overwhelming in their praise. The first notice had come in the February 25 *Variety,* which called it a "warm enjoyable comedy-drama…. It is the type of show that will be liked by both males and distaffers, outside of the baseball fan…. Historical diamond fact is blended nicely with screen drama, and it's all told with such an infectious good humor that audience holds steady."

Variety reviewer *Brog* found much to like in Dailey's performance: "Dailey enjoys one of his better roles in impersonating Dean."

Time also liked Dailey: "[He] makes a likable Huck Finn in spikes." The magazine called the film "an amiable, minor league movie biography of major-league baseball's Jerome Herman Dean."

The Saturday Review agreed: "The story is pretty standard

Hollywood biography, put together by that old hand Herman Mankiewicz, but it does stay close to the main outlines of the fabulous Dean career, finding in it what I guess the front office would call a nice mixture of humor and sentiment.... A likable picture, all in all, and one that should do no one any harm."

The *New York Times'* venerable movie critic Bosley Crowther was astounded—and pleased—that a baseball movie would actually conclude with something other than a ninth-inning home run or a sizzling pitcher's duel: "Baseball itself, while it runs loudly and rampantly all through the film, is not the major interest in this picture about Dizzy Dean. The magnetic thing is the nature of a great big lovable lug who plays baseball for a living and lives just to play—or talk—baseball.... And with Herman Mankiewicz writing him in a howlingly humorous script and Dan Dailey playing him in high gear and in accents that reek of the hills, he is an utterly fascinating blow-hard, a delightfully entertaining clown, but also a warmly sentimental and genuinely ingratiating guy."

But in St. Louis, where Diz had usually received kind notices, his film did not. The *Post-Dispatch*'s film critic Myles Standish wrote, "It may be impossible to do justice to the great Dizzy Dean in one mere movie biography but in 'The Pride of St. Louis' 20th Century-Fox hasn't made a particularly impressive attempt. Dan Dailey comes about as close to portraying the Dean personality as I suppose any actor could but he is left hanging by a rather trite and tepid screenplay."

Standish then went on to tell Hollywood what it should have done with the Dizzy Dean story: "The Dean characteristic that caught the public imagination was that he not only bragged but he made good on his boasting. This isn't emphasized enough—stuff such as his prediction he and Paul would win 50 games in 1934, which they only missed by one. It isn't demonstrated what a really extraordinary pitcher Dean was. The point of his character is missed by persisting in showing him throughout his career as an amiable, rather child-like buffoon; it would be much more interesting to point out that his uninhibited country boy was smart enough to exploit his personality and eccentricities to the point where, 15 years after his pitching career is over, he is earning, I am told, three times what he did at his peak as a pitcher."

Also weighing in with a discouraging word was *The Nation,* which called the movie "another ultra-civic-minded work [that] manages to kill the idea of baseball as the national pastime. The script-writer (H. Mankiewicz) decided that Dizzy Dean is a democratic Ozark peasant, more important for his clean habits and civic behavior than for his fast ball. He has confined the movie to shots of Dizzy (Dan Dailey) glad-handing customers and developing, via talk, into a good citizen, while his career is described by radio announcers and newspaper headlines. When the movie occasionally gets around to baseball, it shows Dailey doing a hammed-up burlesque of pitching so intricate that he doesn't seem to be throwing the ball. Odd note: Dailey, in certain profile shots with his hair dry and bushy, looks a bit like Dean's old-time rival, Carl Hubbell."

Viewed three decades later, the film is more a curiosity than an entertainment. Dailey doesn't resemble Hubbell so much as he does brother Paul, and his baseball scenes are embarrassingly awkward. But the story of Diz and Pat holds as close to fact as Hollywood ever allows.

When it does stray, it does so in odd ways. For instance, the movie Pat calls Diz "Jerome," something the real Pat never did. And when Diz tells Pat he doesn't drink or smoke, you want to howl with laughter. That might have been a nice bit of role modeling for the nation's youth in '52, but the real Diz was a chain smoker from his teens and a great fan of his Falstaff Beer.

Many names were changed to save money. The real Houston Buffaloes manager was Joe Schultz, not Ed Monroe, but to call him Joe in the movie would have required securing the real-life

Schultz's permission, a permission that might have entailed the transfer of funds from the Fox account to the Schultz account.

Many events were left out: his half season in St. Joe, his first stint at Houston, that big-league debut at the end of '30. But that is standard operating procedure in Hollywood. Too many facts, too much confusion.

For those who knew Dizzy Dean as an announcer first, the omission of any scene with Diz singing "The Wabash Cannonball" seems unrealistic.

All in all it's a mildly entertaining version of the Dizzy Dean story, especially considering its unpromising introduction: "This is a true story. A story of a few years in the life of one of the most colorful figures of our time. His name is Jerome Herman Dean."

Makes you want to ask: But what's the true part?

Credits for the Movie

The Pride of St. Louis, directed by Harmon Jones; screenplay by Herman J. Mankiewicz, based on a story by Guy Trosper; produced by Jules Schermer for Twentieth Century-Fox.

Dizzy Dean..Dan Dailey
Patricia Nash Dean..Joanne Dru
Johnny Kendall...Richard Hylton
Paul Dean..Richard Crenna
Horst..Hugh Sanders
Moose...James Brown
Manager Ed Monroe...................................Leo T. Cleary
Castleman..Kenny Williams
Delaney...John McKee
Frankie Frisch..Stuart Randall

Herbie..William Frambes
Johnnie Bishop.......................................Damian O'Flynn
Pittsburgh Coach..................................Cliff Clark
Alexander..Fred Graham
Chicago Manager...Billy Nelson
Ella...Pattee Chapman
Connelly...Richard Reeves
Eddie..Bob Nichols
Western Union Boy.....................................John Duncan
Mike...Clyde Trumbull
Waiter..John Butler
Doctor..Freeman Lusk
Voorhees...Jack Rice
Joe...Al Green
Louis...Phil Van Zandt
Kendall, Sr..Victor Sutherland
Mrs. Martin..Kathryn Carl
Roscoe...George MacDonald
Miss Johnson...Joan Sudlow
Chicago Third Base Coach...........................Fred Scannell
Tom Weaver...Chet Huntley
Benny...John Doucette
Hotel Clerk..Harris Brown

Announcers: Larry Thor, John Wald, Hank Weaver,
William Forman, Jack Sherman, Tom Hanlon.

18

A Game of the Week

On June 13, 1953, ABC debuted a television program that would affect the ways people spent their Saturday afternoons. Before that day none of the networks carried any Saturday afternoon programming to speak of. CBS had a summer horse-racing show that ran from four to five, but the entire afternoon, up to then, was filled by the local stations, which ran a potpourri of old cowboy movies, hillbilly music shows, teen dance parties, and "Industry on Parade" featurettes. If they ran anything. Some stations in small towns simply signed off, returning to the air in the evening.

"The Game of the Week" debuted that day with a game between the Yankees and the Indians.

In the early fifties "The Game of the Week" was one of the few things ABC did right. ABC in 1953 was the bottom of the network heap. It ran the army production "The Big Picture" and the Lutheran Church production "This Is the Life" in prime time. It had no programs in the top twenty in the ratings and never had had since A. C. Nielsen began surveying television audiences in 1949. Even the DuMont network had had one hit show, "Cavalcade of Stars," the number-ten show of 1950. Comedian Fred Allen would call ABC the number-five network in a four-network race.

"The Game of the Week" fit right in on ABC. Like "The Big Picture" and "This Is the Life," it was free programming. The show cost ABC nothing. It was produced by Griesedieck Bros. Breweries, brewers of Falstaff, and supplied to ABC at no cost. It filled time on the network's schedule and helped the network gain name recognition. The only thing it didn't do was provide revenue.

Major-league baseball was cool to the idea of a nationally televised game of the week. They were fearful, as they had been three decades earlier when radio came on the scene, that it would hurt the live gate. Baseball commissioner Ford Frick even convinced Colorado senator Edwin Johnson to introduce legislation in the '53 session of Congress that would ban broadcasts or telecasts within a fifty-mile radius of a major- or minor-league park, effectively blacking out the entire country except for sparsely populated areas of the west. Johnson's bill died in committee, after "The Game of the Week" debuted.

But that didn't mean baseball's powers-that-be were giving up. In fact, the producers of "The Game of the Week" were able to convince only three teams—the Phillies, the Indians, and the White Sox—to allow it to televise games from their home stadia.

It was not a promising start, and baseball had laid one more obstacle in the path of "The Game of the Week." No game could be televised into a major-league city. Not just a blackout when the local team was at home or televising a road game back home, but a blanket blackout of all big-league cities, eleven of the largest cities in the country. (Three cities—Philadelphia, Chicago, and St. Louis—had two teams. New York—including Brooklyn—had three.) Those eleven cities held only about 14 percent of the country's population of 150 million. But according to the June 1,

1953, issue of *Broadcasting-Telecasting* magazine, those eleven cities had 10,766,051 television sets, 47.6 percent of the television sets in the entire country. "The Game of the Week" would be starting out with one strike.

Although ABC claimed 114 affiliates at the time, the effective coverage of the network was much smaller. In many cities ABC was a secondary affiliate, sharing a station with CBS or NBC. And since the two bigger networks had the hit shows, ABC programs were seldom carried. When you consider the fact that the few full-time ABC outlets were generally the weakest—often UHF stations that could be picked up by only those households whose TVs had UHF converters, a fraction of the TV sets manufactured in the early years—it was strike two.

But Diz knew all about being behind in the count.

Diz was a natural choice as announcer on the games. After all, he'd been working for Falstaff for twelve years already and the relationship had profited both parties. In Missouri and the surrounding areas, Falstaff, once a what's-that beer, was now the beer of choice in many taverns.

Nineteen fifty three was turning into a grand year for Dizzy Dean. On January 21 he'd learned that he had received 209 votes in the Hall of Fame election, eleven more than the 75 percent required for election to baseball's most select group. He and Philadelphia Athletics' batting champion Al Simmons were elected on the same ballot. Bill Terry, whose biting remarks about Brooklyn nineteen years earlier had led to the Gas House Gang pennant, finished third, seven votes short of election. Joe DiMaggio, appearing on the ballot for the first time, surprised observers by finishing so poorly. He was eighth in the voting, behind Bill Dickey, Rabbit Maranville, Dazzy Vance, and Ted Lyons. Among those also receiving votes was the man who'd jousted with Diz during '31 spring training, eventually farming Diz out to Houston, former Cardinal manager Gabby Street. Street received one vote.

Diz's election was, like his career, not without controversy. His credentials were considered impeccable, but thin. He'd led the league in strikeouts four times and at the time was the last pitcher to win thirty games in one season, but he'd won only 150 games in his career, a total only half that of Lefty Grove, more than a hundred less than his contemporary Carl Hubbell, and far below any other pitcher in the Hall.

"He got in the Hall of Fame because he was Dizzy Dean," Jim Murray of the Los Angeles *Times* would rightly declare years later. Murray was not disparaging Diz's election; on the contrary, he was pointing out the rightness of it. If baseball were to have a Hall of Fame without Dizzy Dean, why have one at all?

On July 27, 1953, Diz became the sixty-third player enshrined in the Cooperstown institution. His speech was simple and to the point. He called the election his "greatest honor," lauded his former teammates, who "stopped them line drives and got some runs for me," and closed, "The Good Lord was good to me. He gave me a strong body, a good right arm and a weak mind."

"The Game of the Week" began its second year on a mixed note. More stations were on the air; more television sets were in homes; more stations were carrying the game. But the game was losing a big city. The Browns moved from St. Louis to Baltimore that winter, and because of the blackout rule that eliminated yet another town—and another half a million TV sets.

The other networks had been watching "The Game of the Week"'s growing success story during its first two seasons with trepidation; network television is, after all, a war. In the winter of '54 CBS lured the game away from ABC by promising more stations, bigger stations, bigger audiences.

It was what Falstaff—and Diz—wanted.

It was the big leagues of television.

Diz kidded reporters, "The thing I've got to guard against is improvement. If I start talking better, they'll throw me out."

Diz got a new network and a new "podnuh." Actually, it was an old partner recycled for television. Diz and Bob "Buddy" Blattner, the light-hitting second baseman of the postwar Giants, had broadcast Browns games together on the radio in 1951 and 1952.

It was a partnership that would last five years, until the end of the decade.

As 1956 dawned Diz made a major change in his life. He and Pat packed up and moved to tiny Bond, Mississippi, Pat's hometown. They kept their winter house in Phoenix, but from now on they would call Bond home.

Pat's father, Sam Nash, was in declining health, and she and Diz moved into his home on the outskirts of town. "He took that house and just built around it," says Charles Mathis, Diz's friend and traveling companion during the eighteen years he lived in Bond. "I'd say it was a two-bedroom frame and he just bricked around it, ended up with three or four bedrooms and a big old screened-in porch for his trophies and his draft beer."

It was while sprucing up the Nash place that Diz found his way into the newspapers again. "He wanted his house recarpeted and new curtains," recalls Mathis. "He went down and bought the carpet and he ended up with the carpeting store. That was typical of Diz."

A newspaper account of the purchase reported, "When the [carpet] estimate was presented, Diz yowled to high heaven and finally declared: 'If'n I'm a-gonna have to pay that much for rugs I might as well buy the company.'"

* * *

256

Life in south Mississippi agreed with Diz. "We got a lot of good doves and quail down here," says Mathis. "He loved to hunt and loved his dogs. He liked to catfish, you know, and we got a lot of rivers down here too."

Mathis recalls the times he and Diz went fishing: "We'd go out on these houseboats three or four days just letting the wind blow. He'd get back up there [to New York] and tell [his producer] Gene Kirby, 'Got a eight-inch catfish yesterday,' and Gene'd say, "That ain't big enough to fry.' And Diz'd say, 'Between the eyes. Eight inches between the eyes.'"

Diz often used his new home as a source of humor during his broadcasts. Mathis remembers one tale: "Dizzy always said, 'How do you get off at Bond? The train doesn't stop there.' He said, 'There's a sawdust pile.'"

But it was all joshing: Diz loved the town that would be home for the remainder of his life.

Maybe the bucolic life in south Mississippi was too good.

Before the start of the '57 season Diz told the *Sporting News* he wanted out: "If I'm ever going to start enjoying life, the time to begin is now." Funny thing, but on Opening Day Diz was right there at the microphone, his holdout thwarted by the offer of a $62,500 salary.

Diz had always hated airplanes. Part of it was that fear of flying. But he also disliked the sterile environment. "No one ever talks to you on a plane," he told a reporter. "Folks on trains are much friendlier. When I walk into my compartment, I put on my pajamas and I never get out of them. Porters and conductors and other people come in, and we have a good time all the way to New York."

From the time he moved to Bond he only flew out of necessity. He traveled to all his "Game of the Week" assignments (except

Detroit) by train, taking along a south Mississippi entourage that always included Charles Mathis.

"Diz and I really loved that train. He'd call a fellow at Birmingham who was a big shot with the railroad and he'd get on and make sure it was the way Diz wanted it, food, everything. We'd go to Hattiesburg on Thursday, him and I, and catch the Illinois Central. We'd get a ten-twenty train and get off at noon the next day in New York. We'd get a bedroom suite on the train. It was designed for four beds, three or four easy chairs and two bathrooms. We rode the train so much *Southern Railway System* magazine even did a story on Diz in 1963: 'Big Service for a Big Man.'"

And Diz was a big man by the time he did "The Game of the Week," tipping the scales at 265 pounds. The ample Diz was in stark contrast to the skinny Depression-era Dizzy, and once during a golf game President Eisenhower is said to have remarked on how much bigger Diz was. Diz's response: "Mr. President, I spent the first half of my life not getting enough to eat and I've been trying to catch up ever since."

Diz loved food; hardly a broadcast passed that he didn't talk about a meal he'd had the previous week. And the Southern Railway System made sure his train trips included bountiful helpings of exquisite food.

"Back then they had fine food on that train," says Mathis. "Real first-class stuff." But Mathis says it wasn't just the food and the service that he and Diz loved about rail travel, it was also the atmosphere, the serenity of the train: "Diz and I'd just lay back and watch the folks walking in the fields or watch the sun shining. This train travel, it gives a man a chance to think."

By the late fifties doing "The Game of the Week" was for Diz and his friends a full-time party.

Mathis says, "In Detroit we'd go to Windsor, Canada; we had a place over there we could buy some quail. Diamond Jim's in New Orleans would send Diz pork chops on the plane." There was the Spindletop steak house in New York, Stan Musial's restaurant in St. Louis. And first-class hotels at every stop. "Here's how exclusive this one was: two phones in the bathroom, one by the commode and one by the lavatory. Had a thing you punched to walk your dog."

Life was good for Dizzy Dean.

The tranquillity of it all was interrupted at the end of the '59 season. The National League race ended with the defending champion Braves and the Dodgers tied at the top of the standings, 86-68. There was a play-off set for Milwaukee, the first play-off since the Giants' Miracle of Coogan's Bluff finish in 1951.

Diz and Blattner had finished up the season in Chicago, telecasting the Dodgers-Cubs game. The plan was that they would head on to Milwaukee to do the play-off and Falstaff would sponsor the games.

But Falstaff said it couldn't foot the entire bill and brought in a co-sponsor, Liggett & Myers cigarette company. Because Diz had frequently talked about how lucky he was he had quit smoking, L&M balked at his doing the game.

Blattner headed on to Milwaukee, but when he arrived there he was informed he, too, was being replaced on the telecast. He resigned on the spot. He would later tell UPI that Dizzy had kept him from telecasting the Milwaukee–Los Angeles play-off games and that he quit "The Game of the Week" in protest.

When the story broke—that Blattner had resigned because Diz had told Falstaff he would quit if they let Blattner do the play-off games—Diz was quail hunting on the Arizona desert and couldn't be reached for comment. But Pat wasn't closemouthed. "I'm almost speechless," she told a UPI reporter. "It's the most ridiculous thing I've ever heard of. As far as we know, there's never been a rift. Why, Diz got him his job. I'm amazed." She said the first she and Diz had heard of Blattner leaving the game was when Gene Kirby, the show's producer, telephoned two days earlier and told them Blattner quit because he had another job offer. "Diz said he couldn't understand it," Pat told UPI. "He couldn't believe it. He and Buddy never had any differences. I am shocked." In refuting Blattner's story, she claimed Diz never had any intention of doing the play-off games.

UPI reported Blattner laughed at that claim. "All I know is that if Diz didn't hope to do the playoff, he certainly hung around Chicago 48 hours when he usually grabbed the first plane west. And if he didn't want to do the games, why did he set a price?"

In resigning Blattner gave up a two-year contract that reportedly brought him close to $50,000 a year. He also gave up a friendship that had begun a decade earlier when he and Diz worked Browns games together.

CBS and Falstaff kicked around several names as a replacement for Blattner, but one name was always at the top of their list: Pee Wee Reese. Reese had retired from the Dodgers only a year earlier and had spent 1959 in the coaching box. He was knowledgable, well known, and well respected. And also completely inexperienced.

For that reason Pee Wee was reluctant. "I was making more money coaching than anybody in the majors, and the only reason was because of my playing career. But where are you going as a coach? I would have floundered around in baseball, I'm sure."

So the first week in November, 1959, Reese accepted, giving "The Game of the Week" a pair of announcers with names straight out of Damon Runyon: Dizzy and Pee Wee.

For his part, Diz had reservations, mock reservations anyway. "He talks too good for TV," he told a reporter. "Thank the Lord he got a bowling alley and a couple of other things down in Louisville."

260

Pee Wee recalls traveling to St. Louis, home of Falstaff Brewery, to sign his contract. "Diz was there and he was doing most of the talking. One of the Falstaff folks said, 'Pee Wee, do you have anything to say?' And I said, 'No, I don't.' Diz speaks up, 'Now we have one that can't read and one that can't talk.'"

Pee Wee didn't jump into "The Game of the Week" cold. He recalls, "The [advertising] agency in New York sent a man to Louisville and we worked long and hard in my basement making tapes of mock ball games. Then Gene Kirby and I went to Phoenix during spring training in 1960 to make more tapes of five or six innings of exhibition games. Dizzy was playing a lot of golf and advising me, 'Oh, Pee Wee, don't worry, you can do it.'"

One day Diz showed up to help Pee Wee. "Gene and I were sitting in the stands and I was doing my little broadcast on a tape recorder and Diz walked up. He had on that cowboy hat and boots and everybody noticed him. He said, 'Podnuh, are you having a little trouble? Let me show you how to do it.' He picked up that mike and started singing 'Wabash Cannonball.' 'Podnuh, that's how you do it.'"

Today Reese still believes, "I couldn't have started [in television] with a better man. He'd tell jokes, take stuff out of your pockets, pretend to go to sleep, and stuff like that. It made me more relaxed."

The flap with Blattner was well publicized, and Pee Wee says that, going in, "I didn't know what to expect. Buddy Blattner hadn't gotten along with him at all. But we couldn't have had a better relationship. He was a great guy to work with. I never had any trouble with him. Right after I signed to do 'The Game of the Week' I went to New York and one of the baseball writers told me, 'If anybody can get along with that no good son of a bitch I guess you can.'"

Although Diz was often disparaged for his clownish behavior, Pee Wee says he soon began to respect the job Dean was doing:

"I think Diz was good for baseball. Sure, he was a little corny and I'm corny, too, but when you have one hundred games, you have to give 'em something besides statistics."

Diz and Pee Wee developed an almost instant rapport, and soon "Diz and Pee Wee" was a national catchphrase. It was very much a kidding relationship on the air. "I'd finish my two innings and he'd say, 'Podnuh, that wasn't too bad but I guess I'm going to have to pick things back up.' He'd call Pat after every game. I'd ask, 'What did Pat have to say?' He'd say, 'Well, Podnuh, she said I did an excellent job but she wasn't too sure about that other feller.' When he'd take off a weekend, he'd come back and I'd say, 'Did you hear me last weekend?' He'd say, 'I was out in the water fishing. Couldn't pick you up.' But then all of a sudden, he'd say, 'What the heck was that thing you said last weekend?' He was listening."

Pee Wee barely had his feet wet that first season when he found out Dizzy would miss three weekends. "I was sitting there with Gene Kirby one morning on game day eating breakfast and I say, 'When's Diz coming in?' He says Diz isn't coming. He has three weekends off a season. I'm having pancakes and Gene says, 'You concerned about it?' And I say no, but I am. And he says, 'Then why are you pouring coffee on the pancakes?' "

The six seasons that Diz and Pee Wee were together were the glory years of "The Game of the Week." Pee Wee would go on to work on NBC's baseball telecasts with Curt Gowdy, but, he says, it wasn't the same as the years with Diz. "It was a big difference working with Curt and working with Diz. Curt was a professional but if I made a mistake with him it bothered him. With Diz I didn't have to worry about making a mistake. It didn't bother him. There might be a player with a Polish name. Diz would just call him 'that second baseman.' He wouldn't even try to pronounce his name."

Diz and Pee Wee broadcast more than three hundred games together. And a nation watched, enraptured. One Saturday they saw Diz devour a watermelon. On another they watched him nod off and begin snoring. "He'd pretend to fall asleep while I was doing my play-by-play and the camera would focus in on him. Then he'd come on and say, 'Podnuh, I got to pick things up. You put me to sleep.' Or I'd be doing my inning and he'd go out and get something to eat. I remember in Philadelphia you had to come up in the booth through a hole and they'd have a shot of him the whole time, climbing back up with a hot dog. It was a comical sight because Diz weighed about three hundred pounds then. First thing he'd say when he got back up was, 'Podnuh, want a hot dog? I bought you some peanuts.'"

Diz and Pee Wee were just two old ballplayers, and baseball fans everywhere just knew this was what it must be like on a big-league bench during a game: a little what's-he-throwing, a little where-are-the-outfielders, and a lot of kidding, clowning, even razzing each other:

"Diz, you've watched the pitcher out there for about four innings and he's been throwing that ball and I mean doing a great job. What would you say he's throwing out there?"

"Well, Pee Wee, I have been watching him four innings and after watching him four innings, I believe that's a baseball."

United Press International's Doc Quigg tuned in one July afternoon in 1963 and heard this exchange:

Pee Wee: "Podres has always had a bad back. He stayed out of the service for a while with a bad back…. Where you going, Diz?"
Diz: "Get a steak sandwich. Be back in twenty, thirty minutes, podnuh."

Viewers watched the game *with* Diz and Pee Wee; they didn't tune in to hear the game dissected. It was the closest thing to an afternoon at the ball park for fans in backwater towns far from a big-league park.

When Diz said, "Pass me another hot dog, Pee Wee," viewers in small-town taverns would look at each other and wink: this, they knew, was the secret signal to pass him a Falstaff. But Pee Wee says not: "Diz never drank on the air."

Mathis agrees Diz wouldn't touch alcohol during a game: "Diz would have a Falstaff before he called the game, but he wouldn't drink but one. After the game he'd have a boiler-maker."

Diz never drank on the air. But after the game? Well, that was another story. Mathis tells of one visit to Diz's favorite New York watering hole, Toots Shor's. "We spent all afternoon in there one time with Elizabeth Taylor and Richard Burton. We were all drinking and they asked us to go to the Catskills and spend a few days. I tried my best to get Dizzy to go, and he said, 'Hell, Pat'll kill me.' They had a lodge. I almost had him talked into it. He said, 'We might get up there and not get back; we might get up there and get drunk and not get back.'"

No "Game of the Week" was complete without a chorus of "The Wabash Cannonball." It was Diz's signature as much as "slud" and "throwed." He'd first sung the railroad song during a slow Browns game in '41. It was corny, to interrupt a baseball broad-cast for a little hillbilly ditty. But it was Diz.

Forever more, when things got slow during a game, you could count on Diz puffing up his chest and warbling. One day it might be "John Henry." Another time it might be a gospel spiri-tual. But more often than not, it was this:

> From the great Atlantic ocean to the wide Pacific shore,
> From the queen of flowing mountains to the south bell
>   by the shore,

She's mighty tall and handsome and known quite well by
all,
She's the combination on the Wabash Cannonball.

Roy Acuff, the King of Country Music, had made the song famous in the thirties, and it was Acuff's version that Diz favored. He and Acuff had even become close friends. A North Carolina record producer had talked Diz into cutting the song as a single in 1951. It was released on Colonial Records with "You Don't Have to Be from the Country" on the flip side and was never heard from again.

Over the years Diz acquired a reputation that he would say almost anything on camera. He'd holler hello to his hunting buddies down in Mississippi, read a telegram from a listener in some Georgia outpost who had used cat-whisker tuning to pull in a snowy picture from a distant Atlanta station, plug "The Dinah Shore Show" on rival NBC.

A reporter listening in 1957 even heard Diz do a play-by-play on a blowing hot dog wrapper: "The umpire goes and picks up that hot dog wrapping. He looks in there and they ain't none in there. Some one done eat it, Podnuh."

Reese tells the story of the most famous thing Diz never said. "I bet I've had a thousand people come up and tell me they were watching the time Diz spotted the couple kissing in the right field stands. Even my brother-in-law swears he saw it."

The story has it that Diz says, "Yessir, there's two folks that's enjoying this ball game. He's kissing her on the strikes, and she's kissing him on the balls."

Pee Wee says it never happened. "He didn't say it with me. You know, that was a joke that was going 'round when I was a player. Gene Kirby told me it's not true. I've had so many people tell me that story that I don't even bother to correct them anymore. They want to think it's true."

* * *

Diz had his own vocabulary, a catalog of phrases that might have been well known to his radio listeners in Missouri but was alien to the rest of the nation. It was an amalgam of ballplayer slang, country expressions, and Diz's own inventions.

An easy play might elicit this: "He reached up for it like he was picking an orange off a doggone tree and the man was out."

Once while watching a young fastball pitcher, Diz, whose arm was still suffering the effects of throwing too many fastballs, noted, "Every time he throws one up there my arm goes shreeek!"

One of the most famous was, "He's going for the downs," uttered after a particularly vicious swing—and usually miss—by a batter. That same scenario might also bring Diz to comment, "Brother, he had a ripple."

Pitchers, members of his old brotherhood, took the most guff from Diz. A typical at-bat by a pitcher might hear Diz introduce the hitter thus: "It's the old slugger himself, hitting a cool .105, the pitcher."

But Diz's inventiveness with language was sometimes overshadowed by his illiteracies, malaprops, and wild grammatical constructions. On a '57 telecast he described Alvin Dark's execution of a difficult double play this way: "It's one of them plays you don't see very seldom." And in '63 he told viewers, "Good pitchers can stop good hitters better'n good hitters can stop good pitchers."

Both times viewers knew what he meant. He was just putting his own twist on a cliché. They weren't intentional goofs— although Diz wasn't above recycling a past malaprop, once someone pointed it out to him—they were just a part of Diz's hunt-and-peck acquaintance with the language.

Other of Diz's famous phraseologies were nothing more than the effects of Diz's Deep South slur. "Stanch" was his version of "stance." "It" sometimes came out "hit." It wasn't that he thought there was a difference; it was just a regional pronounciation, much as President Kennedy's "Cuba" came out "Cuber."

But because Diz was from the South, "the land of Bozos," H. L. Mencken would call it in print, his odd pronunciations were fair game.

The cornball humor, the country expressions, the hillbilly singing were all part of the appeal of "The Game of the Week." But what set a Diz and Pee Wee broadcast apart was the way Pee Wee could coax stories out of Diz. Stories were what Dizzy Dean was all about.

And he had a million of them:

If an umpire missed a call, he would remember the flare-up he had during the Gas House Gang years with umpire Beans Reardon: "I was walking toward second, mumbling the whole way, and Beans ran out and asked what I was saying. 'Beans, you been guessing out here all afternoon. Now you just guess what I said.'"

If the Cardinals were the team, he would recall Preacher Roe's formula for stopping Stan Musial: "The best way to pitch to Musial is to give him four straight balls good and wide of the plate and then pick him off first."

Then he might recall the tiny dugouts at Sportsman's Park. "And them two-by-fours we had to sit on in the dugout—I used to get splinters in ... splinters in ... and I hit my head on the beams ever' time I got up."

And when a rookie made a rookie mistake, Diz would hark back to 1935 and a rookie catcher in the Cardinals' camp named Sam Narron: "He asked manager Frankie Frisch if he had any particular orders. Frisch told him, 'You pick out some veteran on the club and do whatever he does. If he runs, you run; if he gets in a pepper game, you get in a pepper game.' About an hour later Frankie's leaning on the batting cage and watching the Cardinals hit. Ducking a foul, he sees Sam leaning on the cage. 'Hey, Sam, what are you doing here? I thought I told you to pick out some veteran on the club and do whatever he does.' 'That's what I done.' 'Who'd you pick?' 'I picked you, Mr. Frisch, and I been doing whatever I seen you doing ever since.'"

A question about what he did the night before could send Diz off on a story about carousing ballplayers: "I won't say what year or what club because it's a true story.... There was one pitcher who liked to stay up late, and he didn't know how to take care of his money either. The manager, knowing this pitcher had a family back home, arranged with the front office to send the pitcher's paycheck to his wife so the family would have some money.... He was liable to give it away he was so big hearted when he got on the merry-go-round.... This important game was coming up and the manager told him to please get home early. But he didn't obey. Well, he got to the ball park the next day and the manager catches on. 'In shape or not I said you're going to pitch and—doggone you—you are going to pitch.' 'I'll be doggone if I pitch, Mac. You send my paychecks to my wife. Let her pitch.'"

A bunt in the wrong situation would send Diz's mind wandering back to his days playing for Gabby Street: "We was playing the Giants at the Polo Grounds. There was a man on third, two out, and the Giants leading two to one in the ninth. The count works to two strikes and two balls.... Pepper [Martin] puts down a bunt and the Giant third baseman throws him out. When he gets back to the dugout, manager Gabby Street says, 'Pepper, I never thought you'd do a thing like that.' 'Gracious Gabby, I was surprised too when I got that sign.' 'Who give you that sign?' 'Buzzy Wares.' 'Buzzy, did you give him that sign?' Buzzy said, 'I just give him the sign you give me.' 'Buzzy, I don't believe you even know the bunt sign.' Buzzy rubs his hand across his face. 'Buzzy, can't you tell the difference between when a man's giving the bunt sign and just chasing a fly off his nose?'"

* * *

As the sixties hit their stride, major changes were brewing on the network sports scene. During the winter of '64–'65 CBS purchased baseball's crown jewel, the New York Yankees. It wanted its new property showcased, and it wanted it showcased on "The Game of the Week." So the venerable baseball broadcast was renamed "The Yankee Game of the Week," and each week Diz and Pee Wee described the exploits of the fading franchise. (The Yankees won the pennant in '64 but wouldn't win again for more than a decade.)

NBC threw in the towel that same season, conceding the baseball audience to CBS and dropping its baseball game. But ABC moved in to take up the slack with its own broadcast, "ABC Major League Baseball."

Charles Mathis says that before the '65 season Diz told him he was broke. But despite his financial situation, Diz put up a tough front in contract negotiations with Falstaff. Of course, when it came to money, Diz always put up a tough front. "He hold me, 'They finally quit sending busboys, they sent a vice president.' He said they finally sent someone with authority to trade with him."

Falstaff agreed to pay Diz $120,000 for the '65 season.

Mathis says it was already decided that 1965 was it. "The Falstaff guy told me, 'This will be our last time.'"

The memory of Sandy Koufax's three-hit shutout of the Twins in the final game of 1965 World Series was only five days old when John Fetzer, the head of baseball's television committee, dropped a bombshell on the sports community. Major League Baseball and NBC had signed an exclusive three-year, $18 million contract that would shut out the other two networks. NBC—and only NBC—would televise twenty-eight regular-season games, the All-Star Game, and the World Series each year of the contract.

After twelve years and some 500 games, "The Game of the Week" was over, r.i.p.

Pee Wee says that Diz wasn't in the least concerned when they heard the news of NBC's exclusive deal. Why should he be? He'd moved with "The Game of the Week" from ABC to CBS. Now *that* was a big move. Moving over to NBC would just be a little sideways step, like in a square dance. "He and I were out at Lake Tahoe at a golf tournament and it came over the radio. I said, 'Podnuh, I just heard NBC has bought the whole ball of wax. We may be in trouble.' He said, 'Podnuh, don't worry about a thing.'"

But it didn't turn out that way. NBC didn't want Diz. They wanted Curt Gowdy, who'd been broadcasting Red Sox games. They didn't want a hillbilly clown. They wanted a professional announcer and a broadcast aimed at a more upscale crowd, like the folks who watched NFL football. Football was the hot game of the sixties, a contest played by college men and watched by professionals; baseball was played by country boys and watched by beer guzzlers.

Falstaff no longer owned the game—it was one of several sponsors—but the brewery pushed for Diz as Gowdy's sidekick. NBC resisted. Pee Wee got the job instead.

In the mind's eye the history of "The Game of the Week" may appear a seamless journey. But, in fact, it was changing almost every year. After two years on ABC, the "Game" made the move to CBS in '55. It would remain on that network for eleven years, but other factors would change. In 1957 it got its first full-scale competition in the form of "NBC Major League Baseball." In '58 both programs lost their Los Angeles and San Francisco affiliates because big-league teams had moved into those towns. To counter the loss CBS added a "Sunday Game of the Week." A year later NBC followed suit. At the end of the '59 season Diz and Blattner would have their falling-out and Blattner would be replaced by Reese. That same summer ABC would return to baseball broadcasting with a late-afternoon game that usually emanated from the home park of a West Coast team. ABC dropped its game a year later, coming up instead with a sports anthology show called "ABC's Wide World of Sports." CBS and NBC went head-to-head with baseball on Saturday and Sunday for the next three years, but in '64 NBC dropped out completely, replaced by ABC on Saturdays. When CBS purchased the Yankees "The Game of the Week" became "The Yankee Game of the Week." The package was not as attractive as it seemed at the time because of the end of the Yankee era. In 1966 NBC began the first year of a three-year, $18 million exclusive contract with Major League Baseball and CBS turned Saturday afternoons back to its local affiliate stations.

"The Game of the Week" was over. It had had a grand twelve-year run but an ignoble end. The result of NBC's contract was less, not more, baseball on national TV: only twenty-eight games a year versus more than a hundred only two years earlier.

The one constant in those dozen years of "The Game of the Week" was the ratings. It trounced the competition. NBC tried everybody they could come up with: Diz's old teammate Leo Durocher, ex-Braves manager Fred Haney, Joe Garagiola, versatile professional announcer Lindsey Nelson. But Diz and "The Game of the Week" consistently won the ratings battle.

Over the years there has sprung up the belief among baseball fans that "The Game of the Week" was so popular because people tuned in to hear Dizzy Dean, the game be damned. However, Bill Behanna of the A. C. Nielsen Company ratings service, one of the major ratings services, says, "Personalities are the least important factor in audience. Something like an event will [affect ratings]. But personalities just don't affect ratings [in a major way]."

The history of TV is littered with failed shows based on personality: "The Frank Sinatra Show" (1950), "The Frank Sinatra

Show" (1957), "The Bing Crosby Show" (1964), "Mary" with Mary Tyler Moore (1978). People watch a show because of the show. Bill Cosby is vital to the success of "The Cosby Show," but it is not Cosby alone who attracts the audience. It is that fragile mix of comedy, drama, and personality that causes people to watch. After all, Bill Cosby had two unsuccessful shows, "The Bill Cosby Show" in 1969 and "Cos" in 1976, prior to his hit. And his movies still bomb at the box office. It's not the singer, it's the song.

Dizzy was immensely popular, and after a lifetime in the public eye, there were bound to be some people who watched "The Game of the Week" for Diz. But it's impossible to believe that baseball fans, no matter how much they loved Diz's patter, would turn to his games regardless of the competition. When it came to the ratings domination of Diz's show, there were other factors.

In the early years of "The Game of the Week," the answer is simple: there was nothing else on. Diz and company had four free years; it was local programming on the other stations from 1953 to 1957.

That's when NBC introduced "NBC Major League Baseball."

Still "The Game of the Week" triumphed. It had a leg up on the competition because it was the established show. But it had other things going for it as well, not the least of which was Dizzy Dean.

I analyzed the competitive schedules of NBC and CBS as listed in *TV Guide* from the time NBC debuted its weekly baseball game. And in the analysis, the first thing that jumped out was how much more savvy the CBS programming executives were. Almost without exception "The CBS Game of the Week" started before NBC's game. Sometimes it was only a five-minute head start, but often it was thirty-five minutes. Most CBS games started at 12:55 P.M. Eastern time, while NBC usually waited until 1:30.

For an easy illustration, let's look at the 1961 season. CBS had had a game for six years, NBC for four. The two networks broadcast forty-four games head to head, and thirty-five times CBS began its coverage first. One reason for this was CBS's Eastern time zone bias. CBS seldom traveled to a Central time zone city, where a later start time was necessary. And it featured only one game from the West Coast. NBC pretty much split its games, between Central time zone cities and Eastern time cities.

But the choice of games was where CBS really shone. NBC tried to give viewers a look at a variety of teams. NBC even telecast the Washington Senators twice. (The Senators finished dead last that season, tied with Kansas City, 47½ games out of first.) During the heart of the pennant race each network broadcast the games of sixteen different teams (there were eighteen in the big leagues that season), but NBC chose to spread its coverage out. No team was shown on NBC more than four times, except the Braves, who were on eight times.

CBS, on the other hand, concentrated on contenders, particularly the Yankees. And in 1961, with Roger Maris and Mickey Mantle both chasing Babe Ruth's single-season home run record, this was a very canny choice. Baseball writers had begun the Ruth countdown in early July. NBC showed only four Yankee games in the last three months of the season. CBS broadcast ten Yankee games.

During the last half of the season CBS focused its coverage on first-division clubs. CBS broadcast the games of first-division clubs thirty-six times, second-division teams only twelve times. NBC's coverage was more evenly balanced. It showed first-division teams in twenty-six games, second-division teams in sixteen games.

Sometimes it was necessary to show weaker clubs in order to broadcast their opponent. The Indians, a fifth-place team, were shown sixteen times on CBS, but six of those were games against the Yankees. Neither network showed the miserable Kansas City A's, but NBC did feature two Senators games, a Saturday-Sunday series against the White Sox, a respectable club that would nonetheless finish fourth, twenty-three games back of the Yankees.

People saw Diz so much because they wanted to see the glory teams.

As important as the ratings were to the network and to the game's sponsor, Falstaff, another thing was more important: beer sales. And in that respect Falstaff was surging. What had been a small Midwestern brand at the beginning of the fifties was a major player in the beer market by the sixties.

There was some talk after the end of "The Game of the Week" that maybe Diz would do a TV show. He'd had offers every year since he'd been on "The Game." After a couple of appearances on "The Dinah Shore Show" in '57, he'd told *TV Guide*, "I tell you if I had to do this stuff for a living I'd starve to death. In baseball I know where the plate is. I know where first base is. I know where the catcher is. I know where the umpire is. And that's all you got to know. But when they give me them scripts to read, well Ol' Diz don't always read 'em so good. I'll do this here stuff for Dinah Shore. But not for anybody else. I ain't afraid of nothing on the ball field, but I'm a rookie in that other league." But by '65 he was no longer a show-biz rookie. Still, the right vehicle didn't come along, so Diz kept busy playing golf and making speeches. "He'd charge twenty-five hundred dollars for a speech," says Mathis. "He'd go anywhere and make a speech for twenty-five hundred dollars and expenses. He'd say, 'I ain't got no education. I might have been cut out to be a speaker but I was sewed up wrong.' "

He and his Mississippi pals would train to Phoenix, where they'd meet up with some of Diz's old ballplayer friends, Bob Scheffing and Earl Grace, and go out in the desert to dove hunt. They'd head on up to Reno for more hunting. "And Diz would make a speech and play golf," says Mathis.

And gamble a bit: "Diz liked the slots. We'd go upstairs. You could go up there and sit and watch and see if the table bosses are cheating you. One time they rolled two thousand dollars' worth of silver dollars in on a dolly cart, dumped 'em in his room, and took pictures of him walking in 'em barefoot."

Back home in Mississippi it was cards that got the guys together. "He liked gin rummy," says Mathis. "That was his game. He loved to play gin rummy, and he was good. 'Course, anything Dizzy did he was good at. In golf he could shoot a seventy-eight to eighty and never over eighty-two. His ball went same place ever' time. He'd knock it two hundred yards. He knew how to win."

And how to stir up trouble. The little boy in him caused him to keep things stirred up in Bond and nearby Wiggins.

"He would go from one group to another causing arguments," says Mathis with a chuckle. "He used to play a doctor golf; 'course, he always had to bet twenty dollars. The doctor thought he was best 'cause Diz wouldn't beat you but one stroke so you'd come back again. When he'd win, he'd take their twenty-dollar check and go to their house and ask their wives, 'Where do I cash this check?' What he was doing was stirring them up, letting them know their husband was losing."

If he missed "The Game of the Week," he didn't let on. Soon he wouldn't have time to miss it. In July of 1966 Pat Dean had a serious heart attack. Before the summer was over she would have two more. Diz was too busy worrying about her to care what happened on NBC's show.

Shortly after "The Game of the Week" ended, he had talked seriously about running for governor of Mississippi. He was popular enough in the state, and there were folks there urging him to run. But when Pat's health began to deteriorate, he nixed the idea. On February 16, 1967, he told reporters he just couldn't run with Pat still down: "If I ran for governor she'd be right in there pitching all the way." He called speculation about his candidacy "the greatest honor that's ever been bestowed on me."

Pat made a slow but gradual recovery, and as she did Diz began to miss the spotlight. He still needed the applause. But it wasn't there anymore. His only appearance in the national media was in the summer of '70 when he was dragged into the federal gambling investigation.

Pee Wee remembers seeing Diz at the Bogey Busters golf tournament in Dayton, Ohio, on Memorial Day weekend of '73. "He kept giving me the needle, telling me about the trees on the right or the rough on the left. It was the same ol' Diz."

A month later the same ol' Diz took the microphone for the first time in almost a decade. NBC had been trying to pump up ratings for its flagging Monday-night baseball telecasts with guest announcers. On Monday, July 16, 1974, the guest announcer was the old right-hander himself. Diz joined Gowdy and Tony Kubek for the fifth inning of the Cardinals-Giants game.

Diz was in rare form. When Curt Gowdy asked where he was living now, Diz grinned, "Why in Bond, Mississippi."

Just where was Bond? Gowdy inquired, as if a student of Mississippi geography.

"Oh, about three miles away from Wiggins."

The trap was sprung, and Gowdy fell into it: And where was Wiggins?

"Oh, about three miles away from Bond."

Same ol' Diz.

He told Gowdy that he had quit school in the third grade "because I didn't want to pass my Pa in the fourth.' "

He tried pronouncing the last name of the Giants' shortstop, Tito Fuentes, but his attempt was so far afield that Gowdy interjected, "Hey, take it easy, will you, Diz? I'm having enough trouble pronouncing 'em myself."

It was as if 1965 were yesterday: he searched for the word "momentum" but found "movement" instead. He lauded pitcher Bob Gibson for throwing the right pitch "ninety-nine times out of ten."

Bob Broeg would say in the St. Louis *Post-Dispatch:* "Ol' Diz still isn't the best-informed or most informative announcer, as he proved again when he did one inning of play-by-play.... That inning ended when Lou Brock lofted a high fly to left center. As if aware Gary Matthews and Garry Maddox were in the game, Dean warbled: "The left fielder goes back ... the center fielder goes back...."

It was classic Dizzy Dean. It was also the end of the trail.

19

1934 Is Gone Forever

Dizzy Dean was in South Lake Tahoe, California, for a few days of golf and gambling in mid-July 1974. It was a trip he made a couple of times a year. On the afternoon of Thursday, July 11, 1974, his chest began tightening up and sharp pains were making it difficult to breathe. He feared the worst; he'd already been through these symptoms with Pat. He was sure it was a heart attack, and he didn't fool around. He went immediately to Barton Memorial Hospital. But by Sunday the pains had subsided and Diz was released. He'd been itching to get back to the golf course, so he headed over to Reno, where his good friend Jimmy Hicks owned the Holiday Hotel. But shortly after arriving in Reno, the pains began again. Diz was rushed to St. Mary's Hospital. During the early-morning hours of July 15, he suffered a severe heart attack. At one point his breathing stopped and he had to be resuscitated. The next day his condition was downgraded from serious to critical. The hospital reported he was being given medication to support his system while his heart healed.

On Wednesday, July 17, at 1:36 a.m. Dizzy Dean died. The decades of high living had caught up with him. At his bedside were Pat, Paul, and Paul's two children. Diz and Pat never had any children.

"Well, we're all 10 years older today," Jim Murray wrote in his column in the July 30 Los Angeles *Times*. "Dizzy Dean is dead. And 1934 is gone forever. Another part of our youth fled. You look in the mirror and the small boy no longer smiles back at you. Just that sad old man.... Dizzy died the other day at the age of 11 or 12. The little boy in all of us died with him."

Diz was sixty-three, the papers said. He'd fooled them all one last time. He was really sixty-four.

Diz's body was returned to Bond, his adopted home. The funeral at tiny Bond Baptist Church drew an overflow crowd, and celebrities such as Roy Acuff and Pee Wee Reese squeezed into the pews next to the common folk of south Mississippi.

"He has left us, but he has not left us empty," the Reverend Bill Taylor, the church's pastor, said in his eulogy. "Few men will be remembered as he will be, a man of kindness and good will. He was an institution it would have been a tragedy to institutionalize.... His speech didn't always follow the rules, but he was better understood than our best grammarian."

They buried ol' Diz in little Bond Cemetery under a simple headstone that revealed in death something he would never reveal in life, the straight story. He was Jay Hanna Dean, born January 16, 1910. The birthright that most men hold dear—their birth name and birth date, the facts that Diz had played loose with his entire life—were now told true.

Why had he done it? What caused him to reinvent his name and birth year, do it before he was even twenty years old, and stick to the invention for the rest of his life?

He was listing his birth year as 1911 at least as early as 1929 when he filled out a job application at San Antonio Power. And in the next forty-five years he would never waver from that. But he knew the truth. He put down 1910 on his marriage license in

1931. Pat told the tombstone carver the truth. Why did he take a year from his age, only three years after bumping himself up a couple of years to enlist in the army? Fonce Burkhardt, his work-mate at the power company in '29, says there was absolutely no advantage to be gained at the power company or in the San Antonio city baseball league by subtracting a year from his age. Diz didn't get easier duty, special benefits, a break of any sort: "You got me on why he changed it. I never knew he did."

Charles Mathis says Diz told him near the end of his life that he was really born in 1912. "He said that everybody thought he was born in 1913 but he was really a year younger. And he was sorry he'd changed it because he wanted to get that Social Security."

No one who knew Diz knows why he changed his birth year. In fact, most were shocked when I told them.

I can only conjecture about his reason. I think it may have gone back to those one-room schools in Arkansas and Oklahoma, where Jay Dean, the lanky, oversized kid who missed as much school as he went to, struggled with lessons other boys, much younger than he, had already learned. To avoid the stigma of being called slow or stupid, this sensitive young man—recall he once cried on the mound in a big-league park when his home fans booed him—erased a year from his life. He wouldn't be a fifteen-year-old, who should have been reading in the *Ninth Reader* but instead was still stuck back in the *Seventh Reader.* No, he was just fourteen, just a little behind.

Why then did he change his name?

We know that his middle name, Hanna, was the first to go. He'd shed that by the time he applied at the power company. Again, no one who knew him then can shed any light on the matter, and we are left to speculate. It could have been that he was ashamed of the name. It was not a normal middle name. It was a surname, taken from a Midwestern politician who had already been washed from the history books by the twenties. It was also—a girl's name! Hanna.

He looked around and snatched the first H name he found: Herman. His stepbrother's name.

The Jerome part came sometime in 1929, and I think we can accept Diz's explanation on this one. Jerome was his catcher's name on the San Antonio Public Service team, Jerome Harris. Because there were other Harrises in the San Antonio city league, Jerome Harris was listed in the box scores as Harris, J.

Harris, J.

Dean, J.

They followed each other in the box score. Besides, Jerome Harris wasn't using his name anyway. Burkhardt says Harris was always called "Jelly," short for Jellybean. "Jellybean was a name for a ladies' man."

The shock of Diz's death was felt nowhere more than in Bond. He had lived there for eighteen years, longer than he ever lived anywhere. He had roots, family, friends. No one expected Diz to die so young. He was the healthy partner in the marriage. It was Pat who had been sickly. She had suffered her first heart attack eight years earlier. Charles Mathis says, "They had their wills all set up for Pat to die first."

Around the country columnists and editors rushed to eulogize and remember ol' Diz. But no tribute was more eloquent, and more incisive, than that of Los Angeles *Times* sportswriter Jim Murray. He captured a lifetime in a mere ten column inches:

> Dizzy was not your manufactured American eccentric. He was the real article. He came out of a time and a place, the Grapes-of-Wrath America, that today's two-cars-in-the-garage, television-aerial America cannot even conceive.... I once had an editor who insisted Dizzy

Dean was the invention of a St. Louis newspaperman named J. Roy Stockton, but not even Ring Lardner could dream up a Dizzy Dean. He had a third-grade education, in his own language, and, fortunately for all of us, he never grew up ...

He was as vain as a movie star, as amiable as a dolphin ...

Dizzy let death dig in on him, something no other batter could do. His life, like his career, was too short. He was still a 60-year-old barefoot boy when he died.

But, for one brief shining afternoon in 1934, he brought a joy to that dreary time when most we needed it.

Dizzy Dean. It's impossible to say without a smile. But, then, who wants to try? If I know Diz, he'll be calling God "podner" someplace today. I hope there's golf courses or a card game or a slugger who's a sucker for a low outside fastball for old Diz. He might have been what baseball's all about.

Dizzy Dean was what baseball's all about: kids gathered in a green meadow on a sunny afternoon, testing themselves and each other, playing and laughing on a field of dreams.

Now baseball players have agents and briefcases and investment portfolios. Pitchers don't smile anymore. Baseball cards aren't for trading and flipping, they're for investing. Baseball is a business.

It never was that for Dizzy Dean. He came within an ace of walking away from professional baseball several times. He wanted to smile on the mound. For him and hundreds of other ballplayers of that long-gone time, baseball was a game.

Because he could play the game, Diz never had to grow up, never had to face the harshness of a life that is real and true. He could be a kid forever. Even when his arm went dead, he found a way to avoid growing up, to stay with the game. He just moved his act to the sideline.

It wasn't always a pretty sight, this grown man with a child's perspective. He could be selfish and ruthless and mean. But afterward he always wanted to redeem himself. Frankie Frisch forgave him a hundred times. Who can't forgive a child?

To a man the old ballplayers interviewed for this book would chuckle about some practical joke Dizzy pulled half a century ago and then, with a shake of the head, smile about how Dizzy loved to kid people. They couldn't even talk about his sense of humor without using that word: kid.

Jim Murray's tribute mentioned for the first time in print what had been whispered all Diz's life, that there wasn't really a Dizzy Dean, that the Dizzy of legend was really the invention of a St. Louis newspaperman named Roy Stockton.

Was Dizzy Dean the real article, as he himself might have put it? Or was he a backwoods comedian, content to let the sportswriters have their way with his legend, as long as they moved it forward and helped put a few more bucks in his back pocket?

There is no arguing that Stockton established Diz's name among the general populace with the publication in the November 1935 *Saturday Evening Post* of an article titled "Me 'n' Paul." This would bring Diz's name, and his story, to people who never read the sports pages, who avoided discussions of ball of any sort, because in the thirties the *Post* was the most widely read magazine in the country. It was the *People* of its day: if you were written about in the *Post,* you had made it, everyone now knew about you. Being the subject of a *Post* story was the equivalent of being a guest on "The Cosby Show," "Cheers," and "The Tonight Show with Johnny Carson" all on the same day.

Not that Diz wasn't well known before the publication of "Me 'n' Paul." He was an established national "character," discussed around the country for his spring-training holdouts and for his audacious predictions. He was an eccentric, but he wasn't even the king bee of baseball eccentrics. The 1935 *Spalding Official Base Ball Guide* noted that he wasn't as eccentric in his behavior as former Athletics' left-hander Rube Waddell, a man who wrestled alligators in the off season.

But with the publication of "Me 'n' Paul," Diz left Rube Waddell laughing in his dust.

"Me 'n' Paul" made Dizzy Dean.

James Roy Stockton was a natural for the assignment because he had been covering Dizzy since the lanky right-hander first made the team in St. Joe. J. Roy Stockton, as he called himself in his byline, was a St. Louis native, born there in 1893 when it was still a frontier town. Stockton began his newspaper career in 1915, while still a student at St. Louis's Washington University. He worked after school as a sports reporter at the St. Louis *Republic,* a morning paper that surrounded a smattering of news with short stories and fanciful accounts of historic events. The next year he moved over to the city's dominant morning paper, the *Globe-Democrat,* where he was low man in seniority on a seven-man sports staff.

Journalism as we know it was not practiced in the first years of this century. Every city was served by multiple newspapers, and competition was the bottom line. A paper's only assets were its printing presses and its subscriber lists, and a newspaper that couldn't sell papers couldn't survive.

The *Globe-Democrat* knew how to sell papers. It was heavy with lurid crime stories and historic reconstructions, such as the April 2, 1916, feature "Pancho Villa's Own Story of Life, as he told it to John N. Wheeler." The same issue had another similar story called "Mexican Adventures with Pancho Villa" by former St. Louis newsman John Paul Dana.

The *Globe-Democrat* had six other sportswriters, so in order to get noticed, and get his stories in the paper, Roy Stockton had to hustle. He soon figured out that what a cub reporter lacked in sources he could make up for in writing style. One early Stockton invention appeared in the April 8, 1916, edition:

"By cricky them there Cards ain't such dubs after all, be they," said Baseball Ben to Popcorn Pete last night. Pete was a typical bandwagon fan and a bit deaf.

"You say the Browns will win the pennant," queried Pete.

He continued on with an imaginary speech by Baseball Ben, who concluded that, despite what some folks were saying, the Cardinals had a chance at the pennant after all.

Stockton already had learned the most basic lesson in a sportswriter's arsenal: no one ever lost readers picking the home team to win.

In 1917 he moved to the *Post-Dispatch*, the largest-circulation newspaper in St. Louis and one of the largest in the country. He would spend the rest of his career at the paper, retiring in 1958.

Stockton began his *Saturday Evening Post* story about Dizzy Dean with a slam-bang, an audacious tale that was guaranteed to jerk any nonsports fan to attention:

Jerome Herman Dean was born at Lucas, Arkansas, Holdenville, Oklahoma and Bond, Mississippi, January 16, August 22 and February 22, 1911, with a golden wisecrack in his mouth, ants in his pants and an abiding faith in humanity, of which he knew that he was the most important part. Aurora was tiptoe on the misty mountaintop and the lucky world all unaware that here was the day of days, when the good doctor, turning to inform Mr. Albert Dean that it was a boy, was startled by a voice from the crib.

"Put it there, doc," said the infant. "Give me five. I congratulate you, doggone it. You'll always be proud to tell your grandchildren about this day's work. I'm Dizzy Dean, and am I good! But wait till you see Paul. He'll be along in a couple of years, and then look out! Doc, there won't be nobody good enough to carry our gloves. It's a lucky couple of days for some big-league ball club. Whoever gets me and Paul is gonna be settin' in the kind row. By the way, doc, get me a blank check on any old bank and I'll write you out what I owe you for this job. Mr. Rickey will be glad to take care of it."

It was the same literary technique Stockton had used two decades earlier in his story of Baseball Ben: invent a character and then give him a voice.

But in the case of Dizzy Dean, he didn't need to do any inventing. Or did he?

The answer lies somewhere in between.

Stanley "Frenchy" Bordagaray, Diz's teammate in 1937 and opponent other years in the thirties, says many of the stories about Dizzy were made up: "Sportswriters put down what they wanted. Stuff written about me was not true. I'd say one thing to a reporter and it would be totally different when it came out in the paper. They did it to sell their stories, I guess."

Raymond Cunningham, who roomed with Diz during spring training in '31 and '32, remembers, "In the mornings he would get up and say, 'I wonder what those dirty boogers have said about me today. I swear I haven't said a word to them.' "

To understand how this could be, you must travel back to St. Louis in the 1930s. The city was only a couple of dozen years removed from the frontier. It was the westernmost city in the big leagues by a good margin. Several factors came into play to create a part of the Dizzy Dean legend. The first was the frontier tradition. The endless prairies that extended west from Missouri across to the plains states, the desolate stretches of acre after acre of open country that had produced Kit Carson, Wild Bill Hickok, and Buffalo Bill Cody, American legends created from whole cloth by newspapermen of the time.

Stockton was born of this region and steeped in its tradition. New York *World-Telegram* columnist Dan Daniel once called Stockton "the little St. Louis sportswriter who takes care of [Diz]." It was a time when many sportswriters took care of athletes. Babe Ruth's drinking and womanizing were winked at, not reported. Stockton's services to Diz went beyond charity in what he reported or didn't report. He told many stories of the services he provided Diz, from ghostwriting to financial advising.

Another thing that came into play in creating Dizzy Dean was a relatively modern invention: the public relations man. The St. Louis Cardinals were the first team in baseball to hire a public relations man. His name was Gene Karst, and he was hired—coincidentally—at the beginning of the 1930 campaign, Diz's first year in professional baseball. Diz himself frequently complained that he didn't say nearly all the things attributed to him.

In a pair of articles in the August 6 and August 20, 1938, editions of *Liberty* magazine, Diz claimed a Houston sportswriter, "a little redheaded grinning fellow named Andy Anderson," invented the braggart Dizzy Dean. "He got the idea that I was something out of Ring Lardner. He kept encouraging me to pop off, but I didn't want to. I was afraid to talk too much around the experienced professionals. But now and then I would say something about fogging my fast one through, and that expression tickled Anderson. He started calling me 'Foggy,' but later he decided that 'Dizzy' was funnier and stuck to that."

Diz claimed Anderson told club president Fred Ankenman that he wanted to write a daily story about him, "but that I wouldn't shoot off my mouth enough. Ankenman told me it would be a good idea, for the publicity, if I let Anderson say things for me and tried to say a few for myself. I agreed to try, and the thing went over big."

In a 1951 story about him in *The Saturday Evening Post*, Diz complained it was Branch Rickey who told him to boast; and, when Diz wouldn't, Rickey boasted for him. Rickey, it appears, dreamed up such quoted pregame boasts as, "If they gets a foul ball off me and Paul, they can call theyselves lucky." Diz said he didn't even make the most famous statement credited to him. It was his preseason statement in 1934 that he and his brother Paul between them would win 45 games.... "'I always just went out there and struck out all the fellas I could,' Diz says now. 'I didn't worry about winnin' this number of games or that number—and I ain't a-woffin' when I say that either.'"

A skeptical reading of many of those early "prediction" stories reveals no dateline and no mention of a phone conversation with Dizzy, just a quote. It could be that Dizzy's prediction of forty-five wins first came from the Cardinals' front office.

But Diz was a-woffin' when he took no responsibility for his legend. If he had been a cardboard caricature, a Branch Rickey invention, he would not have been able to sustain a career in broadcasting. As anyone who listened to Diz on the radio or watched along with him on TV can attest, Diz was the genuine article.

Plenty of the Dizzy Dean stories are true. There are even photographs that prove they happened: Diz and Pepper smoking a peace pipe in 110-degree weather. Diz singing in the Mudcat Band.

Did Roy Stockton create Dizzy Dean? No more than Boswell created Samuel Johnson. The only tales Stockton invented were obvious ones: the baby Dizzy perched up in the crib, talking to the doctor, telling Doc to give him five. Even some of the ones that seemed farfetched were probably true. Stockton's *Post* article had Diz wondering how they knew there would be gas under there when they built those gas stations. Could Diz have been that naive? Or was Stockton indulging in legend making? The story was probably true. Fonce Burkhardt said Diz didn't know people had to pay for electricity when he began working for the power company in 1929. And Paul Enright says that when Diz worked for him at WTMV in the forties, Diz didn't know the difference between his savings account and his checking account. "The bank would call the station and tell him he had bounced a check and he would pull out his bank book and tell them that that was impossible, he had so many hundred dollars in the account. And then they would have to explain the difference between the two accounts to him. He never did get it straight."

Stockton was actually more respectful of Diz's Arkansas slur than eastern writers, who spelled Diz's version of "charisma" "crizzma" and turned his spoken "umpire" into "umparr." Stockton allowed Diz to sound illiterate without looking idiotic.

What Roy Stockton did in the thirties was assimilate Dizzy's own words and disseminate them to St. Louis and the world. Good stories have a way of growing, and maybe Stockton occasionally aided that growing process. If he did maybe catcher Joe Sprinz, who played with Diz at Houston in 1930, has the answer for that: "Some of the stuff Dizzy said was not fit to be printed."

But the one who invented Dizzy Dean was Dizzy himself. Although Diz was often considered a southerner and a hillbilly, he wasn't: he had been born in Arkansas, but raised in Oklahoma, married in Texas, and kept a home in Arizona for many years. He was from the West, where truth and legend often rode the same horse. He even got his nickname in the town where Davy Crockett made his name fighting at the Alamo, San Antonio. And his broadcasting attire was Texas gaudy: ten-gallon hat, cowboy boots.

Diz never denied a good story about himself; he just adopted it, added it to his speechmaking repertoire and, in the process, to his legend.

It is entirely appropriate that Dizzy Dean's ancestors came from Tennessee, the home of Davy Crockett. For Dizzy Dean was Davy Crockett with a fastball and control. Crockett once called himself "half-crocodile, half-grizzly bear and half-snapping turtle." Dizzy was half Walter Johnson, half Muhammad Ali, and half Will Rogers.

His tombstone mentions only that he was a ballplayer and a friend to man. There is no epitaph. Every wild and woolly cowboy needs an epitaph.

Perhaps his old teammate from the minors, Ray "Peaches" Davis, has an appropriate one. "You know, when you get around a bunch of old ballplayers and you mention Dizzy Dean, they all start smiling and nodding their heads. They all knew Dizzy Dean. He was a great pitcher. Even more, he was a great character."

DIZZY DEAN 1910–1974
A great pitcher
A great character

Afterword

Steal a man's money and it's called larceny.

Steal his wife and it's called adultery.

Steal his words and it's called biography.

I've tried to steal as many of Dizzy Dean's words as I could in this book in order to capture a voice unique in Americana.

His longtime broadcasting partner Johnny O'Hara frequently introduced him as "the one and only Dizzy Dean," and he surely was. "There's no other like me," he once said. We can all nod in assent.

My interest in Dizzy Dean began at the same time as my interest in baseball, for in the midfifties they were one and the same. I grew up in a mountain-locked town in east Tennessee, hundreds of miles from major-league baseball. The nearest minor-league team was an hour away. The first big-league game I saw was on TV: Dizzy Dean's "Game of the Week." To others he may have sounded dumb or simple with his backwoods accent and his backcountry expressions. But to me he sounded natural. I heard people all the time who talked like Dizzy Dean. But none of them seemed as funny or, when it came to baseball anyway, as knowledgeable.

It was because of Dizzy Dean that I began a weekly ritual: pedaling my bicycle to the local store to pay twenty-five cents for a copy of the *Sporting News,* then the Bible of Baseball. I pedaled for a couple of years before subscribing in 1958 (I know this because I still have a 1958 *Sporting News Baseball Guide,* a premium they gave away with a subscription), and I've been a subscriber ever since. I need that weekly dose of baseball arcana.

When I began this book in the fall of 1989, I didn't set out to disprove all the Dizzy Dean stories. What I have discovered is that almost everything Dizzy Dean is credited with saying is true: He did say it. He just didn't always say it when he was supposed to have said it. Diz would pick up a story about himself and add it to his repertoire. If it wasn't true, that was okay, as long as it was a good story.

Roy Stockton explained Diz's philosophy this way in a July 29, 1951, column: "There shouldn't be criticism of Dizzy if some of his narratives depart from the strict truth. You see Dizzy isn't bothered about facts, about truth. He'd tell you a whopper and he'd know that you knew it was a whopper and he knew that you knew that he knew that you knew it was a whopper. And he's told so many whoppers so frequently and with such fancy embellishments that for the life of him, no doubt, he can't differentiate between fact and fiction."

Maybe all the Dizzy Dean stories aren't strictly true, but one thing they are: they're Dizzy Dean.

I am indebted to the many old ballplayers, fans, and friends who knew and loved Dizzy and shared their memories. They are mentioned in the text.

In addition I would like to thank Bill Deane and Gary Van Allen at the Baseball Hall of Fame Library; the folks at the Bond,

Mississippi, General Store; the staffs of the Fort Smith, Arkansas, Public Library, the St. Louis Public Library, the Louisville Free Public Library, and the St. Joseph, Missouri Public Library; the public information staff at Fort Sam Houston; the sports information staff at Central State University; Johnny Mayfield and all the folks at the Spaulding General Store; Gertrude Robinson and the staff at the *Holdenville Tribune;* the Holdenville Historical Society; Sandy Brown at San Antonio Power & Light Company; and Jurlean Madlock at the Dizzy Dean Museum.

I would also like to acknowledge the help of Karen Smith, Bob Brought, C. Ray Hall, Bob Hill, David Inman, Billy D. Hope, Roscoe McCrary, Claudia Fitch, Mrs. Charles Mathis, Mrs. Ray Davis, David Ferguson, Jr., Erle White, Betty Ankenman, Vic Vogel, Jim Bailey, and W. R. Hopkins.

Much encouragement came from the Pine Bluff Plowboy, Bob Moody.

And special thanks to my research assistant, Sherri Arnett.

Appendixes

Appendix A:
Major and Minor League Record of
Jay Hanna "Dizzy" Dean

	G	IP	W	L	H	R	ER	K	BB	ERA
1930 St. Joseph	32	217	17	8	204	118	89	134	77	3.69
1930 Houston	14	85	8	2	62	31	27	95	49	2.86
1930 St. Louis (N)	1	9	1	0	3	1	1	5	3	1.00
1931 Houston	41	304	26	10	210	71	52	303	90	1.57
1932 St. Louis	46	286	18	15	280	122	105	191	102	3.30
1933 St. Louis	48	293	20	18	279	113	99	199	64	3.04
1934 St. Louis	50	311.2	30	7	288	110	92	195	75	2.65
1935 St. Louis	50	325.1	28	12	324	128	112	190	77	3.11
1936 St. Louis	51	315	24	13	310	128	111	195	53	3.17
1937 St. Louis	27	197.1	13	10	206	76	59	120	33	2.70
1938 Chicago (N)	13	74.2	7	1	63	20	15	22	8	1.80
1939 Chicago	19	96.1	6	4	98	40	36	27	17	3.38
1940 Chicago	10	54	3	3	68	35	31	18	20	5.17
1940 Tulsa	21	142	8	8	149	69	50	51	19	3.17

1941 Chicago	1	1	0	0	3	3	2	1	0	18.00
1947 St. Louis (A)	1	4	0	0	3	0	0	0	1	0.00
Totals	317	1967.1	150	83	1924	776	663	1163	453	3.02

World Series Record

	G	IP	W	L	H	R	ER	K	BB	ERA
1934 St. Louis	3	26	2	1	20	6	5	17	5	1.73
1938 Chicago	2	8 1/3	0	1	8	6	6	2	1	6.48

APPENDIXES

Appendix B:
Diz in His Own Words

In 1946 and again in 1947 the Sporting News *published verbatim transcriptions of Dizzy Dean's radio play-by-play account of a game.*

This enabled readers who lived outside the St. Louis area and only heard stories about Diz's amazing game calls to gain a feel for Diz's unique broadcasting style, which was then heard only in St. Louis.

Here is the transcription of the April 27, 1947, game between the St. Louis Browns and the Chicago White Sox as broadcast over WIL in St. Louis and reprinted with permission of the Sporting News.

Diz's partner on the broadcast was Johnny O'Hara.

After Johnny O'Hara provides a brief introduction and tunes in a replay of the broadcast of Babe Ruth's ceremonies at Yankee Stadium, Dean is introduced as "the pitching ace who thrilled you out there on the mound, the one and only Dizzy Dean." Dizzy takes over:

"Yes, this is the first double-header of the year between the White Sox and our Browns ... Floyd Baker is the first batter.... Muncrief warms up ... there's the pitch ... he's out on a grounder to Berardino. Now good ole Loo-oo-oo-k Appling is up ...

"Yep, it was great listening to that Babe Ruth broadcast and here is hoping the Babe lives a long time for the young kids comin' up ...

"There's the windup and a pitch ... he swings ... it drops out there and Walt Judnich picks it up ... that's a single for Loo-oo-oo-k Appling ... Now Philley is up ... he has his right foot 'way in the bucket—it looks like ... he has No. 9 on his uniform.

"We have two distinguished guests in our broadcasting booth today ... Everybody remembers Cy Casper, the great radio announcer ... and that distinguished little feller, little Crispi [Frank Crespi, former Cardinal infielder] ... Crispi helped on that Cardinal pennant in 1942 ... too bad that feller's not out there right now: ...

"Judnich's playin' this feller over in right field, about two or three steps ... Ball one.

"Talkin' to Johnny O'Hara and Luke Appling before the game ... they say they're both the same age ... Johnny says they're 41 ... guess he's right at that.

"Strike one ... strike two. Appling lumbers back to first ... That is the laziest lookin' player to be a great player I ever saw.

"There's the pitch ... it's a drive to shortstop ... Stephens has it, over to second for one out—too late at first. Two men away now an' the next man in there is the right fielder, Kennedy ... Wearin' no. 5 on his uniform ... He stands deep in the batter's box ... Muncrief throws the ball over the first; Philley gets back.

"Playin' this feller slightly for a straight-away hitter ... there's another throw to first an' they almost had Philley; boy, that was clost ... That guy gets as good a lead as any guy I seen in baseball this year ... Ball one on Kennedy ... There's the stretch ... he swung on it ... there's the drive into center field and Judnich goes over a couple of steps to make the catch. No runs, one hit, no errors, one left.

"The Browns are now at bat ... there's Bob Dillinger at bat an' Lopat's on the mound, smoothing it out, lookin' around at his infield and outfield.... Last time he pitched—I believe it was in Detroit—they hit five home runs offa him an' we wanna hit five home runs offa him here ... Mike Tresh was hurt yesterday slidin' into third ... nothin' broke ... leeglemints torn, we hear ... so Dickey is ketchin'.

"Ball one ... ball two ... ball three. Johnny, keep yer head out

of the grandstand ... yer always lookin' for pretty bonnets....
Strike one ... strike two ... Earle Combs is a-coachin' over thar at
third and Freddie Hofmann at first ... Boy, after comin' back to
St. Louis after that road trip to Detroit, an' seein' this sunshine,
Johnny, you won't know how to act ... Whaddaya mean it was
cold this mornin'? ... you wuz dreamin'—it wasn't cold. Hey,
hey—Dillinger hit one to center—he's agonna try for second—
no—he made it a single ... That looked like Johnny O'Hara—26
years ago—runnin' down thar ... Zeke Zarilla's up now ... He
bunts the ball, but Kolloway at first comes in an' takes the pop
fly ... one man out. Vern Stephens is the next batter in there ...
Wind's a blowin' into right field ... Lopat gets the signal ...
Throws to first; put nothin' on it—just a bluff—and Dillinger
gets back ... Ball one ... Gotta nice crowd out here today.

"C'mon, Vern, getta holda one—I wanna see ya tear loose ...
Foul, strike one ... right into the upper deck here, to our right ...
Lopat, with a new baseball, gets another signal ... He throws and
Stephens hits it right through the pitcher's mound for a hit ...
hey, hey ... it gets away from the center fielder an' Dillinger
scores easy ... an' Stephens goes to second ... I believe it'll be a
two-base hit, because the ball took a bad hop when Philley came
charging in at it. Yep, it's a two-bagger.

"Fred Hofmann's bending over down there ... Will he make
it—whoops—don't think so ... Yep, he did ... Boy, when he
bends over, he scares me to death ... I'm afraid he won't make
it ... There's the pitch to Heath an' Heath hits it to left; Taft
Wright takes it ... two out and the next batter is Jerry Witte.
Brownies lead, one to nothin' ... They're gonna walk Witte purposely ... Ball one, outside ... there's ball two; lotta people are
wonderin' why they're walkin' Witte ... Well, here's the reason
why ... Jerry's a righthand hitter; Lopat's a lefthand pitcher ...
Lefthand pitchers has lots of trouble sometimes with righthand
batters an' the next batter is Walt Judnich, a lefthand hitter ...

Come on, Walt, hit one!

"Ball one ... strike one ... swing and missed ... Johnny, jerk the caps offa few of those bottles of Falstaff and we'll sip up some o' those suds ... With your teeth? ... What teeth? ... Too expensive tryin' to open bottles that away ... haw, haw, haw ... Strike two; there's a curve, way inside.

"Lopat has his signal, stretches and throws ... The runners was movin' but Judnich foul-tipped it an' the runners had to go back to their respectable bases ... Crispi says they're not respectable when you cain't git to 'em ... haw ... Boy. Look what Cincinnati did to Pittsburgh ... four runs in the last of the first ... Here's the pitch—ball three ... On the next pitch, Witte an' Stephens'll be movin' ... a two-base hit would score both runners ... there's the pitch and it's foul ... Oh boy, it was just foul; both umpires called it foul, but Freddie Hofmann, putting on the ole decoy act, yelled 'Go on; go for two!' but back they came.

"Here comes the pitch ... he swung on it, a high inside pitch, striking out, retiring the side ... One run, two hits, two left.

"Now, Johnny, it's your turn to take over ... I got those Brownies one run in the first and now its your turn to you to hold that defense ... An' Johnny, I wanna make an apology to Frank Crispi here ... You know, a while ago when I introduced him, I said 'little' and he informs me he weighs 165 ... an' that's not so daw-gonned little after all is it?"

(After O'Hara describes an uneventful second inning, Dean takes over the microphone for the third inning.)

"Thank you, Johnny ... Lopat is the batter ... Strike one ... there's the windup by Muncrief ... there it is ... ball ... there's a smash out by the third baseman but Stephens picks it up an' Lopat's out ... Yes, that Stephens is all over the infield ... Stephens took that behind Dillinger and Lopat was out.

"Now Baker is up ... Strike one, foul into the upper deck ... it bounced into the stands ... Who got it, Johnny? ... A blonde ...

You don't mean my wife, do ya? ... She's a brunette, boy ... Say, I gotta be careful; she's lookin' right up here at me.

"Strike two ... boy, whatta aggitatin' curve ball ... Here's the pitch ... Baker struck out ... Now look at that beautiful green grass out on that infield an' that outfield ... Boy it'd sure look bad if I had my cattle up here eatin' on it for about a week.

"Now we've got LOO-OO-OO-K Appling up ... Strike one ... A fast ball ... he swung ... it goes out to Berardino. He has it ... an' LOO-OO-OO-K is out at first. No runs, no hits, none left. An' while they's a-changin' sides, here's Johnny for good ole-fashioned Falstaff ... go ahead, John."

(After a commercial by O'Hara, Dean returns on the air.)

"Well said, Johnny ... last half of the third and the first batter will be Robby Dillinger, leadoff man for the Browns ... They're playin' Dillinger for a pull-hitter an' fairly deep ... Here's the first pitch ... He hits a line drive into center field, but he's out, for Philley made the ketch ... Rough treatment on that ball ... Crispi leaned over an' said, 'That's the way I useta hit 'em!' ... But now he weighs 186 or 7, four feet six, a little round man ... but he says he's got a long way to go to ketch up with me.

"Zarilla's up an' there's a hit right over the infield ... Those Brownies are agoin' today ... Sometimes a club looks bad becuz they're atryin' too hard ... that's what's the matter with these Brownies ... but if we win two today, we'll be right in there ... It's gonna be a wide-open race ... A pitch-out to Zarilla, but Dillinger fooled Lopat—he didn't run ... There's the pitch ... it's a long drive, but Kennedy goes back for a great catch ... It was hit easily around close to 400 feet ... Yes, as Crispi says, if he had poled that ball straight-away, he'd a-splattered the mustard in one a those hot-dog stands in the left field bleachers ... haw, haw, haw.

"Jeff Heath's up—the big feller.

"One strike ... Lopat gets the signal ... He swung on a high, inside pitch makin' it two an' nothin' … Zarilla's runnin'. There's the pitch but it's a line drive unto the hands of Michaels.

"I was on the air with Harry Heilmann up in Detroit the other day an' he ast me who I pulled for on the road … the home team or the Browns … I says 'I'm always apullin' for the Browns' … An' he said: 'You're not pullin' for the home team, then?' … An' I says, 'when I'm at home. I'm a'pullin' for the Browns' … Now Johnny, take over an' hold that defense, boy."

(While O'Hara is broadcasting an uneventful fourth inning, Dean can be heard yelling in the background: "Hey Jerry Witte, hit one, boy!" Finally Dizzy takes over for the fifth frame.)

"Thank you, Johnny … An' the first batter will be Kolloway … Here's Catcher Moss givin' the signal … Muncrief goes to the resin bag … They're playin' Kolloway straightaway … Here's 'the pitch' … low an' outside … one ball … The next pitch … there's a line drive over the shortstop's head into left field … Heath's pickin' it up … Kolloway's tryin' for second … he's safe. White Sox now have a man on second an' nobody's out … Here's Michaels up … Guess I'd better tighten up my defense, huh Johnny? … Strike one on Michaels … Yeh, they's somethin' like 16,000 people out here today—maybe more … There's the next pitch … hit right back to Muncrief; he knocked it down with his bare hand … he throwed Michaels out … he couldn't get a glove on it but caught it with his bare hand an' Kolloway held second.

"Time has been called while Muncrief throws a couple up to the plate to see if he's all right … He says he's all right … Now he steps off the mound and Muncrief an' Moss is gonna have a little meeting out there in the middle of the diamond to see if they're gonna have a nice cold bottle of Falstaff an' a nice steak after the game … We used to do that … The ketcher'd walk out to me an' say: 'Have ya decided where we're gonna eat after the game?' … I'd say: 'We've got a game on,' but he'd say: 'Whatcha worryin' about—everything's under control' … haw, haw, haw.

301

"There's Dickey at bat ... Up goes the arm, the pitch ... an' there's a hit into right field ... way out there, up against the screen ... Kolloway scores and Dickey goes to second an' the game's all tied up, 1 an' 1 ... Somethin' was wrong about that conference, at that, John ... Lopat's now up ... a lefthand hitter, an' Dickey's on second ... Here's the pitch—swung and missed ... Muncrief has another signal, gets all set an' throws ... Lopat tried to hold back, but the umpire says, 'Strike two, ya went all the way around ... If he'd a hit it, he'd a hit it outta the ball park ... Scores all tied up, 1 and 1.

"Muncrief gets a new ball—rubs it up. Goes to the resin bag here's the pitch ... it's a curve, inside for ball-one ... One ball an' two strikes ... Moss, the ketcher's, givin' the signal ... There goes Muncrief's arm ... a line drive—ow—whata play this Stephens made ... a line drive, Stephens jumped up, pulled it down and ran over to double Dickey ... Listen to the crowd ... an' the guy who hit it is mumblin' as he goes down to first: 'Look in your pocket, ya lucky stiff, an' see if you have a diamond' ... We used to say that ... Lotta hard ridin' an' kiddin' in baseball ... we'd say mean things to fellers on the other clubs, but after the game, we'd go out an' eat an' drink together ... One run, two hits, no one left.

"Now the Brownies come to bat an' SLUGGER Muncrief is the first up ... Yes, I said SLUGGER ... These pitchers look dangerous at the plate don't they, Johnny? ... It's a pop fly an' Philley comes in for a ketch of the pop fly.

"Dillinger's the next batter ... One strike ... Lopat gets all set ... Yes, Johnny, I see my big fat wife sittin' down in the box ... oh, that woman gettin' big ... Dillinger's out on a grounder to Baker ... Zarilla steps up ... There it goes ... I believe it yes: ... Yeowie ... Yes it is ... it's a home run ... Look at that feller go around second, he' a-roundin' third ... there he come with a home run ... look at those big arms ... he'll walk into the dugout an' say: 'Boy, that guy's gotta lot of stuff'... You know, Al Zarilla was the guy that got the only hit off Feller over in Cleveland, an' when they was akiddin' him he said: 'Boy, that Feller had lotsa stuff!' ... Stephens up ... he flied to Kennedy ... That makes it Browns 2, White Sox 1 ... an' now comes Johnny O'Hara ... An' oncet again, John, I got 'em out in front.

"Yes, that happens to all ball players ... When a guy's got a lot on the ball an' they hit him, they say he's got lots on the ball, but when he's got nothin' an' they're not hittin, they say he hasn't got nothin atall on the—"

—seventh inning, Dean breaks in, "Johnny, they's a elephant down there, walkin' around in the stand ... Look at 'im ... But I ain't agonna say who he is."

O'Hara cuts in with: "I know who he is; why that's——. He's looking for you to play gin rummy."

Dean chirps in: "Yeah, I was cut out to be a great gin rummy player, but I was sewed up wrong."

(Dean takes over to broadcast the seventh inning.)

"Thank you, Johnny ... The Browns is out in front, 2 to 1, as we take over the first half of the seventh inning ... The first batter will be Taft Wright ... Ball one ... There's a drive to deep right field ... It goes against the screen ... Zarilla recovers the ball, but Wright goes into second with a double ... The White Sox have made six hits an' three of 'em has been doubles ... Kolloway, first baseman, up an' nobody out ... Denny Galehouse starts warmin' up for the Brownies.

"Muncrief throws ... C'mon Bob, ole boy ... Ball two on Kolloway ... An' nobody's out in the first of the seventh ... Next pitch ... he swung on it an' hit it through the pitcher's box, but Stephens runs over, picks up the ball an' throws him out at first ... Meantime, Wright runs over to third ... Next batter is Michaels—an' it looks like they might walk him purposely ... Ball two, ball three ... there's ball four ... They do that to set up a double play, but you might say: They're aputtin' the winnin' run on first'... But they play the percentages.

"That brings up Dickey ... Runners on first an' third ... There's the pitch. Strike one on Skeeter Dickey ... Muncrief's again set ... Here comes the next pitch—a line drive right into the hands of Johnny Berardino, who made a nice ketch on the ball an' threw over there to Witte an' they easily doubled up Michaels ... Oh boy, oh boy, oh boy ... these infielders of the Browns is shore playin' heads-up baseball today ... No runs, one hit, one left ... Here's Johnny for Falstaff."

After O'Hara's commercial, Dean resumes.

"Those breaks certainly even up ... All of a sudden your luck turns after you're agoin' bad ... We got a nice break on that line drive ... Moss, the catcher, is the first hitter ... There it is ... it looked like it was—left field seats—went back to the 358-foot sign and pulled it down ... The wind helt it back ... Johnny says when the summer comes, the wind will blow them out ... Well, we wished the summer had come on that one.

"Muncrief's now up ... Johnny, when's the Falstaff an' food comin' down? I'm gettin' kinda hungry here ... Ten minutes? ... Guess I can take it ... Muncrief walks ... free ticket to first base ... You're listenin' to WIL, 1230 on your dial ... one minute past three—Falstaff time.

"Dillinger's the next batter ... here's the stretch ... swung on an' missed ... Ball one ... that evens it up ... Here comes the next pitch, low an' over the plate for ball two ... Bobby Muncrief on first ... First time this year we've seen a pitcher on first without a jacket on ... Brother, you don't need a jacket today ... Ball three ... Dickey yells something at Lopat ... maybe 'C'mon get the ball over the plate.' ... n' Lopat probably says, 'Well, what in the world do you think I'm tryin' to do?'

"Johnny, it's now three and two ... What'll Muncrief be

doin'—runnin'? ... We'll bet a bottle of Falstaff on it ... Yep, he runs on the pitch ... a hard smash to Michaels, who throws to Appling to get Muncrief an' the throw to first doubles Dillinger ... No runs, no hits, none left ... Come on in, Johnny, for the eighth innin' ... n' all the folks they's a lotsa seats still, available out here.

"Whoops, that word 'available' almost throwed me ... Now don'tcha ast me to spell it—haw, haw, haw."

O'Hara: "That new umpire, Hurky, does all right behind the plate."

Dean: "I'm good behind the plate, too."

O'Hara: "But we mean the plate down there on the field; not the dinner plate."

Dean (yelling at the top of his voice): "Come on Jerry [Witte], hit one, boy."

O'Hara: "Here comes Caldwell to pitch for the Sox ... He's 42 years old and weighs only 182 pounds. Diz is two years younger and outweighs him by 100 pounds."

Dean: "The program says this guy won 13 an' lost only four last year, but what I wanna know is how's his hittin'?"

After the Browns score two runs, Dean takes over for the ninth inning.

"Thank you, Johnny ... We're gonna have a change in the lineup for the Browns ... Denny Galehouse, a righthander, is now pitchin' in place of Muncrief an' Lehner goes to left field ... Kennedy is up ... Strike one ... ball one ... Yes, these Brownies look great ... Nothin' wrong with Muncrief ... it's early in the season an' Manager Ruel doesn't wantta take a chancet gettin' Muncrief hurt ... No sense in hurtin' him.

"That's my opinion as to why Muncrief is not out there now ... Sam Zoldak is warmin' up in the bullpen ... Muncrief's nobody's dummy ... Kennedy singled ... an' that brings up Wright ... nobody out.

"Galehouse gets set ... Wright's in the batter's box ... Here's the pitch—high and inside for ball one ... ball two ... They're playin' Wright for slightly a pull-hitter in right field ... Ball three ... three an' nothin' ... Here's the pitch ... it's inside for ball four an' Wright gets a free ticket to first.

"Time has been called and Denny Galehouse an' Moss is havin' a little conference out in the center of the diamond. Come on, Denny boy ... Edgar Smith, lefthander, is warmin' up for the White Sox now ... There's the pitch, fast ball, in there for strike one called on Kolloway ... Nobody out in the first of the ninth ... There's the pitch ... He hits a little pop in front of the plate, Moss has his mask off and he makes the catch ... one man gone. Michaels is the next batter ... He's a righthanded hitter ... C'mon, you Denny boy ... you need only two more outs before the Brownies win the first game of their first doubleheader here at Sportsman's Park ... They're having another conference ... I guess it's something about the signal.

"Strike one ... Very tense moment right here ... Galehouse pitches ... here's the smash into center field ... Judnich, at the crack of the bat, took off an' made a catch with his face toe-ward the wall an' his hands above his shoulders ... Boy, oh boy ... That really helped the pitcher ... No question about it, but as the feller says: 'That's what them outfielders is out thar for.'

"C'mon Galehouse ... Powder river ... Don't give this Dickey nothin' ... Pour that fast one in thar ... Strike one ... thass a boy ... Fast ball, swung on, foul ... into the upper deck ... Who's gonna get it? Looks like a little boy with a blue shirt on ... Two an' nothin' on the batter, Dickey ... One more pitch ... Galehouse has his signal, here's the pitch; it's a base hit into left field for a single ... Lehner makes a great stop an' holds the runners on their base ... Two men away ... Three on ... Caldwell's due, but we're definitely gonna have a pinch-hitter.

"Who's this guy? ... Number 12—Wallasea—from Philadelphia ... The White Sox got this guy from the Atha-letics during the winter ... He's a switch-hitter, so he'll bat lefthand against Galehouse ... He's six feet four an' an infielder.

"Time has been called ... They're gonna send in a runner for Dickey at first ... Tucker for Dickey ... an' this guy Tucker can really fly ... Boy, here comes them sandwiches an' I'll tear into 'em at the end of this game ... Lay them hamburger sandwiches right down there.

"Come on, Denny ... One ball an' one strike ... Ball two ... Runners all over the sacks—first, second an' third ... let me enjoy my hamburger an' Falstaff after this, Denny.

"Come on, boy ... Set down, John, set down, John, will ya? ... There's the signal ... Swung on an' missed ... That's a way to throw ... Rare back an' throw that ball right through the middle with plenty on it ... Galehouse looks down for the signal ... Starts the windup ... It's a fast ball ... it gets away from the ketcher ... here's one run scorin'—an' the other two movin' up.

"That makes it four and two ... The tyin' run's now on second ... Wham ... Wow ... boys, I'm atellin' ya right now, if this won't give you ulcers, I don't know what will ... Ball three ... Strike one ... Now they're agonna walk this guy purposely ... again the bases are loaded and it looks like we might have another pinch-hitter for Baker ... Jones is the guy ... I know this guy ... He was with Shreveport in 1940 when I was down there ... he can hit that ball a country mile ... You gotta pitch high, inside, or low, outside to him ... He's a first baseman ... Oh man, this is brutal ... [he whistles] ... Come on, Denny.

"Four to two ... two men out in the first half of the ninth ... Galehouse looks down for a signal. Here's that pump-handle windup.

"Strike one, called ... one an' nothin' ... Galehouse has another signal ... The next pitch ... swung on an' foul ... strike two ... Come on, Denny everything you've got, boy ... Fast ball, swung on, foul into the upper deck ... The empire goes around and sweeps off home plate; he realizes this is a tense moment and he certainly doesn't want to miss one now.

"Galehouse has the signal ... the windup ... the pitch ... fast-ball ... swung ... and Jones went down swinging, to retire the side ... One run, two hits ... the Browns win the first game of this double-header, 4 to 2 ... Now, I understand I'm supposed to pick the hee-ro of the day ... I'm definitely gonna pick Bobby Muncrief.

"So now I can go ahead with my hamburger an' Falstaff ... Due to the fact that he held the White Sox from tyin' the score, that's due to the fact that I'm givin' him the honor of the hee-ro of the day!"

Appendix C:
A Log of Diz's 30 Wins in 1934

1. April 17—Diz beat Pittsburgh, 7-1, on 6 hits. Opening day of season.
2. May 5—Philadelphia, 7-1. 7 hits. 7 strikeouts.
3. May 9—New York, 4-0. 5 hits. 7 Ks.
4. May 13—Brooklyn, 12-7. 7 hits. 4Ks.
5. May 20—At New York, 9-5, 7 hits. 3Ks.
6. May 27—At Philadephia, 5-2. 8 hits. 4Ks.
7. June 2—At Pittsburgh, 13-4. 8 hits. 6 Ks.
8. June 10—Pittsburgh, 3-2. 9 hits. 3 Ks.
9. June 17—Philadelphia, 7-5. Diz got win in relief. 1 K.
10. June 21—Brooklyn, 9-2. 7 hits. 7 Ks.
11. June 23—Brooklyn, 5-4. In relief. 3 Ks.
12. June 27—New York, 8-7. 12 hits. 5Ks.*
13. July 1—At Cincinnati, 8-6. Diz pitched 18 innings. 7 Ks.
14. July 8—Cincinnati, 6-1. 7 hits. 10 Ks.
15. July 12—At Philadelphia, 8-5. In relief.
16. July 15—At Brooklyn, 2-0, 4 hits. 5 Ks.
17. July 19—At Boston, 4-2. 7 hits. 4 Ks.
18. July 23—At New York, 6-5. 10 hits. 8 Ks.
19. Aug. 3—Pittsburgh, 9-3. 11 hits. 1 K.
20. Aug. 7—At Cincinnati, 2-0. 6 hits. 4 Ks.
21. Aug. 8—At Cincinnati, 10-4. In relief. 1 K.
22. Aug. 24—New York, 5-0. 5 hits. 6 Ks.

*Controversial scoring decision. The official scorer gave Diz the victory, even though he was no longer the pitcher of record when the winning run scored in the bottom of the ninth. Diz pitched 8 2/3 innings but gave up three straight singles that produced a run and tied the score. He was replaced by Lefty Mooney, who retired the final batter. The Cardinals won in the bottom of the ninth on a homer by Bill DeLancey, but scorer Martin J. Hanley gave the victory to Diz.

23. Aug. 31—At Chicago, 3-1. 6 hits. 6 Ks.
24. Sept. 5—At Brooklyn, 2-1. 3 hits. 3 Ks.
25. Sept. 10—At Philadelphia, 4-1. 5 hits. 7 Ks.
26. Sept. 16—At New York, 5-3. In relief. 2 Ks.
27. Sept. 21—At Brooklyn, 13-0. 3 hits. 7 Ks. (Paul pitched no-hitter in second game of doubleheader.)
28. Sept. 25—Pittsburgh, 3-2. 6 hits. 5 Ks.
29. Sept. 28—Cincinnati, 4-0. 7 hits. 7 Ks.
30. Sept. 30—Cincinnati, 9-0. 7 hits. 7 Ks.

Appendix D:
Diz on Video

The Pride of St. Louis (CBS/Fox, $19.95) is the authorized film biography of Dizzy Dean. Dan Dailey stars as Diz with Joanne Dru as wife Pat and Richard Crenna as brother Paul. If you can't find it in your local video store, you can order it from Movies Unlimited: 1-800-523-0823. The mailing address is 6736 Castor Ave., Philadelphia, PA 19149.

The St. Louis Cardinals—The Movie (St. Louis National Baseball Club, $24.95) traces the history of the Cardinals franchise from its founding in 1876 to the tape's release date, 1985. There is one clip of Diz pitching. A sportswriter at the time described his windup as an unusual corkscrew motion, but it seems normal on the tape. There is also an interview with Diz from the sixties. He is wearing his trademark cowboy hat and spinning tales. You can order *St. Louis Cardinals—The Movie* from the St. Louis Sports Hall of Fame by calling 1-800-421-FAME. The mailing address is 100 Stadium Plaza, St. Louis, MO 63102.

The Batty World of Baseball (Major League Baseball, $39.95), a humorous look at baseball and its characters hosted by Harry Caray, has about forty-five seconds of footage of Diz. Most of it is stock newsreel stuff shot on the sideline with Diz looking at the camera. There's only one action shot, but it's a telling one: it shows him in his Cubs uniform throwing with the sidearm motion he tried after his arm gave out.

Appendix E:
Dizzy Dean's Annual Salaries for Playing Baseball*

1932	$3,000
1933	$3,000
1934	$7,500
1935	$18,500
1936	$17,500
1937	$25,500
1938	$25,500
1939	$20,000
1940	$20,000
1941	$15,000 (including coach's salary)

Total major-league baseball earnings, including World Series shares: $162,036

The day in 1941 that he signed a coach's contract with the Cubs, he told Chicago newspaperman Charles Dunkley he had earned $258,036 during his eleven years in baseball. That would mean he earned $96,000 in outside endorsements and appearance fees.

*Sources: Associated Press accounting, May 15, 1941; Milton Gross's North American Newspaper Alliance column, April 7, 1963.

Appendix F:
Dizzy Expressions

Here are some of the baseball expressions that Diz made famous on his broadcasts. He didn't invent them all—many were well-known clubhouse terms—but he popularized them on his daily radio broadcasts.

These are adapted from *The Dizzy Dean Dictionary*, published by Falstaff in 1943.

Diz	Definition
A La Carte	Catching the ball with one hand
Annie Oakley	Base on balls; free pass to a game
Around the Horn	Sidearm curve
Barbering	Conversing or chewing the fat
Belly-whopper	Headlong slide into base
Big Bertha	Club's cleanup hitter
Blooper	Fluke hit over infield
Boarding House	Hotel where big-league clubs stay
Broadway	Flashy dresser or show-off
Busher	Raw recruit
Butter Cup	Weak hitter
Butterfly	Knuckleball
Can of Corn	High, lazy fly to the outfield
Chuck Wagon	Dining car
Cockeye	Left-handed pitcher
Confidential	Confidently
Consumed	Assumed
Cousin	Pitcher easy to hit
Cripple	Ball pitched when count is 3-0, or 3-1
Cunny Thumb	Pitcher with nothing but slow stuff
Cup of Coffee	Short trial in the big leagues
Daily Win	Club meeting before each game

Daisy Cutter	Sharp grounder that skims infield grass
Dick Smith	Player who keeps to himself and seldom ever treats
Dipsy-do	Slow, tantalizing curve
Duster	Beanball thrown to drive batter back from the plate
Dust Sprayers	Player sliding into base
Ear Bender	Hotel stranger who talks to the players
Fat One	A pitch right down the middle that is easy to hit
Fireman	Player who takes shower and dresses quickly
Fish Cakes	Low pay
Fishing Trip	Swinging at a bad pitch
Fluffy Duff	Player easily hurt
Fog It Through	Fastball
Foot in the Bucket	Batter pulling away from the plate as he swings
Gillette	Fast pitch thrown near the batter's whiskers
Glass Arm	Weak arm
Grandstand Player	One who makes easy plays look hard
Guesser	Umpire
Gully Jumper	Train
Heifer	Step 2½ feet
High Pockets	Player with long legs
Hitterish	Team or player in the midst of a hitting streak
Horse Collar	Zero in the hit column
Horseshoes	Lucky catch or stop
Hot Corner	Third base
House Dick	Player who spends most of his time in the hotel lobby
Humpty-Dumpty	Person held in contempt

Jaker	Player who is frequently out of lineup because of imaginary ailments
Jesse James	Uncomplimentary term for an umpire
Jockey	One who constantly rides or ribs others
Keystone Sack	Second base
Lallapalooza	Spectacular play
Lawyer	Player who blabbers a lot in the club-house
Leather Players	Good fielders who are weak hitters
Meal Ticket	Club's winningest pitcher
Monkey Suit	Baseball uniform
Morning Glory	Early-season hitter
Moxie	Guts, courage
Nonchalotted	Play made with great ease or indifference
Nub	Sore finger
Nuthin' Ball	Slow ball with no curve on it
Ole Rubber Belly	Veteran player with a bulging waistline
Pebble Picker	Infielder who alibis for making an error by picking imaginary pebbles, which he pretends caused the ball to hop
Pickpocket	Signal stealer
Pistol-whipped	Disappointed, dejected
Portsider	Left-hander
Powder the Ball	Make long, hard hits
Prayer Ball	Pitch with nothin' on it
Rabbit Ears	Player who tries to hear everything said about him
Round House	Sweeping curve
Rubber Arm	Pitcher who works often
Rubnoff	Player in need of a haircut
Scatter Arm	Player who throws hard but wild
Sidewheeler	Left-hander
Skipper	Manager

Smack Dab	In the center
Strawberry	Bruise from sliding
Sunday Pitch	Pitcher's best delivery
Sun Field	Outfield position where sun shines most
Take Button off His Cap	Dust off the batter
Tee-off	Hit a hard one
Toehold	When batter crowds the plate and digs in to swing
Tools of Ignorance	Catcher's equipment
Truck Horse	Very slow runner
Uncle Charlie's Got Him	Can't hit a curveball
Union Hours	Nine-inning game
Waste One	Pitch thrown wide to the catcher to permit him to make a quick throw to try to catch a runner stealing
Whammy	Jinx, hoodoo
Wig-wagger	Coach
Wooden Indian	Player who waits out pitcher
Yodeler	Coach at third base
Zebra	Fleet outfielder

Index

Abbott, Charles, 44
ABC, 269-71; "Game of the Week," 252-53
Abramson, J. P., 131
Acuff, Roy, 265, 279
Adair, Jimmy, 48
Adams, Sparky, 76, 89-90
Ahearn, James, 154
Alexander, Grover Cleveland, 131, 135
Ali, Muhammad, 290
All-Star games, 91-92, 167, 181-83, 185-86, 206
Allen, Ethan, 115-16
Allen, Lee, 14
Allen, Mel, 239
Allen, Newt, 152
Allen, Fred, 253
American League, 107, 139, 183, 224, 228; 1935 pennant, 170; All-Star games, 91-92, 186-87
Anderson, Allie, 119
Anderson, Andy, 66, 287
Ankenman, Fred, 41-42, 44-45, 62, 66, 119-20, 287; contract signing with Diz's father, 69-71, 81-82; on Diz's practical jokes, 64-65
Appling, Luke, 212
Army, U.S., 26-34
Associated Press, 137-38, 139, 169; Diz on lack of schooling, 223; on Diz's sore arm **before** All-Star game, 182; on Rickey's trading of Diz, 191
Auker, Eldon, 148, 149
Averill, Earl, 181, 186

Bachelor, Eddie, 142
Bailey, Eugene, 44-45, 50
Baker, Floyd, 212

Bancroft, Billy, 72
Barnstorming and exhibition games, 152-54, 170-72
Baseball Hall of Fame, 3, 9, 22, 32, 130-32; Dizzy elected to (1953), 254-55
Baseball players: 1934 prize money, 138; Diz's stories about, 267-68; fans of Diz and Pee Wee broadcasts, 263-64; and gambling, 234; interviewed about Dizzy, 283; language of, 209; and superstitions, 128; of today, contrasted with yesteryear, 282
Bauer, Hank, 240
Beaumont Exporters (Texas League), 73, 141
Becker, Sam, 66
Behanna, Bill, 271
Bell, Beau, 40
Bell, Cool Papa, 171
Bendix, William, 245
Benge, Ray, 134
Benjamin, Jerry, 171
Binning, John, 9
Birmingham Barons, 71-73
Blair, Hattie, 9, 16
Blattner, Buddy, 256, 259-60, 261, 270
Bond, Ford, 137, 155
Bond, Mississippi, 256-57, 275-76, 279, 281
Bondurant, Dewey, 48
Booe, Everett, 50
Bordagaray, Stanley "Frenchy," 286
Bost, Dr. J. R., 64
Boston Braves, 83, 96, 97, 124, 132, 161-62, 163; 1959 pennant play-off, 259; Diz pitching with sore arm (1937), 181, 187
Boston Red Sox, 72, 84, 190
Bottomley, Sunny Jim, 100
Boyle, Ralph, 129

Bradenton spring training camp: 1932 season, 61-62, 75-77; 1934 season, 103-7; 1935 season, 162-63
Bradley, Hugh, 241
Breadon, Sam, 66, 78, 83, 106, 109, 111, 122, 138, 154, 166, 186, 190-91, 224; Diz on, 225;
Bridges, Tommy, 139, 143, 146
Bright, Mort, 106
Broadway show (Dean brothers), 154-55
Brock, Lou, 277
Broeg, Bob, 277
Brooklyn Dodgers, 84, 94, 95, 127-28, 168, 175, 239; Diz brawling with (1932), 83-84; and loss of doubleheader (1934), 128-31, 132, 134-35
Brought, Bob, 30
Brought, Sgt. James, 26, 28-31, 37
Brown, Bullet Joe, 45
Brown, Mace, 47
Brown, Mordecai, 4
Brown, Vera, 11, 67
Brown, Warren, 98, 99
Brundidge, Harry, 66
Bryant, Clay, 192, 195, 234
Burkhardt, Fonce, 36-42, 280-81, 288
Burton, Richard, 264
Byrd, Rear Admiral Richard, 142

Caldwell, Ray "Old Man," 72
Calverton, May, 17
Caray, Harry, 207, 224
Carey, Max, 95
Carleton, Carl, 121
Carleton, Tex, 74, 107, 127, 192, 210
Carmichael, John, 146, 208, 233
Carpenter, Claude, 245
Carrasquel, Chico, 217
Carroll, Ownie, 100
Carson, Kit, 286
Catfish story, 257
CBS, 223, 254, 269-71; "The Game of the Week," 3, 252-74, 291
Chandler, Albert B. "Happy," 230-31, 234
Charboneau, Joe, 88
Chicago baseball teams, 253
Chicago Cubs, 5, 55, 62, 83, 85, 88, 93, 108, 116, 118, 133, 163, 166, 174, 179, 205; 1938 season, 190-95; 1939 season, 195-96; 1935 winning streak and pennant, 168-69, 170; Diz recalled (1940), 199; Diz vs. Manager Hartnett (1940), 196-97; Diz's retirement (1941), 200
Chicago White Sox, 30, 44, 198, 274; tele-

casts, 253; transcript of Diz's broadcast, April, 1947, 211-16, 297-309
Chilcote, Ken, 59-60
Cincinnati Reds, 62, 76, 78, 93, 100, 108, 117, 132, 134, 175, 184, 187, 192, 193, 214, 239-40; trades with Cardinals (1933), 90
Clarke, Jack, 224-25
Clarkson, John, 4
Cleveland Indians, 88, 181, 252, 253
Cobb, Ty, 179, 231
Cochrane, Mickey, 138-39, 141, 143, 147, 149-50
Cody, Buffalo Bill, 286
Collins, James "Ripper," 92, 101, 121-22, 140-41, 173
Combs, Earle, 194, 213
Comorosky, Adam, 56, 78
Conniff, Frank, 241-42
Cooper, Gary, 245
Cooper, Mort, 217
Corum, Bill, 99, 139
Cosby, Bill, 272
Cosell, Howard, 6, 210, 225
Cousins, Norman, 222
Crabtree, Estel, 100
Crawford, Pat, 89, 143
Crenna, Richard, 245
Critz, Hughie, 128
Crockett, Davy, 289
Cronin, Joe, 190
Crosetti, Frank, 76, 195
Crowder, Alvin, 138, 139
Crowther, Bosley, 248
Cuccinello, Tony, 94, 129
Cummings, Candy, 3
Cunningham, Raymond, 286
Curtis, Don, 41-42

Dailey, Dan, 244-50
Daniel, Dan, 166, 287
Davis, Curt "Coonskin," 190-91
Davis, L. C., 75, 89
Davis, Ray "Peaches," 52, 290
Davis, Spud, 173
Davis, Virgil, 110, 118, 131, 144
Dean, Albert Monroe (father), 9, 11, 12-15, 17, 32-34, 36; Diz's underage contract, 68-71, 82
Dean, Alma Nelson (mother), 13, 16; death of, 19
Dean, Bland (uncle), 197
Dean, Charles Monroe (brother), 13
Dean, Elmer (brother), 13, 16, 21; as peanut

vendor at baseball games, 118-20; separated from family, 31-33

Dean, Jay Hanna "Dizzy": 1930 season with St. Joseph Saints, 44-52, 287; 1930 season with Houston Buffaloes, 52-54; 1931 season with Houston Buffaloes, 62-73; 1930 season with Cardinals, 56-58; 1931 season with Cardinals, 59-62; 1932 season with Cardinals, 74-87; 1933 season with Cardinals, 88-96; doubleheader strike-out record, 93; exhibition games, 91, 93-94; 1934 season with Cardinals, 101-36; Dodger doubleheader wins, 129-31; fines and suspension, 120-26; and Gas House Gang, 97-101; high jinks and practical jokes, 115-16, 128; on chance of winning pennant, 132; pennant race, 127-36; and publicity, 114-15, 128; salary disputes, 100, 104-6, 109-12; wins credited to and record, 113-14, 130, 138, 310-11; World Series, 137-51; 1935 season with Cardinals, 161-70; autograph seekers and promoters, 162; fans turn against, 161, 165-67; high jinks and practical jokes, 168; and marshmallow pitches, 165-66; record wins, 170; as tired-ball pitcher, 170; 1936 season with Cardinals, 173-80; high jinks and practical jokes, 174-79; and lucky rabbit's foot, 174-75; 1937 season with Cardinals; broken toe and sore arm, 181-83; 1938 season with Cubs, 189-95; end of fastball pitch, 191, 193-94; high jinks and fans, 195; World Series and record, 194-95; 1939 season with Cubs, 195-96; 1940 season with Cubs, 196-99; 1941 season with Cubs; coaching and retirement, 200, 201, 205; army days and baseball, 26-34; barnstorming (1934), 152-54; barnstorming (1935), 170-71; baseball beginnings, 18-20, 24-26; baseball career, 3-4, 183, 255, 295-96, 310-11; birthdate conflicts, 1, 8-10, 21, 37, 81, 279-80; in Bond, Mississippi, 256, 276-77; box scores (1930), 49-50, 57-58; Broadway vaudeville show, 154-55; carpet store purchase, 256; character and personality; behavior problems, 51-52, 61-62; borrowing and losing clothes, 52, 53; bragging and boastfulness, 59, 59-62, 127, 143; egotism of, 5; extravagance and over-spending, 61, 159; fun with opposing teams, 94-95; growing up (1936), 176; and Hollywood film, 248-49; humor and generosity of, 40-41; staying a kid forever,

282-83; childhood and schooling, 16-26, 280; courtship and marriage, 65-69; earnings; from endorsements, 156-59; from film, 244; from playing baseball, 112, 156, 158, 174, 313; from radio broadcasts, 206, 228; from speech-making, 274; from telecasts, 257, 260, 269; epitaph for, 290; fear of flying and train travel, 257-59; fighting and brawling; with Dodgers (1932), 83-84; with other ballplayers, 48, 63, 90, 165, 192-93; Tampa hotel and sportswriters, 184; films; movie offers, 219; *Pride of St. Louis*, 30, 245-51; Warner Brothers short, 155-56; funeral, 279-80; gambling and, 230-37; betting on games (1937), 232-33; federal investigation, 231-32, 276; golf games, 106, 235, 237, 243, 275; horse racing, 235-36; Hall of Fame election (1953), 254-55; heart attack and death (1974), 278-79; innings pitched (lifetime), 183; job with San Antonio power company, 36-41; language and grammar, 2-3; English teachers' objections and, 208, 219-23; "If I start talking better, they'll throw me out," 256; list of expressions, 314-17; mispronunciations, 217, 239-40, 262, 267; Ogden Nash's poem on, 220; and publicity, 223-24, 256; "respectable bases," 215; "slud" and "throwed," 2, 209, 264; lawsuits, 158-59, 175-76; legendary stories about, 44; couple kissing in stands, 265; lucky sock, 295-96; multiple room-rentals and clothes borrowing, 52, 53; profile of Diz in *St. Joseph Gazette*, 46; rabbit's foot, 174-75; removal of scored run on scoreboard, 63-64; and love of food, 258-59; and Lubbock baseball team, 243; major and minor league records, 183, 255, 295-96, 310-11; and Mississippi governorship, 276; and mother's athletic ability, 13; Murray's tribute after death, 283; name conflicts, 1-2, 37, 279-81; nickname origins, 30-31, 44; on Anderson's creation of Dizzy sayings, 287; on being misrepresented, 286-87; on Breadon being skinflint, 225; on getting out of army, 34-35; on improvement of baseball, 104; on Pee Wee Reese, 260-61; on pitching a no-hitter against Dodgers, 131; poetic tributes to, 201-4, 220; "Poppin' Off" column, 219; predictions; 1933, 92; 1934, 103-4, 106-7, 130-32, 288; product endorsements, 156-59; radio broadcasts, 205-29; English teachers

Dean, Jay Hanna "Dizzy" *(continued)*
objections to, 219-223; as entertainment,
209-10, 217-20; grammatical inventions,
209; play-by-play style, 214-15; and rain
delays during war, 218; stage fright and
popularity, 207-8, 219; "telling it like it
is," 210-11; as reflection of what baseball
once was, 282; and sidearm delivery, 198-
99; speech-making, 274-75, 289; television broadcasts, 218, 238-43, 252-53,
255-72, 274; with Blattner, 256, 259-60;
contrasted with radio, 241; and Diz's stories, 267-68; hillbilly singing, 264-65,
267; N.Y. critics and, 240-42; phrases,
grammar, malaprops, mispronunciations,
239-40, 262, 266-67, 314-17; with Reese,
260-65; story of couple kissing in stands,
265; as television interviewer, 240-41;
Texas League most valuable player award,
73; true stories about and photos, 288;
with Tulsa Oilers (1940), 198-99; TV
show possibility, 274; in U.S. Army, 26-
35; videos of, 312; weight gain in 50s,
227, 258. *See also* Bradenton spring training camp; Chicago Cubs; St. Louis Cardinals
Dean, Jerome Herman, 1, 11-12, 81-82,
244. *See also* Dean, Jay Hanna "Dizzy"
Dean, Matt (grandfather), 12-13
Dean, Moses (great-great-grandfather), 12
Dean, Patricia Nash (wife), 103, 154-55,
175, 184, 224, 235, 262; control of family
finances, 67-69, 71; courtship and marriage, 65-69; and Dean brothers' fines and
suspension, 122, 124; and Diz's death,
279, 281; and Diz's gambling, 230-31;
Diz's love for, 116; and Diz's popularity,
162; Diz's practical joking and, 64-65; and
Elmer as Cardinal vendor, 119; heart
attack, 275-76, 278; move to Bond, Mississippi, 256; on Blattner's resignation,
259-60; on Diz entering army, 27; on
Diz's childhood and youth, 16, 18, 24-25;
on Diz's reinstatement with Chicago Cubs
(1940), 197-98; on Diz's taking Jerome
Herman name, 11-12; on finding Elmer,
33; as portrayed in Hollywood film, 249
Dean, Paul (brother), 1, 13, 16, 17, 21, 33-
34, 36, 69, 158-59, 184, 246; 1934 fines
and suspension, 120-26; 1934 salary
negotiations, 103, 104-5, 109-12; 1934
season, 108, 117, 129-31, 133-35; 1935
season, 168-69, 170; 1936 season, 180;
1934 World Series, 143, 145, 146; barn-

storming with Diz (1934-35), 152-54,
170-71; Broadway vaudeville show, 154-
55; with Columbus farm club, 93-94, 96,
104; and Diz's broken toe, 182; and Diz's
death, 279; failure of comeback (1941),
204; film short for Warner Brothers, 155-
56; with Houston Buffaloes, 119; and loss
of Elmer, 32-33; and Lubbock baseball
team, 243; nicknames for, 105; on becom-
ing a pitcher, 105; on Dizzy's schooling,
23-24; and signing of movie contract,
244; strikeout-to-walk ratio, 180
Dean, Robah, 21
Dean, Sarah May (sister), 13
Deck, Vernon "Lefty," 45
DeLancey, Bill, 114, 130, 142, 162, 173
Derringer, Paul, 61, 74, 90, 167, 193
Detroit Tigers, 25, 120, 133, 170; 1934
World Series, 137-51
DeWitt, Bill, 157-58, 225
Dickey, Bill, 254
Dickey, Glenn, 131-32, 213
Dickson, Paul, 97-98
DiMaggio, Joe, 186, 194, 240, 243, 254;
hitting streak, 207-8
DiMaggio, Vince, 233-34
Dixie Series (1931), 71, 119
"Dizzy and Daffy" (film short), 155-56
Dizzy and Daffy Tour, 152
Dizzy and Daffy trademarks, 158-59
Dizzy Dean All-Stars, 170-71
Dizzy Dean Day (1933), 95-96, 246
"Dizzy Dean" radio show, 228-29
Doan, Ray, 152
Dru, Joanne, 245, 246
Dugas, Gus, 56
Durocher, Leo, 90, 92, 106, 107, 168, 173,
174, 193, 236, 243, 271; 1934 World
Series, 141, 144, 146-48, 149, 151; and
Gas House Gang, 97-98, 99, 102; on
Dean brothers' pitching (1934), 133; on
Diz and Tigers' batting practice, 140
Duvic, Frank C., 236

Ebbets Field, 84, 94, 129
Eisenhower, Dwight D., 258
Elmira, NY exhibition game, 91
English teachers, 208, 219-223
Enright, Paul, 224, 225; on baseball broad-
casts in 40s, 206-7; on Diz and bank
accounts, 288-89; on Diz's betting on
games, 236
Erickson, Paul, 200
Exhibition games: Diz against Paul (Colum-

bus 1933), 93-94; Diz sleeping through Elmira stop (1933), 91; Diz's behavior in St. Paul (1935), 167. *See also* Barnstorming and exhibition games

Falstaff Beer, 17, 19, 35, 216, 249, 253, 256, 261, 263, 269; co-sponsor Liggett & Myers, 259; and Diz's radio broadcasts, 205-6; increased popularity of, 254, 274
Fans (baseball), 114, 124-25, 127, 134-35, 241-42, 263-64
Farrington, Dick, 114
Fast ball pitching, 104, 191, 193-94
FCC, 221-22, 223
Feller, Bob, 4
Ferguson, David, Jr., 20
Ferrick, Tom, 227
Fetzer, John, 269
Filipowicz, Steve, 239-40
Ford, Whitey, 4
Ford Motor Company, 137-38
Fort Sam Houston, 26, 28-29
Fort Smith baseball team, 14-15
Fort Worth Panthers, 198
Foxx, Jimmie, 59, 167
French, Andrew, 66
French, Larry, 56, 87, 133, 170, 192
French, Oliver, 59
Frey, Benny, 100
Frey, Linus, 129
Frick, Ford, 164, 219, 253
Frisch, Frankie, 89, 99, 100-101; **1933** as Cardinals' manager, 92-93, 95, 102; **1934** season, 102-33; Dean brothers' fines and suspension, 120-23; and Dizzy's walkouts, 111-12; and Dodger doubleheader, 129-31; and Gas House Gang tricks, 116; pennant race, 127-28, 133; and team resentment against Deans, 114; World Series, 138, 140-42, 144, 146-48, 150-51; **1935** season, 166-69; injured leg, 163; warning Diz re marshmallow pitches, 165-66; **1936** season, 173-75, 177-78; **1937** season; hotel brawl with sportswriters, 185; on Diz's pitching after broken toe, 187; Diz's estimation of, 210; on Diz's emerging maturity, 175; on Dizzy's disposition, 118; rookie advised to follow veteran, 267-68
Fry, Stanley, 133
Fuentes, Tito, 277
Fullerton, Hugh, 135

Gallagher, Jim, 200

Gallico, Paul, 210
"Game of the Day" (Mutual Radio), 243
"The Game of the Week." *See* CBS
Garagiola, Joe, 271
Gas House Gang, 5, 90, 110, 160, 163, 167-68, 170, 190, 204, 254, 267; during 1936 season, 174-79; beginnings and name origin, 97-102; jokes and tricks, 115-16; Martin as embodiment of, 101, 174-78; and Missouri Mudcats Band, 147, 177; verbal taunts, 143
Gehrig, Lou, 76, 91, 160, 186, 195, 245
Gehringer, Charlie, 141, 144, 149
Gelbert, Charley, 89, 90, 101, 173
Gibson, Bob, 4, 277
Gibson, Josh, 171
Gill, Ernest, 20
Gill, Ray, 16-17, 17, 20
Gillespie, Ray, 121, 122
Gillespie, Ray J., 111
Goetz, Larry, 178
Gomez, Lefty, 4, 76, 195
Gonzalez, Mike, 112, 117, 184
Gordon, Joe, 194
Goslin, Goose, 149
Gould, Jack, 242
Gould, Jay, 11-12
Gowdy, Curt, 239, 262, 270, 276
Grace, Earl, 275
Graham, Frank, 94, 97, 99, 138, 148
Grammar and mispronunciations. *See* Dean, Jay Hanna, language and grammar
Grantham, George "Boots," 56
Green, Doc, 42
Greenberg, Hank "Mo," 140, 141-42, 148-51, 155, 170
Gregory, Lloyd, 45, 66
Grimes, Burleigh, 56, 61, 108
Grimm, Charley, 93, 169, 191, 194
Grove, Lefty, 4, 53, 86, 131, 255
"Gunga Dean" (poem), 201-4
Gutteridge, Don, 175, 193, 224

Hack, Stan, 169
Hafey, Chick, 100
Hahn, Noodles, 93
Haines, Jesse "Pop," 55, 61, 74, 84, 112, 127, 133, 210
Haley, Martin J., 105, 106-7, 113-14, 120
Hall of Fame. *See* Baseball Hall of Fame
Hallahan, Bill, 61, 74, 85, 86, 91, 107, 112, 113, 114, 146; 1934 World Series, 143, 146-48
Haney, Fred, 271

INDEX

Hanna, Mark, 12
Hanner, Jay, 10
Hanyzewski, Ed, 217
Harper, Blake, 118
Harris, Jerome, 281
Harris, Riley, 36, 39-40, 41-42, 42
Harris, Vic, 154
Hartford Blues baseball team, 14
Hartnett, Gabby, 186, 194, 195, 199-200
Hasty, Bob, 72
Hauser, Joe, 171
Heath, Jeff, 214, 225
Heath, Mickey, 94
Heinrich, Tommy, 194
Hendrick, Harvey "Gink," 100
Henry, Dutch, 90
Herman, Billy, 169, 186
Herman, Jerome, 10-11
Heydler, John A., 86, 113
Hickok, Wild Bill, 286
Hicks, Jimmy, 278
Hofmann, Freddie, 213-14
Holmes, Joe, 31
Holmes, Tommy, 1, 8, 130
Holt, John, 17
Holway, John, 152-53
Hornsby, Rogers, 89, 102, 164
Houston Buffaloes, 41-43, 45, 71, 87, 198,
    249-50, 289; Diz with (1931), 52, 62-64,
    71-73, 141; Diz's problems and tricks,
    126; and Elmer Dean, 118-20
Hoyt, Waite, 133
Hubbell, Carl, 4, 53, 87, 91-92, 108, 132,
    138, 183, 249, 255
Hunt, Jodie, 76
Hyland, Dr. Robert, 176

Ireland, John, 246

Jackson, Reggie, 2
Jackson, Travis, 179
Jacobus, George, 235
James, Byrne, 95
Jenkins, Burris, 201-4
Jensen, Jackie, 240
Johnson, Roy, 199
Johnson, Senator Edwin, 253
Johnson, Syl, 61, 74
Johnson, Walter, 53, 72, 104, 107, 290
Johnson's Carnu and Wax, 228-29
Jones, Fleeda, 25-26
Jones, Harmon, 245
Jorgens, Arndt, 76
Judnich, Walt, 212, 214, 217

Kaese, Harold, 129
Kamm, Willie, 44
Kansas City A's, 273-74
Kansas City Monarchs, 152
Karst, Gene, 103, 287
Kaufmann, Tony, 76
Kearney, Tom, 77
Keener, Sid, 103, 107, 110, 127
Kelly, Mike, 44
Kennedy, John F., 10, 267
Kieran, John, 10
Kimball, Newt, 171
Kirby, Gene, 257, 261, 262, 265
Kite, Ila Maude, 223
Klem, Bill, 179
Kluszewski, Ted, 239
Knowles, Dr. Harry, 66-67
Koenig, Mark, 135
Kolp, Ray, 117
Koufax, Sandy, 3, 4, 269
Kubek, Tony, 276
Kunes, Blaine, 45
Kupcinet, Irv, 184-85, 192, 193

Landis, Judge Kenesaw Mountain, 80-82,
    125-26; Diz removed from broadcasting
    1944 Series, 218; and gambling in base-
    ball, 234; ruling on Diz's agent's fee, 157
Lardner, John, 128
Lardner, Ring, 287
Lavagetto, Cookie, 108
Lazzeri, Tony, 160, 194
Lee, Big Bill, 168, 192
Lemon, Bob, 4
Leonard, Buck, 171
Leslie, Sam, 129
Lindsey, Jim, 61, 62, 74, 84
Lindstrom, Freddie, 163, 170
Lloyd, Clarence, 61, 112
Lombardi, Ernie, 135
Lopez, Al, 130
Los Angeles Dodgers, 259, 260
Lotshaw, Lot, 196
Lyons, Leonard, 220-21, 223
Lyons, Ted, 254

McCarver, Tim, 217
McCovey, Willie, 88
McCullough, Bill, 1, 8, 127
McDonald, Webster, 171
McGinnity, Joe, 183
McGoogan, W. J., 233-34
McGowen, Roscoe, 1, 8-9, 131

322

McGraw, John J., 79, 91
McGrew, Slim, 40
Mack, Connie, 91, 100, 195
McNamee, Graham, 137, 141
Maddox, Gary, 277
Malone, Pat, 84
Mankiewicz, Herman, 245, 248, 249, 250
Manning, Tom, 137, 138
Mantle, Mickey, 240, 273
Mapes, Cliff, 240
Maranville, Rabbit, 254
Marichal, Juan, 4
Maris, Roger, 273
Martin, Pepper, 89, 92, 98-99, 100-101,
    144-45, 149, 160, 268; 1936 season;
    Philadelphia hotel high jinks and Missouri
    Mudcats Band, 174-78; on Diz's trade to
    Cubs, 191; smoking peace pipe under
    blanket on hot day, 175, 288; staged
    fights and pranks, 115-16; wrestling with
    Diz, 168
Martin, Stu, 173
Mathewson, Christy, 3, 4, 93
Mathis, Charles, 6, 237, 243, 256, 264, 269,
    274, 281; on Diz and train travel, 258-59;
    on Diz hunting and fishing, 257, 275; on
    Diz's birthdate, 280
Matthews, Earl, 51
Matthews, Gary, 277
Mayfield, Ornie, 24-26
Mayfield, Riley, 21
"Me 'n' Paul," 243, 283-86
Meany, Tom, 11, 15, 155, 198-99
Medwick, Joe "Ducky," 92, 101, 160, 175,
    190; 1935 fights with Diz, 165, 192-93;
    1934 World Series, 141-42
Mencken, H. L., 267
Milan, Clyde, 72
Miley, Jack, 184-85, 192
Minor-league farm teams, 43, 189. See also
    names of minor-league teams
Missouri Mudcats Band, 147, 177, 288
Mize, Johnny, 173, 193
Montana, Joe, 156
Mooney, Jim, 107
Mooney, Lefty, 114, 127
Moore, Mary Tyler, 272
Moore, Terry, 162, 163, 173
Morgan, Joe, 217
Mosolf, Jim, 93
Movies, 246, 247. See also Pride of St. Louis
Mulbry, Walter, 230
Mullin, Willard, 98
Mungo, Van Lingle, 134, 180

Murphy, Edward T., 155
Murray, Jim, 255, 279, 281-83
Murrow, Edward R., 219
Musial, Stan, 267
Mutual Radio, 243
My Greatest Day in Baseball (Dean), 149
Myers, Billy, 62

Narron, Sam, 267-68
Nash, Ogden, 220
Nash, Sam, 256
National League, 77, 96, 116, 240, 259;
    1934 pennant race, 132-36; All-Star
    games, 91-92, 167, 185-87; Dizzy's
    record wins (1934), 135-36
NBC radio: "Dizzy Dean" show, 228
NBC television, 254, 269; competitive sched-
    ules vs. CBS, 272-74; contract for baseball
    telecasts (1965), 262, 269, 271; Diz as
    guest announcer (1974), 276; "Major
    League Baseball" (1957), 270, 272
Negro Leagues, 152-54, 171
Nelson, Lindsey, 271
New York Black Yankees, 153
New York City, 253, 257-58; and Diz's pop-
    ularity, 241-42
New York Daily News, 109, 184, 210, 211
New York Evening Journal, 99, 114, 139; on
    the new Dizzy after suspension (1934),
    126
New York Giants, 77, 78-79, 83, 91, 95, 97,
    108, 109, 113, 116, 122, 139, 179, 193,
    268, 276; 1934 pennant race, 126-35;
    1916 winning streak, 170; Diz's needling
    of, 161; and Paul Dean, 204
New York Times, 5, 10-11, 55, 77, 79, 98,
    131, 190, 248; on Deans' Broadway
    salaries, 154; praise for Diz's telecasts, 242
New York World-Telegram, 107, 155, 166,
    191, 198, 209, 241-42, 287
New York Yankees, 2, 76, 121, 190, 207,
    252, 273; 1938 World Series, 194-95; and
    Babe Ruth, 190, 297; decline of, 269,
    271; Dizzy's TV broadcasts, 6-7, 238-43;
    Murderers' Row, 160, 194
Newman, Zipp, 72
Newsom, Buck, 164
Nielsen ratings, 252, 271
No-hitters, 130-32

Ogden, Jack, 90
Ogrodowski, Ambrose "Brusie," 173, 233-
    34
O'Hara, Johnny, 5, 224, 226, 228, 291; on

O'Hara, Johnny *(continued)*
Diz's mangling of Polish names, 239;
radio broadcasts with Diz, 207, 211-16,
297-309
"Old Sport" columnist (Philadelphia
Inquirer), 101, 110-11, 116-18
Opalinski, Sergeant Obie, 29
Orsatti, Ernie, 92, 101, 106, 144, 163, 173
O'Shea, Bernie, 117
Ott, Mel, 95, 179, 193
Owen, Marv, 151
Owens, Brick, 149

Page, Ted, 171
Page, Vance, 193-94
Paige, Satchel, 171
Parham, Claude, 26-27, 36
Payne, George, 53
Perkins, Johnny, 233
Pershing, General John J., 28
Petersen, Leo H., 61
Pfirman, Cy, 179
Philadelphia Athletics, 59, 72, 76, 100, 253, 254
Philadelphia Phillies, 83, 85, 108, 109, 113, 121, 122, 124, 128, 132, 133, 164, 178;
lucky rabbit, 118; television broadcasts, 253
Phillips, Elmer H., 158
Pitchers: of fast ball, 104; left-handed, and right-handed batters, 299; sore arms, and innings pitched, 182-83
Pittsburgh Crawfords, 154
Pittsburgh Pirates, 47, 50, 55-57, 62, 78, 83, 86, 108, 112, 118, 127, 132, 133, 163, 185, 194, 205, 214, 219
Polo Grounds, 85, 128, 134, 164, 170, 193-94, 268
"Poppin' Off" column, 164, 219, 235
Povich, Shirley, 225-26
Powers, Jimmy, 109, 116
The Pride of St. Louis (film), 30, 65, 245-51;
reviews, 247-50
The Pride of the Yankees (film), 245

Quigg, Doc, 263
Quigley, Ernie, 84, 86

Ramsey, Thomas (Toad), 93
Reardon, Beans, 267
Redbirds. *See* St. Louis Cardinals
Redner, Arthur, 158-59
Reese, Pee Wee, 260-65, 270, 276, 279;
respect/admiration for Dizzy, 261-62

Republic studios, 219
Reynolds, Carl, 44
Rhem, Flint, 61, 74
Rice, Grantland, 138, 144-45
Rickey, Branch, 43-44, 49, 117, 138, 168, 172, 180, 219; 1933 season, 89-90, 92, 102; 1934 season, 103; and Dean brothers, 96, 105-6, 111; and Diz's weight gain, 104; trades, 101-2; as author of Dizzy quotes, 287-88; baseball innovations and contributions, 189; Dean brothers suspension, 123, 126; disbanding of Missouri Mudcats, 177; Diz traded (1938), 167, 189-91; Diz's 1935 contract, 159; Diz's first contract, 70-71; and Diz's retirement, 188; and Elmer Dean as vendor, 119; on Diz's wedding plans, 66; and young Diz, 59-60
Rigler, Umpire, 165
Ring, Jimmy, 102
Ripple, Jimmy, 193
Rizzuto, Phil, 241
Robinson, Murray, 211, 242
Roe, Preacher, 267
Rogell, Billy, 145, 150
Rogers, Roy, 219
Rogers, Will, 6, 220, 290
Rose, Pete, 231
Rossie, Dave, 2
Rothrock, Jack, 149, 173
Rowe, Schoolboy, 139, 143, 155
Rowland, Clarence, 190-91
Royal Giants, 191
Rucker, Nap, 93
Ruether, Dutch, 198
Ruffing, Red, 195
Ruth, Babe, 2, 11, 53, 91, 121, 156, 160, 163-64, 190, 194, 212, 245, 273, 287;
Diz's bet in golf tournament, 235; and Diz's telephone call, 139-40
Ryba, Mike, 170, 182
Rye, Gene, 53

St. Joseph Gazette, 44-52, 59
St. Joseph Saints (Class A), 96; Dizzy pitching for (1930), 45-52, 59, 126, 250, 284
St. Louis, Missouri, 253; Dizzy legend and frontier, 286
St. Louis Browns, 6, 40, 107, 190, 207, 255, 260, 264; Diz's radio broadcasts, 205-16, 224-28, 238; in last place and Diz pitching for (1947), 216, 227; transcript of Diz's radio broadcast, 1947, 211-16, 297-309
St. Louis Cardinals, 2, 5, 89, 194, 267, 276;

1930 season; Diz as pitcher of last game, 55-58; 1932 season, 74-75, 77-87, 100; 1933 season, 88-96; 1934 season, 103-36; Dean brothers' suspension, 120-26; fans and Dean brothers, 114, 124-25, 127, 134-35; final week, 132-36; front office publicity, 114-15; Gas House Gang, 97-102; Paul Dean's contract, 104-5; pitching staff, 107; September schedule switch, 128-29; team resentment of Deans, 114, 123; World Series, 25, 137-51; 1935 season, 161-70; fans against Diz, 161, 165-67; records and Diz's wins, 161, 170; 1936 season; Diz and Pepper's high jinks, 175-79; 1937 season, 183-88; Tampa hotel brawl, 184; 1938 season; Diz traded, 190-91; team feud with Diz, 192; Diz broadcasts of, 6, 205-16, 224; Diz publicity and, 210, 287-88; and Diz's marriage, 65-66; Houston Buffaloes farm team, 41-42, 43; pennants, 43, 100; team record after Diz, 205. *See also* Dean, Jay Hanna "Dizzy"

St. Louis *Globe-Democrat*, 105, 120, 122, 145; support for Dizzy's language, 221-22; type of newspaper, 284-85

St. Louis *Post-Dispatch*, 53-54, 75, 89, 96, 109, 131, 132, 145, 235, 277; Diz's gambling in Boston game, 233-34; Diz's "Poppin' Off" column, 164; Dizzy's letter to fans on suspension, 124-25; Elmer Dean in St. Louis, 118; review of Dizzy's movie, 248-49; Stockton writing for, 285

St. Louis *Star-Times*, 67, 103, 110, 111, 120, 121, 145

San Antonio Public Service Company, 22, 34-41, 279-81

The Saturday Evening Post, 9, 10, 148, 239; 1935 Dizzy article, 10, 16, 22, 30, 283-86; 1951 profile of Diz, 22-23, 68, 245, 287-88; on Paul's signing movie rights, 244

The Saturday Review, 222, 244-45, 247-48

Scheffing, Bob, 275

Schermer, Jules, 245, 250

Schuble, Agnes, 115, 220, 224

Schuble, Heinie, 115, 176, 220

Schultz, Joe, 62-64, 66, 249-50

Schumacher, Garry, 114, 126

Schumacher, Hal, 92, 1676

Scoring decisions, 113

Shanks, Linda, 21

Sherdel, Wee Willie, 96

Shiell, Vic, 48, 193

Shore, Dinah, 274

Shoun, Clyde "Hardrock," 190

Simmons, Al, 91, 167, 254

Smith, Constance, 246

Smith, Hilton, 153

Sober, Howard, 236

Sophomore jinx year, 88, 96

Southern Railway System, 258

Spahn, Warren, 4

Spalding, Al, 4

Spaulding, Oklahoma, 21, 23

Spence, Stan, 226

Spink, J.G. Taylor, 9

Sporting News, 9, 23, 33, 45, 52, 114, 257, 292; Diz named Announcer of the Year (1944), 218; Diz's broadcast transcript, April 27, 1947, 211-16, 297-309; on 1934 pennant race, 136

Sportsman's Park, 119, 127, 135, 205, 246, 267

Sportswriters: and Dizzy, 1, 2, 5-6, 9; Dizzy on their need of him, 127; and Gas House Gang origin, 97-99; and Tampa hotel brawl with Cardinals, 184-85

Sprinz, Joe, 289

Squirrel-hunting story, 17-18

Stainback, Tuck, 190-91

Standish, Myles, 248-49

Starr, Ray, 74

Stengel, Casey, 134, 239; Diz's interview of, 240-41

Stephens, Vern, 213, 214

Stevens, Chuck, 227

Stewart, Jimmy, 245

Stockton, J. Roy, 8, 10, 16, 22, 30, 74, 76, 86, 98, 104, 112, 118, 131, 182, 282; background and career, 284-85, 287; Dean brothers fines and suspension, 120-21; Diz as invention of, 283-89; Diz's "Poppin' Off" column, 164; on Diz and truth, 292; on Diz's earache, 176; on Diz's squandering of earnings, 159; on Diz's taunts to Greenberg, 148; on Dizzy's offers, 152; tribute to Dizzy, 204; and young Diz, 60

Stout, Allyn, 74, 84, 90

Stratton, Monte, 245

Street, Charles "Gabby," 55, 61, 62, 75-76, 80, 84, 89, 117, 224, 255, 268; fining of Diz, 91; firing of (1933), 92, 102

Sugden, Joe, 59-60

Suhr, Gus, 56, 78

Sukeforth, Clyde, 83-84, 193

Summers, Bill, 226

Susce, George, 154

Tate, Bennie, 44
Taylor, Elizabeth, 264
Taylor, Reverend Bill, 279
Taylor, Sec, 49
Taylor, Zack, 72
Television: baseball broadcasting, 252-74;
    283
Terry, Bill, 79, 91-92, 95, 109, 178, 254;
    crack against Dodgers, 132, 134-35; on
    Diz's trade to Cubs, 191
Texas League, 41-43, 45, 52, 54, 71-72,
    141, 198-99
Thomas, Bob, 92
Thornton, Wiley, 13, 19-20, 32, 145, 182
Tips, Kern, 66
Todd, Al, 63, 193
Tolbert, Francis X., 9, 28, 32, 245-46
Topping, Dan, 238-39, 243
Traweek, Roger, 45
Traynor, Pie, 56, 78, 91
Trebelhorn, Tom, 2
Trosper, Guy, 245, 250
Tulsa Oilers, 198-99
Twain, Mark, 6
Twentieth Century-Fox, 244-46

Umpires, 178-79
UPI, 259-60, 263

Vance, Dazzy, 90, 144, 254
Vergez, Johnny, 5, 224
Vogel, Victor, 27, 33-34

"The Wabash Cannonball" (song), 177, 222,
    250, 261, 264-65
WABD radio station, New York, 239
Waddell, Rube, 93, 131, 284
Walker, Bill, 107, 167
Walters, Bucky, 163
Waner, Lloyd, 78
Waner, Paul, 56, 91
Wano, Chief, 48

Ward, Arch, 91
Wares, Buzzy, 112, 149, 268
Warneke, Lon, 92
Warner Brothers, 155-56
Washington Senators, 40, 72, 139, 190, 216,
    273-74
Watkins, George, 92
Watwood, Johnny, 44
Weiland, Al, 199
West Texas–New Mexico League, 243
Western Association, 14-15, 43
Western League, 45, 48
White, Joyner "Jo-Jo," 141
Wiggins, Mississippi, 275, 276-77
WIL radio station, St. Louis, 207, 221, 223
Wilhelm, Hoyt, 3
Williams, Joe, 61, 63, 107, 191; and Diz's
    grammatical inventions, 209; on Dean
    brothers' wage strike, 109-10; on Diz
    reading commercials, 242-43
Williams, Mary (aunt), 12
Wilson, Boojum, 171
Wilson, Hack, 84, 171
Wilson, Jimmie, 92, 93, 94, 113
Wilson, Raymith, 20-21, 33, 66
Woodling, Gene, 240
World Series: 1930, 59; 1931, 100; 1933,
    139; 1934, 2, 11, 15, 67, 69, 137-51;
    players' bonuses, 129; 1938, 194-95;
    1965, 269; 1981, 2
World War II weather regulations, 218
Wotowicz, Clarence, 239-40
Wray, John E., 109, 132
Wright, Taft, 214
Wrigley, Phil, 190, 197
Wrigley Field, 163, 191
WTMV radio station, East St. Louis, 206,
    221, 224, 225, 289

Young, Cy, 3, 130
Young & Rubicam, Inc., 156-57

Zanner, Oscar, 225